Cooking up a Storm

Abby could not let herself indulge in wishful thinking – not with this man who could reduce her to jelly with both hands tied behind his back. He had placed himself at her mercy and he had offered his body as a personal playground. The more she restrained him the better he seemed to like it. In the past few days Abby had faced more sexual firsts than in her entire adult life. That was all she needed to know for now.

Cooking up a Storm
Emma Holly

BLACK LACE

Black Lace books contain sexual fantasies.
In real life, always practise safe sex.

This edition published in 2002 by
Black Lace
Thames Wharf Studios
Rainville Road
London W6 9HA

Originally published in 1998

Design by Smith & Gilmour, London
Printed and bound by Mackays of Chatham PLC

ISBN 0 352 33686 2

To MFW and ERA:

For inspiration and information, for friendship and laughter – and for the courage to persevere.

1

Abigail Coates never would have guessed it, but she looked great in leather.

She turned from side to side in front of the cheval glass in her old-fashioned bathroom, trying to see if she'd misled herself. But, no, the tiny black bikini still hugged her bottom in its loving clasp, showing off her high, rounded curves and baring the crease between her cheeks and thighs. Despite her diminutive five-foot-two-inch height, her legs looked long and strong; her reward for many early-morning runs along the dunes of the Outer Cape.

She put her hands on her hips. She didn't have a wasp-waist, but she didn't have love handles, either. Her belly was another matter. She touched its gentle swell. With all the sit-ups she did, you'd think she'd be flat by now. Still, it wasn't too bad. Sucking it in, she slid her palms up her ribcage and over her breasts. She pressed them together and watched the soft flesh swell over the edge of the bra. This bikini made her look like she actually had something up top. Better yet, her skin glowed milky pale against the dark leather, its translucence washed with pink.

She'd always thought someone as fair and blonde as she was should stick to pastels, but maybe she'd been wrong. Maybe Bill knew something she didn't when he'd bullied her into wearing this get-up – or perhaps 'pestered to death' was a better phrase.

Her Cupid's-bow mouth flattened into a frown. Abby loved Bill dearly but there were times when letting her long-time boyfriend have his way really put her back up. The fact that she liked the leather outfit, that it warmed her sex like a little electric coil, made her resentment all the more noticeable.

Why does it bother me? she wondered as she tugged the bra straps higher. A baby-fine lock of hair drifted over her eye and she absently smoothed it back. Everything she'd read said men needed visual stimulation to light their erotic fires. Why should she resent accommodating Bill now and then? Certainly, he could have asked for worse – a French maid's outfit, or having her dress him in diapers. She loved him, right? She shouldn't mind wearing this flattering leather bikini.

A quiet tap on the door told her she'd kept her partner waiting too long.

'Don't forget the shoes,' he said, his voice muffled by the thick old wood.

Abby bit back a sigh. She cast a reluctant glance at the five-inch, patent-leather heels she'd kicked under the pedestal sink. The same day she'd agreed to Bill's request to dress up he drove all the way to Boston to buy the things. He was like a five-year-old at Christmas when he returned, so excited he'd wanted her to ditch work and try everything on. He'd forgotten she couldn't leave the restaurant this close to tourist season, not when she was doing double duty as manager and chef. But today was Saturday. She'd caught up on stocktaking and balanced her accounts – such as they were – and renewed her chef-wanted ad in *Restaurant Monthly*. Short of getting on her knees and scrubbing the already spotless kitchen floor, she had no excuse for not being here.

'Ab?' Bill said, sounding worried now. She wished the worry were all she heard, and not his underlying petulance.

'Just a minute. I'm almost ready.' Ordering herself to be a good sport, Abby strode to the open window and slid up the screen. A delicious gust of late-May Cape Cod air blew a few blonde wisps off her face. She drew a deep, calming breath. This side of the cottage faced the ocean. She smelt salt and fish – the fresh, living kind – and some indefinable scent she could only call sunshine. Fat yellow roses climbed the weathered cedar shingles at the back of the house, then flowed in lush billows over the roof trellis. Honey bees hummed among the blooms, furry with pollen, giddy with spring.

She smiled at their drunken swoops. She'd never been stung and considered, perhaps irrationally, that she and the bees were friends.

Grabbing a face cloth to protect her hands, she leant out and carefully snapped off one perfect bud. A quick rinse under the tap washed off any blackfly and nail scissors dispatched the thorns. She tucked the flower between her breasts and stepped into the tottery black shoes.

Her toes pinching already, she checked her reflection. The brief minute in the breeze had blown her upswept hair into disarray, but she supposed it didn't matter. Her big green eyes blinked sleepily behind the tousled fringe. She looked different, sensual, not like her normal self at all. Following an inexplicable impulse, she removed the rose from her cleavage and slid it into the front of the black leather panties. The petals nestled against her navel, a fragrant, floral kiss.

For some reason, the change satisfied her nascent rebellious streak. The rose was her choice, not Bill's. She would wear it as she wished.

I'm ready now, she thought, and pushed the door open before her.

* * *

3

'Oh, sugar, can you cook!' the woman purred as she thrust narrow hips off cream satin sheets and up his thick, driving cock.

Storm Dupré chuckled low in his throat, though he'd heard the joke so many times he was tempted to roll his eyes. Yes, he was a chef whose hobby was making love to women, but couldn't any of his partners be original?

Unaware that she had made a misstep, the woman lifted her arms and gripped the pale wooden rails of his headboard. The bed was a queen-sized futon, low to the ground and very firm. He and the woman filled it nicely. Storm had to admit she was lovely. The thighs that clasped his hips were long and muscular. The breasts that cushioned his chest were as full and firm as science could make them. Her skin was spa-perfect, with an all-over tan that suggested regular jaunts to European beaches.

Forgetting his annoyance, he nuzzled her professionally depilated underarm. His cock hardened a fraction more at her shiver of pleasure. He would have trailed his tongue over the sensitive skin but for the fact that she reeked of antiperspirant.

Zut alors. What was wrong with the women of Los Angeles? Either they refused to shave at all or doused themselves in scent until a man could hardly smell the woman beneath the stink. Storm loved a woman's natural perfume – the musk under her arms, between her legs, the way it changed not just with her arousal, but with her emotions. Nothing got him harder faster than the smell of a woman who wanted him – although a perfectly grilled plate of garlic shrimp came close.

He slowed his thrusting, ashamed of his lack of focus. This woman was who she was. No one had forced him to accept her advances. The least he could do was coax her body through its full range of pleasure. Aside from preparing soul-delighting food, helping women explore the true depths of their sensuality was his gift – his mission in life, he sometimes thought.

Storm smiled at his own hubris and shifted angles to catch the top of her cunt. The woman sighed with pleasure as the bulb of his cock massaged her hidden sweet spot. His smile broadened. He'd warm her up this way, nice and slow, then pull out and coax her up the slope again. He'd ply her with kisses and strokes, with pinches and whispers, with the sights and sounds of his own arousal. He'd show her how sweet delayed gratification could be.

But the woman had other ideas. She crossed her ankles behind his gently rolling buttocks. 'Harder, darling,' she demanded, arching her long, tanned throat. 'I'll never come unless you do it harder.'

Storm sighed to himself even as he obliged. Lately it seemed they all wanted it harder: harder and faster. Why did people treat sex like a cheap burger they had to wolf down between appointments or, worse, a notch on the bedpost of their self-esteem? To his mind, sex was a feast, and orgasm a treat best savoured after much anticipation. The palate, he believed, should be teased slowly, lingeringly, with an ever-changing assortment of *hors d'oeuvres*. Each bite should be allowed to melt in the mouth: this bite tangy, that bite sweet, each one worthy of appreciation. When it came to sex, hunger was a gift, not an inconvenience. It should be stoked to excruciating heights, not sated as soon as it rose.

Why was everyone in LA in such a goddamn hurry?

The woman groaned, picking up still more speed. Her hands slid up and down his back. Her long nails pricked his buttocks. Her cunt gripped his cock like a blood-pressure cuff. 'Ooh, you're so big and hard. Oh, yes. Ram it home, darling. Ram it hard.'

Storm rammed, his body delighting despite his philosophical disapproval. Since he knew he wouldn't last long at this pace, he slipped his hand between their bodies. Her clit was a wet, hard berry swimming in cream. He should have been rolling it against his tongue. He should have been suckling it to screaming, jangling longing.

'Harder,' she said as he rubbed the slippery jewel. 'Harder!'

Fine, he thought. I'll give you harder. He jammed his thumb over her clitoris and slammed in full force, full speed. She began to wail in a way that sounded practised, though he didn't doubt the genuineness of her body's response. A flood of juice washed over his churning cock. He closed his eyes and put all his awareness into his penis, into the tight hug of her body, the warmth, the pre-orgasmic flutters. His glans squirmed happily against the hot, wet folds of her sheath. He could smell her now, tangy and rich. The pressure in his balls increased, the sense of impending crisis. His thigh muscles tightened.

Yes, he thought, ready to catch the wave. Yes.

'Yes,' she screeched, distracting him. 'Yes, darling, yes!'

She sounded like a starlet auditioning for a pornographic film, rather than the successful caterer she was. In direct contrast to his usual pattern, he lost the urge to come entirely as she climaxed. Mindful of her needs, he continued thrusting until her shudders died, then pulled out and discarded his empty condom. The woman followed him to the edge of the bed.

'Mm,' she said, rubbing her naked front across his naked back. 'You're every bit as good as Sheila said.'

How the hell would you know? he wondered, less than impressed with his own performance. He eased her roving hands off his chest, consoling them with a gentle kiss. The last thing he wanted was for her to discover his erection and suggest a second round. He grabbed his silk robe off the sand-coloured chaise longue and tied it, careful to keep his back to her.

'I'm sorry,' he said, struggling not to let distaste creep into his voice. 'But I've got to be at work in an hour and I need to shower.'

'Oh, sure.' She sounded disconcerted. 'You won't forget my offer, though, will you? I think we'd work well together.'

He looked back over his shoulder. She was pulling her bra on, a filmy green stretch-thing. Under other circumstances, he would have enjoyed the show, but now he felt empty – not to mention a little grimy. He was reasonably certain the bump and grind they'd just shared had been his real job interview.

'I've been thinking of opening my own restaurant,' he said, though until this moment the thought had been no more than a daydream.

'Oh,' she said, startled again. She wriggled into her matching green panties and smoothed her flat stomach with an air of satisfaction. 'Well, you definitely should, darling. You're much too gifted to be languishing at that dinky place on Melrose Avenue. Spago's I could see. Of course, everyone is in Wolfgang's shadow there and you're not the shadow-standing type, are you?'

'No,' he said, amused by her combination of name-dropping and insult. For the past eight years that 'dinky place on Melrose' had paid him a salary so astronomical he could almost afford his own place – not in LA, he supposed, but somewhere.

The woman cocked her head at him, clearly gauging his prospects. He was personable, he imagined her thinking – charming as well as talented, determined, self-disciplined. She knew his boss and had probably heard stories of how Storm occasionally strong-armed

Jimmy into letting him have his way – always to the eventual benefit of the restaurant. Storm's culinary flair had put Jimmy Dee's on the must-visit map. Producers ate there now; starlets, agents, people who mattered.

The woman fluffed her tastefully streaked hair and smiled. Storm knew the verdict had come out in his favour.

'I'll leave my friend Nancy's card,' she said, no doubt hoping to ingratiate herself with a man whose name might be worth dropping in the future. 'She's an estate agent. When you're ready to scout locations, she'll be happy to take care of you.'

I'm sure she will, he thought, pasting a fake smile over the queasy feeling this conversation was giving him.

To his relief, the woman was gone when he emerged from his shower. Rubbing his dark, shoulder-length hair with a towel, he paced to the open window and looked out over busy Santa Monica Boulevard. The ubiquitous palm trees wávered behind a haze of car exhaust. Fronds drooping, they looked more like weary drabs than harbingers of paradise. The same smoggy, salty breeze that set their fronds swaying blew sheer white fabric against his naked chest.

His decorator had chosen these curtains, along with the beige Berber carpets and the sleek modern furniture. 'Serenity,' she'd intoned, 'minimalist earth- and sand-toned serenity'. The end result was serene and uncluttered and even, to a certain extent, him. But his flat felt more like a picture in a decorating magazine than a home.

He'd assumed a professional would do better than he could. With his upbringing, he didn't know how a home was supposed to look. He only knew it didn't look like this.

Something on the bedside table caught his eye: a

glossy magazine. He picked it up. *Restaurant Monthly*. The woman must have left it. He hoped she wouldn't use it as an excuse to return. He paged idly through the issue, calmed by the pictures of gourmet cuisine. A flaming banana rum cake made him smile like a woman at a particularly adorable baby. He'd made his first flambé at the age of thirteen. How Mrs Kozlakis had clapped. A favourite recipe is like a trusted friend, she'd said, and she'd been right. Flipping ahead, he admired the presentation of a fan of chargrilled chicken breasts. Then, near the back, where the cheaper ads clustered, a black and white photograph caught his eye. It showed a woman standing in front of a quaint two-storey house.

Without warning, his heart gave a great pound and his face flashed hot, as though his blood was rushing to his extremities. Love at first sight, he thought, one finger rising up the clapboard siding to the picturesque widow's walk on the roof. He smiled at the overflowing window boxes, at the fat brick chimney, at the bird-filled bird's nest in the shady oak. Now this was a home.

THE COATES INN, said the hand-painted sign next to the blurry little woman – the owner, he presumed.

'The Coates Inn,' he murmured, and a second flush of excitement warmed his chest. Fate, he thought, having lived in California too long not to believe in such things.

He scanned the copy beneath the picture.

'Prime Cape Cod location,' said the header. Cranberries fresh from the bog, he thought, his imagination beginning to spin. He read on. 'Competitive salary and benefits ... room and board ... fabulous opportunity to put your stamp on a thriving family concern ...' Ah hah! The Coates Inn was looking for a chef.

Storm laughed out loud and kissed the photograph. It was perfect. So what if Massachusetts was clear across the country? From what little he knew, they had a nice ocean, fresh air, no crazy actor types, and all the oysters you could eat. Best of all, the tone of the ad sounded a mite too cheery, as if they were desperate for a good chef, as if they might go belly-up if they didn't get one.

Unless his business radar had failed him entirely, the Coates Inn was a cherry ripe for plucking. Lucky for Storm, he knew all about plucking cherries, plucking them and letting them stew in their own juice.

Abby's room was done up country-French style with big overstuffed chairs, lots of chintz and ruffles and purposely 'distressed' secondhand furniture. The walls above the white wainscotting were painted a rich, cinnamon pink. Bill fitted the flowery decor like a bull in a china shop, but he'd been here so many times in the last four years, Abby hardly noticed. Now he sat on the edge of her high tester bed and stared. His eyes trailed over every scrap of clinging black leather before fastening, spellbound, on the yellow rose that hugged the lower curve of her belly. His mouth fell open.

'Jesus,' was all he said, his butcher's hands kneading and releasing his hairy, trunk-like thighs.

Bill was a big man, a big ol' teddy bear, according to Abby's two sisters, who didn't understand why she kept declining his marriage proposals. At six foot three, two hundred who-knew-what, he made Abby feel slim and delicate rather than short and solid. His size was no small part of what had attracted her to him, along with his unfailing gentleness. Even now, with his chest heaving and his cock bouncing in his boxers like a toddler on a bed, she knew he'd make no move towards her until she indicated she'd welcome one.

'Jesus,' he said again. 'Ab, you look . . .' He shook his head, completely dumbstruck.

Suddenly self-conscious, Abby crossed her hands over her belly. 'You don't think this makes me look fat?'

As soon as the words were out, she could have kicked herself. She wasn't fat. She knew she wasn't. She was a healthy young woman with the sense not to diet down to stick-hood, but sometimes she just couldn't believe in her bones that she was attractive.

'Ab,' Bill said, shaking his head again. He lumbered off the bed and went to his knees before her. He kissed her belly on either side of the rose, reverently, gratefully. His neatly trimmed beard brushed her skin. 'You're the most beautiful woman I know. You're smart and kind and you cook the best clam chowder in New England.'

Her nervousness abating, Abby laughed and stroked his short dark hair. The way to Bill's heart had definitely been through his stomach. Taking her caress as permission, his hands roved up the back of her legs and cupped her bottom cheeks through the butter-soft leather. He growled against her belly. Like an animal, he opened his mouth and nipped its curve between his teeth.

'You look so sexy I could scream,' he said, then grabbed her up and tossed her on to the bed as if she weighed no more than a child.

Abby let out a shriek of startled delight. One of her heels tumbled with a clatter to the floor. Bill gasped and picked it up. As though the shoe had been hurt and needed soothing, he rubbed it across his chest before slipping it back on her foot. It was a strange gesture; one she was sure he made without thinking.

She glanced at his crotch. His cock was so erect the head was poking through the vent of his pale-blue shorts. Bill didn't usually get this hard until they'd engaged in a bit of foreplay – a good thing, too, since his family jewels were proportioned to the rest of him: big, thick and meaty. Intrigued, she stretched her leg, caught his testicles on her pointy toe and lifted.

To her surprise, Bill moaned and clasped her ankle. Holding the back of the shoe with his other hand, he rubbed her foot over his joggly sac, working the point over and into his hidden curves. His boxers felt warm and sweaty, his balls taut and full. A trickle of pre-come rolled down the head of his cock. Abby's womb tightened at the sight, despite the fact that his behaviour unnerved her. This outfit really turned him on. She liked knowing she could reduce this big, strong man to jelly with a flick of her toe; she just wished she had more to do with it than the spike-heeled shoes.

'Oh, God,' he said, suddenly dropping her foot and yanking down his shorts. His cock stood straight out from his body, as red as if it had been dipped in a lobster pot. It jiggled with his movements as he climbed on to the bed. It hung and swayed as he straddled her. It pounded as he kneed her thighs apart. It bobbed as his hips swung down to take her.

'Bill,' she said nervously, because she wasn't sure she was ready to be taken.

'Right,' he said on a heavy breath. 'Got to make you wet.'

He looked at the bikini top and stroked his moustache. Abby loved having her nipples sucked. She was small, it was true, but very sensitive. Unfortunately, she had a strong suspicion she wasn't going to get any suckling today, not if it meant removing Bill's arousal aide.

Sure enough, he avoided her breasts and began kissing his way down her belly.

Well, all right, she thought. I like that, too.

The crotch of the bikini was narrow but, rather than push it aside, he took it in his mouth and licked her around the barrier. Like a dog with a chew toy, she thought, and had to scold herself again. As usual, he didn't get the pressure or the positioning quite right. To give Bill credit, he often asked what sort of touch she preferred. The problem was, if she said anything besides 'that's great, keep it up' he got defensive and invariably forgot her instructions.

You can't blame him if you don't speak up, she told herself, but at the same time a little voice said: there's something wrong here if you don't care enough to speak up anymore.

Nonsense, she thought. Bill was a wonderful lover – considerate, vigorous. If the earth didn't shake when they made love, that was because the earth only shook in romance novels. Count your blessings, she ordered, and buried her hands in his thick, straight hair. Her nails were clipped short for kitchen work, perfectly safe for a good scratching. She raked them from his temples to his nape, firm, scalp-warming strokes. Bill uttered a deep, pleasured sound and licked her harder.

'Oh, yes,' she gasped, as he inadvertently hit the right spot. 'Don't stop. That's perfect.'

'You're perfect,' he said, lifting his head and crawling up her body. 'I can't wait, sweetheart. I've got to have you now.'

He looked so desperate she didn't have the heart to protest. Instead, she lifted her knees. Pushing the damp crotch of her bikini to the side, Bill took his big banger in his hand and guided it to her gate. He dropped on to his elbows.

'Ah,' he sighed, surging halfway in. 'Tight. You're always so...' His words dissolved into moans as her body gave way before his steady pressure, sooner than it usually did. She was wet and slick inside. His arousal had aroused her, in spite of her ambivalence.

She hugged his hovering bulk and he grunted, already starting to thrust. He rarely spoke once he'd entered her, as if the act of penetration precluded all but the most primitive communication. Abby didn't mind. She liked grunting, actually; it was sexy. Sometimes, though, she wished she knew what was going on inside his head when they made love, that she didn't have to guess – and that he didn't, either.

'Mmph,' he said, pushing up straight-armed so he could swing his hips faster. 'Agh, Abby, Abby.'

The sound of her name, not to mention the panic in his voice, startled her from her thoughts. She looked up at him. His face was red, twisted with effort and so sweaty his beard had gone damp. His eyes were glued to her breasts, joggling now behind triangles of snug black leather.

My God, she thought. He can't hold back. He's going to come already. The realisation sent a quicksilver flash of excitement through her sex. Her sheath tightened. He groaned again and pushed harder.

'Ab. Jesus.' He jerked his thighs wider, spreading her, stretching the tendons near her groin to the edge of pain. The bikini's gusset, shoved aside in his haste, cinched her left pussy lip flush to his cock. She could feel her own wetness on his skin, feel his grossly swollen veins. 'Ab. I can't –'

The telltale ache of impending orgasm swelled between her legs, stronger than she could ever remember feeling it.

'It's all right,' she gasped, throwing her hips off the mattress to meet his choppy thrusts. 'I'm almost there. Keep going. Keep going. Oh, Lord –' She came a second before he did. The long rolling spasm seemed to go on and on, as if his noisy, heartfelt groans were keeping it going. Finally, though, they both finished shaking.

He collapsed on top of her like a ton of bricks. Squeaking under his weight, she pushed hard until he rolled to the side. He sighed sleepily and captured her breast in one meaty hand, covering both it and the bikini.

'Thawasgood,' he slurred into her neck. 'First time we came together.'

Abby stroked his big, damp shoulder and wondered why that fact didn't seem more momentous. She hummed a noncommittal response.

'Told you you'd like it,' he said. 'Next time you can wear the boots.'

Abby's afterglow faded with the tightening of her neck. Was she supposed to wear his little costumes all the time now? Was that the price of today's better-than-average pleasure? For once, she didn't push back her annoyance but let it swell into full-fledged anger. With a huff of effort, she pushed Bill off her chest and sat up. He goggled at her, his mouth hanging slack within his beaver-coloured beard.

'I think we need to have a break from each other,' she said.

Bill gasped. She almost gasped herself. She hadn't known she was going to say that. The hurt in his eyes made her wince but, rather than take the words back, she fisted her hands in the rumpled bed covers.

'But I thought you liked it,' he said. 'You came harder than you ever have.'

Abby blushed and stared at her clenched hands. She wondered how she was going to explain this abrupt and rather intense urge to have him out of her life.

'If it's about the boots, we don't have to –'

'It's not about the fucking boots!' she shouted, then covered her mouth in shock. She never cursed, never.

Bill's face turned soft and compassionate then, as if she were a child having a tantrum. He laid his hand over her knee. 'What's this all about?'

Abby felt sick to her stomach. Suddenly she knew she'd been wanting to do this for a long time. But how was she going to tell him? How was she going to make her wishes clear? 'It's . . . It's just . . .'

'What, sweetheart?' His palm squeezed her kneecap.

God, did he have to be so nice? She took a deep breath and forced herself to look him in the eye. 'It's not about the boots. It's about the fact that I don't want to wear the boots for you.'

'Oh,' he said. She could see his mind working, trying simultaneously to decipher and deny. 'Well, I understand, I suppose. Some women don't feel comfortable –'

'Bill.' She covered his hand. 'I'm saying I resent wearing the boots for you, but I might not mind wearing them for someone else.'

'But –'

'Our relationship isn't working for me. I think I need something else.' There. She'd said it. Despite her discomfort at hurting one of her oldest friends, she experienced a wonderful sense of exhilaration, like a spring rainstorm blowing through a musty attic.

'You need a break,' he said, returning to the one statement that now seemed tolerable. He pulled his hand out from under hers and swung his heavy body off the bed. Visibly in retreat, he gathered his clothes and began pulling them on. The change he always kept in his trouser pockets jingled. The sound was so familiar it brought an unexpected tear to her eye.

'I might need a permanent break,' she warned.

Bill looked up from fastening his belt. For a moment he just stared. When he spoke his voice was low and controlled. 'I'm not giving up on you, Ab.'

'Maybe it would be better if you did.'

He blinked, then covered the distance between them in a single stride and lifted her by the back of her neck. Legs bent, feet dragging sideways on the bed, she clutched his shoulders for balance as he pressed a hard, angry kiss into her startled mouth. His tongue filled her, thick and choking. If this was meant as a display of sensual mastery, it failed miserably. Abby began to cry, not because he was hurting her, but because she felt so sorry for him.

Her tears made him break away. He gave her a little shake, then let her fall back on to the mattress. 'I'm not giving up,' he repeated through gritted teeth. 'I love you, Ab, as much as you love me.'

Which probably isn't saying much, she thought as she watched him storm out the door.

Marissa ducked into the bathroom in time to miss being run over by Abby's angry boyfriend. She sagged back against the cool pink-and-black tile wall, her body shaking with a fine, rapid tremor. She could still see Abby's face as she'd climaxed, the adorable preparatory pucker between her flaxen brows, the flush on her peachy skin, the final gasp for air and then her look of childlike wonder as the pleasure rolled through her and her muscles went slack with relief.

Oh, God. Oh, God. Curling both hands into fists, Marissa pressed them hard between her legs, grinding them over the awful, throbbing ache. She wanted Abby so bad it hurt.

She swore under her breath. Don't do this to yourself, she ordered. Gemma warned you Abby doesn't swing both ways. Just because she gave poor old Bill the boot doesn't mean your chances are one iota better than they were before.

Gemma had been Abby's roommate at college and, later, Marissa's lover. Gemma liked to joke that Marissa was her mid-life crisis, even though Marissa was just five years younger, and Gemma was only thirty. Since they never fell in love, the relationship ended amicably. When Marissa fled Boston for the Cape, Gemma was happy to recommend her for employment to an old school chum.

Marissa called her former lover a week after she started working at the inn.

'I think she's the one,' she'd gushed with a naivety that made her cringe today. 'She's got a boyfriend but he's a jerk and I don't think she really loves him. Oh, Gemma. Every time I see her I get butterflies. I've never met anyone so pretty and sweet. Last night we talked until two in the morning about the most incredible things and she really listened; she really understood.'

That's when Gemma warned her what a straight arrow Abby was.

'If I couldn't seduce her, no one could,' Gemma said, 'and, believe me, I tried.'

This was probably true. Gemma was a wisecracking, redheaded Amazon with a knack for coaxing people past their normal comfort zones. She often said that, given time, she could joke a nun into bed.

So Marissa had tried to stop dreaming about Abby; had tried not to notice the baby-soft curve of her cheek, the strength of her hands as they worked side by side in the kitchen, the compassion in her limpid green eyes whenever anyone came to her with a problem. Her efforts were all in vain. Her throat tightened twenty times a day with an urge to explore her employer's rose-pink mouth. Her hands itched to touch her. Her cunt ached to be touched.

Abruptly overcome, Marissa slid down the tiles and worked both hands under her skin-tight black cycling shorts. Her fingers delved between her swollen lips, spreading her wetness, brushing the hard, hot button of her clit. Her knees sagged to either side and she closed her eyes. The image of Abby's orgasming face drifted through her mind. Swallowing a moan, she thrust two curled fingers into her sheath, searching out the sensitive cushion behind her pubic bone. She pressed it hard and pinched her clit with her other hand, a machine-gun rhythm that never failed to bring her, or her partners, off.

'Abby,' she mouthed, recalling the brief glimpse of shiny, pink pussy she'd seen through the open bedroom door. How delicate it had been, how plump and sumptuous. I'd suck you till you came, she thought, remembering how Bill had mounted her too impatiently, too roughly. You'd never go wanting with me.

God, she could almost taste Abby on her tongue – soft, smooth, musky-briny like the ocean. Abby would touch Marissa's hair the way she'd touched Bill's. She'd stroke her shoulder, touch her breast with shy, trembling fingers . . .

A climax wrenched Marissa's pussy tight around her fingers. She bit her lip, a little grunt the only noise that issued from her throat as the contractions came and came.

Stupid, she thought a minute later as she pushed to her feet and splashed water on her face. Stupid, stupid, stupid. She looked at herself in the bathroom cabinet mirror, at her sharp bones and hard brown eyes, at her spiky hennaed hair, at the pretty gold ring in her nose and wide thin slash of her mouth. Gemma said she was striking; said she had the kind of looks no one could ignore. Her mother said she'd be pretty if only she'd take more care. Marissa herself thought she'd do, but she'd never stop traffic; not like Gemma and not, in a quieter way, like Abby.

Not that devastating looks carried much weight with her boss. Bill was, at best, pleasant-looking and, at worst, a clod.

'Idiot,' she told her reflection.

She found Abby slumped in the centre of her bed, blowing mightily into a Kleenex. Looking up in surprise, Abby gave her nose one last swipe and tossed the crumpled tissue into a small wicker bin. The tip of her nose was pink and her eyes were swollen. Her hair, fine as spun sugar, draggled off her head like a bird's nest after a storm. Marissa still thought she was the prettiest thing she'd ever seen.

She sat next to Abby on the flowery coverlet and took a second to look around. She loved this room. It made her feel safe and pampered even though she'd never choose anything so feminine for herself. The air still smelt of sex, but Abby had pulled an old pink T-shirt over the leather bikini. Marissa tried not to stare at the long, clean curves of her thighs.

'I saw Bill tearing out of here,' she said. 'I take it you finally dumped him.'

'Yes,' Abby admitted, too upset to ask what Marissa was doing there. She pulled another tissue from the box on the bedside table and began to worry it between her hands. 'I'm pretty sure it was the right thing to do, though I dread telling my sisters. Fran would marry him herself if bigamy weren't illegal.'

Marissa patted her knee and tried not to notice how silky it was. 'You did the right thing. Bill wanted a caretaker and you already do too much of that. Speaking of which . . .' Reluctantly, she released Abby's knee. 'I'm here because Francine is over at the restaurant. She wants you to babysit tonight.'

'Oh,' Abby said, already beginning to rise.

'No.' Marissa caught her shoulder and pushed her down again. 'The last thing you need right now is an evening with those squalling brats. Your sister has to learn to plan ahead. It's not as if no one else on Cape Cod could take care of her kids – your other sister for one. I mean, she can only spend so many hours a day writing that awful poetry.'

'Even so,' Abby said, 'I should tell her "no" in person.'

Marissa scratched her temple and laughed. 'That's hard to do when she's got one monster hanging from either hand, both bouncing with excitement at the thought of spending the night with their Auntie Abigail.'

Abby's eyes widened. 'Francine brought the kids? She must be desperate.'

'Most likely Richard got his bi-monthly erection and she doesn't want it to go to waste.'

Abby gasped out a laugh and smacked Marissa's knee. 'You are so bad!'

'Bad but wise,' Marissa said, her chest warming painfully at the moment of female bonding. 'Why don't I tell her you're suffering from a killer sinus headache? Then you and I can drive up to Provincetown and drown our sorrows in a pitcher of margarita.'

Abby smiled gently and Marissa knew the answer was no. Her face stiffened to hide her disappointment.

'The headache story sounds fine,' Abby said, 'and I thank you for looking out for me. I think I need some time to myself, though. Bill and I went together for four years and, tempting as your invitation is, I don't think a gallon of margarita would help me sort out my feelings.'

'Sure,' said Marissa. She stood and began backing towards the door. 'I understand. We'll take a raincheck.'

'Absolutely,' Abby agreed.

Marissa hoped to God the look she saw on Abby's face wasn't pity.

2

Storm could not get from LA to the Cape in one go. He had to take a puddle jumper from Boston to Barnstable. The little plane touched down in mid-afternoon. To his disappointment, the overcast sky prevented him from observing the peninsula's famous 'beckoning arm'.

The Cape was an island – just barely. In 1914 the Cape Cod Canal freed the peninsula from the geographical tyranny of Massachusetts. He knew from his research that the pilgrims spent their first months in the New World here. Nowadays, the pilgrims had cameras round their necks and sand in their shorts. Between the fourth of July and the dog days of August, they came to spend the few precious weeks or weekends they could spare from their jobs. While they remained, they tripled the population. Locals called them the Summer People.

Sometimes Summer People fell in love with the Cape. They returned year after year and then, if fate had blessed their bank accounts, they retired here. The harsh winter weather did not dissuade them, nor the creeping incursions of developers. They knew where to find the Old Cape, the real Cape.

Storm understood their obsession. After dog-earing one smudgy photograph of a 250-year-old house and a handful of tourist guides, he'd been infatuated enough to follow his impulse out here. Now the feel of new ground under his feet set his heart racing. He covered the distance to the hire-car firm in no time. He'd leased a French green convertible, a celebration of his new start. For a moment – but only a moment – the manager's gloomy demeanour cut through his excitement. The big, bearded man looked as if he'd lost his best friend.

Woman trouble, Storm deduced as he tossed his luggage in the boot. He was glad he had arranged his life, and himself, to circumvent the annoyance of a broken heart – unless it was someone else's broken heart, and even that could be avoided if one was honest about one's intentions from the start. A dedication to sexual exploration required that one's heart remain warm but mild. If more men acknowledged that home truth, there wouldn't be so many dragging about with their tails between their legs.

Pleased with his own wisdom, Storm manoeuvred the sporty green Miata on to 6A, the mid-Cape highway. He was headed for a village called Picker's Hollow, nestled – according to his guide book – just above South Wellfleet and happily ensconced within the Cape Cod National Seashore Project. In essence, his future home was protected by federal law from overdevelopment.

Yet another sign of his supremely good sense, he thought as he checked the lay of the land. Flying in to Provincetown would have shaved an hour off his drive time, but time wasn't the issue. The longer Barnstable route allowed him to see what traffic this resort area supported during the off season – and to run his eye over his restaurant's potential competition.

Steering with one hand, Storm brushed his long hair back from his face. The early-June day was cool. A pearly fog blanketed the roadside motels, lending them an unearned, nostalgic air. Between these gentle reminders of the modern day, he spotted salt marshes and pine groves, open moors and tiny quicksilver ponds complete with patient fishermen. Narrow back roads led off from the highway. Along their shady verges he saw houses of similar vintage to the one that had lured him here.

Some were covered in crisp white clapboard, others in weathered cedar shingle. All stirred a pleasant pang of longing in his chest – pleasant because his dream of owning such a place seemed for once achievable.

He had investigated the local property values. They were high, but so was the balance in his brokerage account. If he played his cards close to his chest and chose the right moment to bid, he'd take the pot with no trouble.

As a further sign of serendipity, he rolled into the car park behind the Coates Inn in time for the evening meal.

He knew the ocean was near. He could hear the meditative shush-shush-shush of breakers on the shore. The air was sharp with sea smells, and the heady scent of roses blooming nearby was dizzying to a man with his sensitive nose.

He climbed out of the low-slung car and donned his linen jacket. Shaking the kinks out of his legs, he looked around. Two rectangular wings extended backwards from the black-shuttered white house. Between their stiff embrace a tidy herb garden sloped to a windbreak of hemlock and pine. The paint on the wings was peeling. They looked sturdy enough, but uninhabited. Apparently, the inn was not currently fit for guests.

On the lookout for further flaws, he ambled to the front of the eighteenth-century house. Here the view did not disappoint. The past seemed imprinted on the pristine clapboard: a soft vibration tingled seductively over his skin. In his mind he heard games of tag and a rope swing creaking in the shady oak. For generations, children had played here and squabbled and had their boo-hoos kissed by loving parents. He looked up at the widow's walk and pictured a whaling captain's wife standing braced on the railing, her hair and dress whipped back by the wind, her eyes fixed on the endless expanse of the Atlantic, waiting for her man.

His cock stirred within his trousers as he imagined reunions after months at sea. What would it be like to do without sex that long? From the age of seventeen he hadn't gone more than a week between encounters. After a month, would you rip off your clothes and do it on the doorstep? Would your woman drag you to the bedroom and lock you in? An image formed in his mind: tiny mother-of-pearl buttons marching up a slender female back. A single forceful wrench would scatter them, creating music to accompany deep kisses of homecoming.

I want this place, he thought, and his arousal surged as much at the idea of owning the inn as for his fantasy.

Shaking his head at himself, he crunched up the oyster-shell path. A border of yellow and purple irises led him to a brass-handled front door. He filled his lungs with sweet Atlantic air and tugged it open.

He smiled. The interior was everything he'd hoped, homey and warm with a collection of worn but not ragged antiques. The floor was oilcloth painted to resemble marble, the old-fashioned version of linoleum – in good condition, too. One of the local craftspeople must have restored it. He nodded in approval, then frowned.

PLEASE WAIT TO BE SEATED, said the sign beside the empty hostess station.

Eh bien, he thought. It will be interesting to see how long this takes. He crossed the hall to examine a photograph of dunes iced in snow and fringed with golden beach grass. The hand-lettered card beneath the frame said JACK WESTON, $575. A bargain at any price, he thought, though he wasn't one for acquiring art. Something about the image moved him, the purity maybe, or the sense of timeless peace. He was promising himself he'd consider buying it when a small, smiling woman with astonishingly blonde hair bustled out to greet him.

His first impression was that she was soft all over, from the wisps of hair that escaped her French braid, to the humour in her clear green eyes, to the pink cashmere twin set whose sleeves she'd pushed to her elbows. Her flowing flowered skirt hid all of her legs except for a pair of trim, tapered ankles. His eyes slid back to her chest. Her breasts jiggled as she walked. She wore no brassiere. No doubt she considered her attributes too small for containment. He appreciated the oversight. Her nipples had a lovely pouty shape, their areolas swollen though not erect.

He wondered if this was a sign that they were sensitive. Perhaps she was one of those rare women who could orgasm from being suckled. He had never met one, but it would be interesting to find out. Already verging on tumescence, his cock pushed against the confinement of its skin, a sleepy animal squirming awake.

Coming to a halt before him, the cuddly little blonde clapped her hands to her cheeks. 'Oh, dear,' she said, looking him up and down. 'I bet you're hungry.'

For a second, he thought she had spotted his erection, but her expression was far too innocent for that.

'Come with me,' she said, taking his elbow and steering him into the airy dining room. Her touch sent a fierce pulse of awareness to his groin. 'I'm afraid our hostess called in sick today and we're a bit short-staffed. Let me get you settled and I'll have the waitress come by in a few minutes for your order.'

She led him to a white-draped table in a corner between two tall windows. His elbow tingled when she let it go. She handed him a menu, took his drink order and disappeared in the same flurry with which she'd arrived.

Storm's erection subsided with her departure but did not disappear. He could still smell her, a light, spicy mingling of lavender and orange blossom which enhanced her underlying scent. If a woman had to wear perfume, he thought, it ought to be a perfume like that.

He flipped his napkin into his lap and wondered if she might be the owner. If she was, the negotiation process could be more interesting than he'd expected.

He perused the menu with a practised eye, then gazed at his fellow diners. Off season or not, the place was woefully under-patronised. He counted two married couples, a silver-haired fisherman type scribbling in a notebook between bites of oyster stew, and three giggling college girls who were making a meal of salad and side dishes.

The skinny, spike-haired waitress seemed to know these women weren't likely to tip. She was ignoring their nearly empty water glasses in favour of picking lacquer off her nails. Storm narrowed his eyes. She wore a gauzy, mud-brown smock over a pair of tight black cycling shorts – hardly professional garb. Considering her appearance, he was pleasantly surprised when she arrived to take his order. Her manner was polite and efficient and she answered all his questions about the entrées with accuracy and aplomb.

Perhaps she wouldn't have to be fired after all.

He waited longer for the food than he considered ideal, but it was hot. The portions were huge – laughably so – and the preparation competent, if uninspired. Storm consumed his entire lobster, which was wonderfully fresh, ignored a despicable iceberg lettuce and tomato salad, and picked dubiously at an overheavy crab cake. He ordered three desserts, which earned him a raised eyebrow from the rake-thin waitress, but he was on a research mission here, not a diet.

The quality of the desserts was considerably higher than the main course. The lemon meringue tart melted in his mouth, the bittersweet chocolate rum cake caused his cock to lift its head in wonder, and the caramel-pecan crumble tasted so decadent he actually cleaned the plate, despite being quite full already. He concluded that the owner either had a good supplier or she let her sweet tooth set her kitchen priorities. Remembering the woman's soft pink cheeks and rounded build, he suspected the latter.

The dining room had cleared by the time he finished, which suited his purposes perfectly.

'I'd like to speak to the owner,' he said when the waitress arrived with his bill.

She immediately crossed her arms beneath her pointy, high-slung breasts. 'Why do you want to talk to the owner?'

He smiled reassuringly. Perhaps she thought he had a complaint. 'I'm a chef. I've come to apply for the position she advertised.'

'Oh,' said the waitress. Her arms uncrossed but she did not relax. 'You might have called ahead, you know. I'll have to see if she's got time to talk.'

Protective, aren't we? he mused, and made a note to watch his step around this young female Cerberus.

Abby ran the damp, soapy cloth down the counter, so lost in her thoughts she wasn't aware that she was lost. The stranger was more exotic than handsome. His jaw was too long, for one thing, and his mouth was unusually shaped. She touched her own, trying to re-create it in her mind. Yes, his upper lip was almost triangular. It looked temptingly soft. His nose was on the large side. It matched his jaw, but not his pretty blue-grey eyes. His clothes were expensive, but his hair was shaggy – shiny, though, so he must care for it.

He was a misassembled puzzle, she thought. His face made one want to stare, to figure out what made it so appealing. Of course, it didn't hurt that from the neck down he was drop-dead perfect.

She ran the cloth the other way, heedless of the soapy drips trickling to the floor. Out in the lobby, she'd caught him staring at Jack's photo as if he wanted to crawl inside. The expression of naked yearning disappeared the moment he caught sight of her, but it lasted long enough to brand itself on her memory. She knew it was stupid, but she couldn't suppress the urge to soothe him, as if he were an injured puppy rather than a full-grown man who probably ate women like her for breakfast.

He had that heartbreaker's look; that 'I can have any woman I want and I've proved it' look. Was he ever sexy, though! Just holding his elbow, she'd marked the heat of him, the sexual electricity. Her pussy felt swollen even now. Every so often it gave a little twitch of longing.

Ridiculous, she thought, crouching down to swipe a soapy puddle off the floor. Bill hadn't been gone a week. Her body ought to be in mourning, not panting after a man who probably wouldn't give her a second look. He probably went for fashion-model types who wore designer gowns to the grocer's, women who read the *New Yorker* and never got grease under their nails. If she had the least bit of sense, she'd keep her interest hidden and save herself some embarrassment.

Marissa's unexpected entrance made her gasp and jolt to her feet.

'One of the customers wants to talk to you about the chef's position,' she said.

A little shiver tickled the back of Abby's neck. She

just knew it was him, Mr Sexy in the linen jacket. Heart thudding in her chest, she asked Marissa which customer she meant.

Marissa studied her fingernails. 'Shortish guy. Long hair.'

Abby pressed her lips together to hide her smile. The man had been of average height and his shaggy brown hair did hang to his shoulders, but Marissa had to be blind to think that description did him justice.

'Bedroom eyes?' she added, succumbing to her urge to tease.

Marissa shrugged. 'He didn't make an appointment. Want me to show him the door?'

'Of course not.' Abby pulled the soiled apron over her head and tossed it on to a stool. 'I'll talk to anyone who'll get me out of this kitchen.' She peered at her reflection in the door to the microwave. 'Lord, look at my hair!'

Marissa's disapproving stare seemed to follow her to the dining room, but she forgot it as soon as she saw him standing by the corner table, waiting for her. He'd taken off his jacket. He wore a grey silk T-shirt beneath it and snug black trousers. She could see every lean, curved muscle through his clothes. He must work out. Nobody's genes were that good.

He reached towards her with a beautifully shaped tan hand. She put her own hand into it. A tingle shot up her arm at his firm, dry grip. A tiny muscle in her pussy quivered and, a second later, her panties were wet. Good Lord, she thought, this man was dangerous.

'Thank you for taking time to see me,' he said, smiling down at her, but not very far down. 'My name is Storm Dupré.'

He had a slight, delightful accent – soft consonants, sensual 's's and half-swallowed 'r's. French maybe, she thought, which would go with his surname. As she stared, the corners of his mouth curled upward and he lowered his silvery-blue eyes, as if his smile were a secret he couldn't share. A fan of black lashes shadowed his sculpted cheekbones.

Abby shook herself. 'Abigail Coates,' she said, her voice embarrassingly breathy. Alarmed at the sound, she released his hand. Hers was damp. She dried it on her flowered skirt. 'Marissa tells me you're a chef.'

'That's right.' He pulled out a chair and gestured her towards it. 'Why don't we sit and I'll tell you what I have in mind.'

Though his tone was not overtly suggestive, Abby couldn't suppress a blush. She cleared her throat. 'Have in mind for what?' she asked.

He proceeded to tell her. New menus, he said, with fewer dishes per night, but more variety from night to night. He'd go over her old receipts, keep the most popular dishes and jettison the rest. He'd want uniforms for the staff, nothing fancy – black trousers and clean white shirts would do. Advertising was advisable or, at the very least, press attention for the change in personnel. He was an award-winning Californian chef; he was certain they'd find him newsworthy. He didn't see any reason why the Coates Inn shouldn't be a place people ate at all year round.

'And the portions are too large,' he said, holding her with his soft, burning eyes. 'I don't propose we switch to *nouvelle cuisine* but, when it comes to eating out, a little too much is just right. People should go home feeling pampered, not pained.'

Abby nodded, just as she'd been nodding all along. The man named Storm waited.

'Oh,' she said, jerking out of the warm, floaty place where his voice had sent her. 'That all sounds very interesting. I should warn you though –' she smoothed the edge of the table cloth '– I'm on a limited budget. I can only afford to pay the salary I promised for six months and, if we aren't making money by then, I'll have to let you go. If I do all the things you suggested, we'd have to turn a profit much sooner.'

He leant back in his chair. 'Ah,' he said. The single syllable rang with foreign charm.

'Where are you from?' she asked, unable to restrain herself.

'Montreal,' he said, the word very Gallic on his lips. 'But I moved to the States when I was sixteen.'

A silence fell then, a repressive silence that did not encourage further questions. Abby fidgeted. She wondered if she ought to tell him the extra operating capital existed, but her sisters – who owned the restaurant in common with her – had dithered endlessly about freeing it up. Nervous, she looked up at him. His face gave nothing away, though in repose he appeared sad. The corners of his beautiful mouth turned down, as did his lambent eyes. No, she told herself, family business was family business. It wasn't meant to be shared with strangers, no matter how alluring and competent they seemed.

Finally, the man sat forward and rested his forearms on the table. Perhaps he'd come to a decision. Abby held her breath. She realised she wanted to hire him. Looks aside, he sounded like the sort of go-getter she needed.

'I don't think money will be a problem,' he said. 'Tourist season starts at the end of June, yes? I suspect we'll be turning customers away before July draws to a close.'

'You do?' she breathed, captivated by his confidence.

He smiled the slow, close-lipped smile she already knew must be habitual. Again, he lowered his eyes. He smoothed the edge of the table just as she had, but the gesture was different when he did it – sensual, as if it weren't a table he was touching. 'I have a secret weapon.'

'You do?' she said again, then pinched her thigh for being such a ninny. She managed this place, for goodness sake. She had a business degree from a respected university. Her family counted on her to keep her head and make sensible decisions. 'I mean, I'd need to know the secret weapon before I hired you.'

'Have you eaten?'

She shook her head. 'I usually grab something after I've finished cleaning up.'

'Well you won't have to grab anything tonight.' His eyes twinkled with devilment. 'Tonight I will lay the secret in your hands.'

The delectable Abby Coates led him through the dining room and past the servers' station. She tripped twice on the wide pine floorboards and stammered when she tried to speak. Her flusterment, obviously the result of a budding attraction, turned Storm's cock to hot, pounding stone. She was enchanting, adorable, fresh as the first spring crocus. He could hardly wait to slide between her plump pink thighs and drive them both to completion.

He would wait, though, of course. He liked to prolong the process of seduction as much as possible. No afters without starters was his motto, even if the afters were ready to leap on to your plate at the first crook of a finger.

He nodded in approval at the spotless, well-appointed kitchen. Too many owners, tired at the end of a sixteen-hour day, left the mess until morning. He was glad to see this woman shared his passion for cleanliness.

Clearly, she deserved a special reward.

Without asking permission, he walked into the

unlocked storeroom; that would have to change, too, he thought, and pawed through the materials on hand. When he found a bag of pine nuts, the decision was made.

'Angel-hair pasta with fresh fennel pesto,' he said.

She responded with a squeak. He knew the cost of the ingredients alarmed her. He silenced her protest with a level stare, one that said: Don't you think you deserve it? She backed down with a nervous smile.

He made quick work of the sauce, pouring boiling water over the tomatoes and throwing the fennel, garlic and basil into the food processor. He'd been cooking professionally since the age of sixteen – twelve if you counted his apprenticeship with Mrs Kozlakis, their neighbour in Montreal. At this stage of his career, preparation was more art than mechanics. He didn't measure. He didn't fuss. He always knew precisely what he was doing, no matter how many pots he had going.

The pasta he cooked *al dente*. He drained it with a flourishing toss better suited to a *Teppanyaki* chef. Show-off, he thought, but he couldn't restrain himself.

Abby had long since pulled a stool over to the workstation, where she watched his every move with wide-eyed awe. Her nipples had puckered like currants beneath her pink cashmere twin set. He knew some women thought watching a man cook was sexy. He was glad she was one of them, even if his trousers had grown uncomfortably tight.

He pursed his lips in amusement as he tossed pasta and pesto together. Should he warn her precisely how many aphrodisiac ingredients this fragrant dish contained? The pine nuts, the basil and the olive oil were loaded with boron, vitamin E and zinc, libido boosters all. The fennel contained trace amounts of estragole, a mild hallucinogenic. Moreover, if Mrs Kozlakis could be trusted – and Storm thought she could – the merest whiff of raw garlic was guaranteed to get anyone's blood pumping.

But perhaps it would be more scientific not to tell her. As he well knew, suggestion itself was a powerful aphrodisiac.

'*Voilà*,' he said, transferring a small, steaming mound on to a plate. With a twist of his wrist, the pasta settled into a beautiful, twining pattern. He garnished his creation with a sprig of fresh basil.

Abby applauded as he set it before her. To his amazement, he blushed.

'Oh, my.' She gazed at her plate. 'It's almost too beautiful to eat. I'm starving, though, so I will.'

She ate the way a woman should eat: slowly but with gusto, savouring each bite and occasionally moaning out her enjoyment. She'll sound good in bed, he thought, surreptitiously tugging the cloth stretched over his crotch. His cock was straining for freedom now, head up, shaft quivering. But it would wait – and thank him for it later.

'How do you feel?' he asked when she'd sucked up the last strand of angel hair.

'Wonderful.' She wiped her chin clean on a napkin. 'Almost glowy.'

Storm smiled at her. Her cheeks were pink, her lips red. She squirmed a little on her stool. *Bon*, he thought. Good. She's ready.

He stepped around the work island, coming close enough to hear the tiny catch in her breath. Reaching out, he eased a strand of falling hair from her face, his touch too light to brush skin. The hair flowed like silk over his fingertips. Her lips parted. Her mouth was a perfect Cupid's-bow, plump and soft and small. His throat tightened with a hunger to plunge his tongue inside, but he kept his voice steady. 'Do you, perhaps, feel as you do when someone kisses you?'

The gap between her lips widened, shock and arousal causing her jaw to drop. 'I don't know what you mean,' she said.

'Don't you?' He moved his hands, let the palms hover an inch from her breasts, just close enough to bathe her nipples in their heat. Her cheeks went as red as plum tomatoes, but she didn't move away.

'You can't do this,' she whispered.

'But I am testing my secret weapon.'

'You intend to treat all my customers this way?'

Laughing silently, he lowered his head until his breath stirred the fine hairs at her temple. 'It's an aphrodisiac.'

'I'm sure it is.' She fumbled for his wrists, catching them in hot damp hands and pushing. 'But it's not exactly professional.'

Her innocence was priceless. Heart warming with amusement, he squeezed the hands that were trying so hard to push his away. 'The ingredients in the pasta are aphrodisiacs. I wanted to see if they really worked.'

'Oh.' She stumbled back off her stool and pulled her cardigan together at the neck. He saw from her face that he'd hurt her feelings, though he didn't know how. 'I'm sorry,' she said. 'I thought you were making a pass at me.'

Now he understood. He was happy her hurt was so easy to soothe. He crossed the distance she'd put between them and laid one hand, very lightly, against her cheek. The feel of her skin made his eyes slide shut for a moment. Her cheek truly was as soft as a baby's bottom. All over, he thought. She'll feel like that all over.

'I am attracted to you,' he said, watching the colour come and go in her face. 'But I would never make a pass at a woman I hope to make my employer.'

'What do you call this?' she squeaked. When he chuckled and dropped his hand, she looked down at her flat-soled shoes. 'I don't think it's a good idea, mixing business and –' she hunched her shoulders '– you know.'

'No,' he said very seriously, without actually agreeing.

'Besides,' she added, 'I'm not your type.'

'But of course you are.' He caught her nervous hand. She gasped as he tugged it slowly, gently towards his bulging crotch. He gave her plenty of time to pull away. She didn't. In truth, she seemed mesmerised.

'Oh,' she moaned as he pressed it home. He decided 'oh' was his very favourite portion of her vocabulary.

'Oh,' she said again, exploring him with a surprisingly strong hand. Her fingers wandered over his swollen balls, then up his thick, stiffened shaft. Icy-hot tingles spread out from his groin as her dainty thumb dragged up the nerve-rich under-ridge. *Mon Dieu*, her touch was incredible, far more arousing than he'd expected. When she reached his glans and pushed the cloth of his trousers into its pulsing curve, he had to gulp for breath.

'You're almost as big as Bill,' she murmured.

Caught by surprise, Storm barked out a laugh.

Abby immediately released him and covered her adorable mouth. 'I can't believe I said that. I am so sorry.'

He wiped a tear of amusement from his eye. 'That's perfectly all right. Size isn't everything.' He grinned at her wail of mortification. 'I take it you have a boyfriend.'

'I used to,' she admitted and scuffed the toe of one sensible shoe atop the other. 'Maybe I should take you to your room now. I mean, just take you to your room, not ... Oh, dear, I really shouldn't have done that, should I?'

He took her trembling shoulders in his hands and squeezed until she met his eyes. 'I'm glad you touched me. I enjoyed it very much and I hope you will do it again. However,' he added, as she bit her lower lip, 'the fact that you did commits neither you nor I to anything. As far as I'm concerned, every stage of a seduction requires permission.'

Her eyes went so wide he could see the whites all around. 'Are you planning to seduce me?'

He swept his thumbs in a half-circle around her shoulders. 'If you give me half a chance.'

'I'm not sure I'm ready to be seduced.'

When he smiled, her eyes followed the curl of his lips. 'Don't worry,' he assured her. 'I prefer to move slowly, to anticipate each small concession: the touch of a hand today, tomorrow a kiss or a smile, the day after that a slow dance under the moon. Hunger is the best sauce, you know.'

She blinked, her thick golden lashes sweeping down and then up. 'You've done this a lot, haven't you?'

The comment threw him off balance, but he was careful not to show it. 'Once or twice,' he admitted because lying could only cause trouble down the road.

'Hah.' She swept loose tendrils of hair off her forehead. 'I doubt it's only been once or twice.'

'Experience can be a lovely thing,' he said mildly.

She cast a doubtful glance from under her brows. With a pleasant skip to his heart, he realised he was going to have a bit of a chase after all. But his smile must have annoyed her. She crossed her arms and set her feet like a diminutive member of the riot police. 'I don't believe there was anything in that pasta but good cooking,' she declared.

He spread his hands as if to say: have it your way.

'Do you want the job or not?' she snapped, as much as a woman with a voice like a kitten could snap.

'Absolutely,' he said, though he wanted much, much more than a job.

With a suspicious frown, she led him on a tour of the

inn, her crisp demeanour intended, he was sure, to keep him at a distance. She pointed out the staff locker rooms, the herb garden and the entrance to the now-closed north wing. He'd be staying in the south wing, she said, along with the waitress he'd met earlier. The rooms weren't anything fancy, but he'd have his own bath and he could change the furnishings however he liked.

'And nothing leaks,' she added, as though that should be the deciding factor.

He looked around the cosy sitting room. 'I like it,' he said, and he did.

An adjoining door led to a bedroom and, from there, to a pleasantly spacious bath. The furniture was all 'found' items, big fat chairs and scratched secondhand tables. Only the upholstery was new, a cheery cream-and-navy check dotted with scarlet diamonds. Another landscape photograph hung in the sitting room, this one of herons flying over a flooded marsh. He could picture himself living here after he bought the place. He needn't reopen the inn, after all. If he could not make a good income from the restaurant alone, he wasn't the chef he thought he was.

'You should air out,' she said, striding by him to fling open the inside shutters and throw up the sash.

A rose-covered cottage sat across the way, no more than a stone's throw distant. Two storeys high, it had a sharp peaked roof and the trademark dark-grey Cape Cod shingles. Swimming with roses, it looked like an illustration from a fairy tale. Its topmost window was lit against the coming night. A sight to welcome a man home, he thought, with an old hitch in his chest. In its own way, the cottage was as seductive as the inn.

'Who lives there?' he asked, coming to stand beside her.

For one telling moment she was silent. 'I do,' she said, and stalked from the room.

Storm unpacked, first his clothes, then his toys. Both bags were equally large and equally well organised. He set his personal massage oil on the small drop leaf table in front of the sitting-room window. The oil was his own recipe – a blend of sandalwood, cedar and other aromatic essences. Much lighter than most people preferred, but effective for him.

He placed his favourite Delft blue saucer on the warming tripod and poured a pool of golden oil into it, making it a private act of grace. The flick of a match lit a small bayberry candle, which he nudged beneath the dish. At once scent rose in the air, sweetness and spice. His thigh muscles heated. His shoulders relaxed.

For a moment, he contemplated pulling out his bondage straps, perhaps the leather cuffs with the Velcro fasteners. He'd noticed a bentwood chair in the bedroom. He could secure himself to it with no trouble. His balls tightened eagerly at the idea and, as a result, he discarded it.

He did not intend to spill his seed tonight, not yet, and perhaps not at all. His passion for bondage was deep and secret. Always he indulged alone, preferring not to bare his vulnerabilities to an audience. The only people who knew of his hobby were the teenage girl-friend who'd given him his first taste, and a psychiatrist he'd consulted briefly when various childhood ghosts rose up to haunt him. Both the shrink and the girlfriend had made their natural exits from his life. Only his love of rope and strap remained. He did not regret the predilection. He could not regret anything that stirred him to such an agonising pitch of desire. Given his purpose tonight, however, the bindings might prove too stimulating.

While the oil heated, Storm removed his clothes and folded them. He looked down the lean planes and curves of his body. He was harder than usual at this stage of the proceedings, angling up a bit. The old-rose colour at the root of his cock darkened towards raspberry by the time it reached the mushroom-shaped head. He was circumcised, which he regretted sometimes, though it did put everything on show. No doubt he was not as large as Abby's former boyfriend, but no woman had ever complained about his looks and he didn't think she would, either.

Smiling to himself, he placed a bath towel over the seat of one of the overstuffed armchairs. He adjusted the storm shutters until they covered two thirds of the window, then turned the chair to face the narrow view. Dusk had fallen as he made his preparations. A standard lamp with a pleated parchment shade lit the room behind him. Though muted, the glow would reveal him to any passerby. That was to the good. Storm hoped he'd be seen. In fact, his erection stretched a good half-inch at the prospect. He did not, however, wish to be obvious about it.

He sat and sank into the chair's embrace, then dabbled his fingers in the warming oil. Excitement crawled over his skin as he gazed at the lone lighted window in Abby's cottage. A shadow moved behind the glass, slim and small. She was home.

Let her see me, he prayed. Let her sense the current between us and welcome its rise. A single evening in her presence told him she was his favourite sort of woman: not a virgin, but virtually unawakened to her erotic potential. Deep down where the self hides its secrets he knew she was hungry even if, on the surface, she merely wondered what the fuss was about.

Oh, love, he thought, how happy I'll be to show you.

He closed his eyes. He must not be caught watching

her watch him. She must believe herself alone and safe in her voyeurism.

He lifted his hand from the oil and moved it over his erection. Fragrant droplets rolled down his fingers. They fell to the bobbing head, a warm, wet patter, then ran in tickly rivulets down his shaft and over his balls. He pulled his feet on to the cushion of the chair, narrow feet with long, agile toes. For an instant, he imagined them digging into her mattress as he pressed slowly inside her. Would her bed be soft like her? Would it smell of lavender and musk? Shaking off the image, he let his knees sag on to the chair's plump arms. A cool breeze slipped between the shutters and ruffled the hair around his anus. He was completely exposed now.

He dipped his hand in the oil again and let fall another rain of drops. His blood seemed to thicken in his veins. With the smallest sigh, he cupped his scrotal sac and began to massage his balls.

Was she watching yet, he wondered behind his shuttered lids, and what would he wish her to see if she was? Something that would shock her a bit. Something that would capture her attention and refuse to let it go.

He dipped his second hand in the oil and curled it into the furrow between his cheeks. Anal play excited him almost as much as bondage, but the risk was worth it. He would like her to know this about him, for the day when she changed from tempted to temptress.

Blowing his breath out lightly, he circled the puckered ring of muscle, then pushed his left middle finger firmly inside, down to the webbing. His thumb he centred over the Jen-Mo spot, an acupressure point midway between his anus and scrotum. Thus poised to halt ejaculation the moment it threatened, he willed his hand to stillness. The two pressures, on his perineum and in his anus, were pleasurable but not unbearably so.

And now to begin, he thought. With his right hand, he grasped his oily shaft, thumb on top and two fingers enclosing the ridge. He pulled upward, easing his grip as he approached the head, tightening it as he neared the less-sensitive root. Despite the precaution, his arousal spiked quickly. He couldn't help but think of her watching; couldn't help imagining how her hand would feel performing this service, small but strong, gentle but curious.

The image was too powerful. He had to back off. He lightened his strokes until his touch barely skimmed the surface of his cock. Even so, his skin stung with sensitivity, especially the drum-tight surface of the head. He felt a drop that was not oil roll down the glans. He forced himself to breath deeply, slowly. When that didn't calm him, he let go altogether.

Relax, he told himself. You've done this hundreds of times. You are not going to lose control tonight. He breathed in. He breathed out. He took hold of his shaft and resumed the massage. This time he allowed his stroke to rise only to the flare of the head. *C'est mieux*, he thought, better.

Just as he was congratulating himself, a bird took flight in the grassy space between the inn and the cottage. He started at the flurry of wings. Adrenaline flooded his bloodstream. He almost opened his eyes. Had Abby's appearance at the window alarmed the bird? Was she truly there? His excitement level surged so abruptly he had to administer a bracing pinch to keep himself from going over the top.

After a short rest, he began masturbating again, then stopped again. Four times, he repeated this pattern, each time rising more swiftly towards the point of no return. Thoughts of Abby disrupted his usual control: her soft pink lips tugging at his nipples, her thick, sun-bright hair sweeping his groin, the arch of her neck as she climaxed – all figments of his imagination but so vivid he realised tonight could be no demonstration of stamina. He must end it, and quickly, or he'd never be able to restrain himself.

Soon, he promised his clamouring cock. He was so hard now he had to pull the shaft back from his belly. He pumped harder, his fingers tight, almost rough. He gave his sensation-starved glans the attention it wanted, enclosing it with fingers and thumb at the top of every pull. His skin was hot and slick, his veins popping in tiny ropes of blue. Ah, it felt good. He never wanted to stop, but his balls were rucking up in preparation, his thighs burning. His anus quivered round the finger that pierced it. He should stop. This second, he should stop.

He squeezed out one more pump. His seed seemed to boil inside him. Out, it wanted out. One more stroke, he pleaded, risking it, loving it, but then his limit was reached. His orgasm was a breath away, a looming pressure, an ache. The first contraction fluttered. He dug his left thumb into the Jen-Mo point, halting his seminal fluid just as it exploded down his urethra.

A single, scalding spurt escaped the tip of his cock, then stopped as he increased the pressure of his thumb. He uttered a curse he couldn't hear over the roaring in his ears. Then he came in earnest – hard throbs of sensation, an orgasm slowed to quarter speed and cranked to quadruple intensity. His cock twitched with each contraction but emitted no more fluid. He came, for one minute, then another. His thighs jerked closer to his chest. He gasped for breath, his body dripping sweat. He flung his head against the back of the chair. He wriggled the finger that nestled inside his anus and came again.

Dieu, he thought, his brain reduced to one-syllable words. God. Sweet.

The contractions diminished, the sea of pleasure calming. He sighed and opened his eyes. He looked out the window towards the cottage...

And saw a slender shadow dart behind a curtain.

3

The memory of his pleasure haunted her. She lay in bed in her T-shirt and panties, with the covers shoved to her waist, and she remembered.

He'd been completely exposed. He'd pulled his feet on to the navy cushion and thrust his knees wide. She'd seen the dark pucker of his anus, and the finger he'd pushed inside. He'd opened his legs like a woman who wants to be filled, and yet she'd never sensed anyone's masculinity more forcefully. She'd been quivering with awareness, dripping with it.

He'd stroked himself. He'd oiled the stiff, thick rod so that it glistened in the lamplight. He loved his own cock; she knew from the way he touched it. He'd lingered, he'd teased, starting and stopping, starting and stopping, until she'd pressed her thighs together on a sharp throb of sympathetic longing.

Her fingers had twitched. She'd wanted to touch his swollen flesh herself, but even more she'd wanted him to come; wanted to see his hard shower of seed. That tiny jet had not satisfied her. She'd wanted fountains, oceans. Instead, he showed her that long, dry, bone-shaking convulsion. The length of it distracted her from her disappointment, and awed her. She'd thought it would never end. She'd thought she might come herself just by watching.

In all her life, she'd had two lovers: a boy in college and Bill. Nonetheless, she knew this wasn't ordinary male behaviour, neither the ritualistic auto-eroticism, nor the orgasm that wracked his body like an electric shock and refused to let go. How long had it lasted? Two minutes? Three? Had she ever seen anything like his transcendent, tormented expression?

Storm was different from other men.

Abby slid her hands down her body and cupped her panty-covered mound. She'd worked herself to three hard orgasms since she'd fled behind the curtain – three, and felt as if she'd had none; she was that hungry. This wasn't like her. Once had always been all she'd ever wanted. Had he put something in the pasta?

'Nonsense,' she said aloud for the reassurance of hearing the word. She'd watched him prepare the meal. There was nothing in that dish that wasn't perfectly ordinary.

No, his exhibition had done this to her. He'd opened his eyes at the end. Had he seen her? Had he meant for her to see? But what sort of man masturbated for an audience? A dirty old man with a raincoat, she thought. Except it wasn't like that. She couldn't say how it was different, only that it was.

She clenched her hands in front of her mouth. Maybe it was different because he'd known she wanted to see. But how had this stranger known what she hadn't known herself? Frustrated, Abby flopped on to her side. This isn't like me, she thought. This isn't me. She turned off the lamp with the fat red roses on the shade. She was exhausted. She needed sleep. But Storm followed her into her dreams.

They were waltzing on the beach under a crescent moon. She didn't actually know how to waltz but she swooped like a feather on the hard, damp sand. As they turned, her gown fluttered, filmy and white with a touch of innocence – like Clara's nightdress in the *Nutcracker* ballet. Like a true prince he danced her through the foamy edge of the waves. He smiled at her and didn't drop his eyes. She wished she could see them better. The dream was misty.

'I can't feel you,' she complained.

He pulled her closer, his palm pressing the small of her back. He was naked. 'Is that better?' he asked.

She squirmed, wanting to brand herself with the whole, hard imprint of him. His hip brushed her hip, his chest her breast. But the sensations wouldn't coalesce.

'It's not enough,' she said.

'Don't worry.' He brushed a wisp of hair from her face. 'Tonight I will lay the secret in your hands.'

She started awake and bit back an unladylike curse. Her body throbbed as though he'd teased her to the edge of satisfaction and left her hanging. The dream seemed so close, so vivid, she could almost hear the echo of his final words.

She shivered and hugged herself, then stiffened at a sudden sense of wrongness. The room was dark. The moon lit the other side of the house. The nearest illumination was the security lamps at the front of the inn. She listened, but heard nothing except her own quickened breathing and the waltz-like sweep of the curtains on the floorboards. The curtains were satin printed in large pink and yellow roses. Their hems pooled on the floor the way the Victorians used to favour, to prove they could afford more than just what they needed.

What had Storm said? 'A little too much is just right.' But how much was too much, and did he mean sex as well as food? Her pussy swelled, heavy and warm.

Something was different. The window was open. She'd left it open, but had she left it open so far? Had the breeze picked up since she went to bed? Was that why the curtains billowed out that way?

The sound made her think of sheets rustling, of making love to a stranger, slowly in the dark, without a word, just push and pull, push and pull, and throaty cries above the rustling of the sheets. She put both hands to one breast and pushed it back against her ribs. Her nipple was so hard.

A shadow detached itself from the shadow by the window.

'Pleasant dream?' it asked.

Abby's shriek was pathetic, a squeaky inhalation no louder than a mouse.

'What are you doing here?' she said, once she'd found her voice. She should have been outraged, or terrified. She was a little frightened, but it was a butterfly-in-the-stomach sort of fear. She knew the intruder's identity, of course. The way he moved gave him away: silent, confident, like an Indian rajah. He even smelt of India: sandalwood and other, more exotic spices, perhaps from the oil he'd used to rub his cock. In her mind she saw his hand again, squeezing up that thick column of flesh. She bit her lower lip.

'I thought you might want company,' he said.

I don't, she tried to say, but he was there, looming over the bed, and the words wouldn't come. Her body was melting, not just her quim, but her breasts, her bones, her tongue. She wanted company all right – his.

He pulled the light blanket down her body, then the sheet, like someone unveiling a work of art. Abby shivered. He laid his palm over her belly, pressing lightly through her T-shirt. Like magic, her shivering ceased. She was hot. His hand was hot. Was it normal to have hands that hot?

'May I remove this?' he asked, touching the hem of the cotton shirt.

She knew that if she said 'yes' to this, she'd say 'yes' to anything that might follow. But how could she refuse? She might never get another chance to sleep with a man like this, a man she'd wanted the instant she met him. Unable to speak, she nodded.

Even in the dark, he saw.

'Thank you,' he said, as though this didn't happen every day, as though he were someone who had to ask. He removed her T-shirt and panties, then folded both and laid them over the foot of the bed. Abby smiled. He was a neat-freak, she thought, liking him better for that small eccentricity.

'Tonight is for you,' he said, his accent even more wonderful in the shadowed hush, 'for your pleasure.'

'And not for yours?' she was bold enough to ask.

He growled. Really, she couldn't call it anything but a growl, soft though the sound was. The effect was delicious, like a finger trailing down her spine. Almost before she knew what he was doing he'd climbed on to the high tester bed. He crouched over her on hands and knees.

'I will definitely take pleasure in this,' he said. 'But tonight I wish to explore, not to experience, to discover what pleases you and what doesn't. For that I need all my concentration.'

'Oh,' she said, and wished she knew how to play his lush, verbal games, how to make him quiver with longing at the sound of her voice. It was probably too much to hope that he would stick around long enough to teach her.

Feeling wistful, as if this were already goodbye, she lifted her arms and lightly clasped his waist. His skin was warm and smooth, his flesh solid. He bent his head and kissed her, a slow, deep insinuation of tongue to tongue. After four years with Bill, kissing a man without a beard felt strange. Storm's lips were soft, his jaw shaved very close. He tasted faintly of anise, perfect for a woman with a sweet tooth. She moaned when he withdrew.

'No promises,' he murmured, the words tickling her lips. 'No obligations. Only pleasure.'

It sounded so appealing when he said it. 'No obligations. Only pleasure.' Hadn't she had enough of obligations, what with Bill and the restaurant and her sisters' children who were, face it, the teeniest bit bratty?

'Only pleasure,' she agreed, and felt him smile against her cheek.

Storm ran his hands down her body, one long sweep from shoulders to feet. She had the most incredible skin, smooth as silk, but not as fragile. More like velvet. The flesh beneath was soft and firm. He circled the gentle mounds of her breasts, then her belly. She tensed. A vulnerable spot, he thought, and bent to kiss it, gently, softly, until she relaxed.

Her legs were longer than he expected, and stronger. He lifted one foot and found a callus behind the heel. Perhaps she ran. That would explain the well-developed muscle of her thigh, the apple-firm round of her calf.

Her feet were small. The length of his hand covered her sole. He sucked a curled toe into his mouth and laved it with his tongue. She squirmed. Her musk rose in the air. She was silent, though, as if shyness held her cries inside. No matter, he thought. The other signs of her pleasure would read all the more clearly.

He kissed a path up her legs and parted her petals with his thumbs. Her sex glistened in the dimness, running like an open honeycomb. He inhaled deeply. Her scent swirled through his head, rich, sweet, and tinged with an exotic spice that was purely her own. That scent called to him, as if some celestial perfumer had designed her with him in mind. He was so hard his skin felt ready to burst. His testicles hung like stones in their drawn-up pouch. The temptation to eat her juicy peach until she begged for mercy was strong.

That, however, was a pleasure for another night.

He continued his upward progress, lips preceding

fingers up arms, across shoulders. He found another sweet spot under her chin, a tender little pillow of flesh. He nuzzled it until her arms came round his back. Then he laid a trail of kisses to her breasts. The lightest touch of his tongue on her nipple broke her silence. Ah, her breasts were sensitive. One cry followed another as he suckled and plucked and nipped the sharpened tips. Her legs scissored on the mattress. Her hips thrust upward, seeking penetration. He had to lift his body to remove his half-crazed cock from temptation's path.

She whimpered at his retreat but he filled her with his fingers – just two fingers, for she was tight. Her warm, thick folds clung to his knuckles as he worked her, his thumb firm on her button, his mouth busy at her breasts.

'Please.' Her head thrashed from side to side on the pillow. She seemed unable to get where she wished to go. 'Please.'

He took her hand and placed it over his. She did not move. She seemed afraid to guide him. 'Show me,' he said, and kissed her full on the mouth.

Her tongue reached for his. She sighed, and then shyly she moved his thumb. She swept it from one side of her clit to the other, rubbing the slippery hood across the shaft. When he'd caught the motion she wanted, she pressed the back of his hand as if to say: a little harder.

Good girl, he wanted to say, but feared she'd take offence.

He brought her off three times, each hard and quick.

'Enough,' she gasped, though her body still squirmed around his fingers.

He let her rest for a moment, then sat back on his heels. 'I want to show you something.'

'I don't think I can stand any more,' she pleaded even as her sheath rippled and clung.

'One more special one,' he insisted, and curled a third finger into her body. After three orgasms, the swelling behind her pubic bone was unmistakable, a delectable, fluid-filled cushion. He pressed upward, slowly increasing the pressure until at the last he was lifting her weight off the bed.

'Oh, my God,' she said. 'What is that? That is so ... oh, my God!'

He chuckled, delighted to be the first to introduce her to this pleasure.

'Abigail Coates,' he said, 'meet your G-spot.'

He covered her mound with his second hand and captured her clit between finger and thumb. She groaned. Lightly, he pinched the hood over the shaft and sleeked it up and down – not her motion, but one he thought she might like.

She did. Her hips struggled towards his hand. Her breaths came in aspirated moans.

'Please,' she said, completely beyond shyness. 'Make me come. Oh, God, I can't stand it!' Before the wail faded, her body bent up like a bow. Her sheath clenched tight. He pressed harder, within and without.

'Oh,' she cried, 'oh ...' and spurted all over his hand.

It was over in five deep shudders. She sagged back against the bed. He petted her gently down before removing his sopping fingers. He was glad she hadn't realised she'd ejaculated. Some women got nervous about that, thought they'd lost control of their bladder. He could explain the difference to Abby some other night.

'That was incredible,' she said. 'I've never felt anything so intense. How did you know I could do that?'

He bent to kiss the tip of her nose. 'I make it my business to know.'

'Your business,' she said, a funny note in her voice.

'My avocation,' he clarified.

She seemed to like that answer better because she twined her arms behind his neck and pulled his head deeper into the kiss. Mm, she had a nice mouth, firm but pliant. He hovered over her, enjoying it, the tip of his cock throbbing painfully in time to his heart. He wanted to spill, needed to, but it would wait; just a little longer, it would wait.

Abby loved his tender exploration of his mouth, that one luscious point of intermingling. She wanted more, though. Every inch of her skin was hungry for contact. She wanted all of him to touch her. Most especially, she wanted to feel his cock. She wanted to feel what she'd done to him. She needed to know he was as hard now as he'd been when he was sprawled in that chair, rubbing himself the way he liked best.

'I want you touch me,' she said, the words bursting out, hot and impetuous.

He reached above her to turn on a lamp, a sudden and shocking exposure. She flushed as he drew back on to his knees, kneeling over her like a conqueror. His hands played lightly over her breasts. 'Where would you like me to touch you?'

Not where, she thought, I want you to touch me with your cock.

'Anywhere,' she said, and could have kicked herself.

He knew she was lying. He knew. He leant down and tutted in her ear. His hair, shaggy and smooth as silk, tickled her cheek. 'Tell me what you want, love. Whisper it in my ear.'

Oh, if only he hadn't turned on the light. But he kissed her eyebrow very gently and the courage came. 'Touch me with your cock,' she whispered.

A shudder coursed through him, a glorious, carnal shudder.

'Ah,' he said, and set his teeth to her earlobe, as

though the tension inside him demanded immediate expression. His knees shifted. The heat of his groin approached hers. 'Where shall I touch you with my cock? Here?'

The satiny tip brushed from her knee to the top of her thigh. There it stilled, pressing softly, rhythmically against the valley that bordered her fleece.

'You're sticky,' she said, then wondered if that was the wrong thing to say.

He chuckled. When he spoke, his voice was rougher than before. 'I am overeager tonight.'

The admission, and the huskiness, thrilled her. 'Touch me all over.'

'With this?' He drew a curve around her belly with the hot, sticky head, then flattened the thick length of it over her hipbone. 'Or this?'

Abby rolled into the pressure. 'Yes. Both. All over.'

This time his chuckle was just an expulsion of breath. 'Want to test my limits, do you?'

'I want you to come.'

His cock jerked. 'Ah,' he said.

She loved that word in his mouth, a sigh of understanding and approval – and pleasure.

He said no more. He rubbed her with his velvet-wrapped hardness, up her thighs, around her belly. He rolled her on to her front and caressed her bottom, every inch of either cheek and then the crease between, with the head, with the shaft, with the soft-hard crush of his balls. He measured the small of her back, and trailed up the sides of her body until he could thrust once, slowly, into the pit of each arm.

Settling his knees beside her shoulders, he smoothed her hair backwards over her head, on to the pillow, and rubbed his cock along the nape of her neck. He probed each side, pushing along the underside of her jaw. Delicious, she thought, like having your whole body fucked instead of just your pussy. She purred at the feel of it, then squirmed on to her back.

'I know what I want now,' she said.

His cock jutted directly towards her face, stiff but tremulous, vibrating with the blood trapped inside. She kissed the swollen cap of the head. Oh, it was so smooth and hot, like living satin. She licked it. It jerked under her tongue.

'No,' he said, and his voice was very low, very dark. 'Not that. Not until you know me better.'

She almost laughed. His cock was straining towards her lips, practically sitting up and begging. But that hadn't been what she meant to do, in any case. The sight of him had distracted her from her original goal. 'This,' she said, pushing her small breasts together to form a shallow channel. 'I want you to come here, where I can see you.'

'Ah,' he said, relief in the word this time. He lowered himself. His hip popped slightly and then he sighed as she embraced him with her breasts.

He thrust slowly but firmly, pacing himself. She tilted her head to watch. His cock and hips filled all her vision. He had tan marks on his hipbones. She guessed he liked revealing bathing suits. He'd look gorgeous in a little Speedo – even a thong. The hollows at the side of his muscular buttocks were well worth showing off. Even his pubic hair was beautiful. A wild thick growth at the base of his belly, it gleamed in tight black curls, as if he'd oiled it along with his penis. His balls rolled back and forth over her ribs as he thrust. She squeezed her flesh tighter, surrounding more of him. He gasped and braced his weight on his arms.

His strokes lengthened until he butted the softness under her chin, the little cushion he'd loved with his earlier kiss. He left his fluid on her flesh; he was dripping now, a clear sweet trail of eagerness.

'Come,' she said.

He choked out something she couldn't understand. Her hands occupied in holding herself around him, she lifted one knee and caressed the sweaty upper curve of his buttocks.

'Come,' she whispered. 'I want you to come all over me.'

'Jesus Christ,' he said, his accent so thick she almost couldn't decipher the words.

He pushed harder, faster. The friction burnt the tender skin between her breasts, friction and his own inner heat. She watched him watch his penis. The muscles of his face tightened. His skin went dark like an Arab's. She knew he was going to come any second, so she shifted her gaze to his cock. Like his face, it was darker and stiffer. The cap was red and shiny, growing even fuller as she watched. He moved faster still. A cry caught in his throat. He held his breath. The eye at the tip seemed to widen, darken, deepen.

Yes, she thought, yes, and he came, an explosive burst of white, hot against her chin, wet running down her neck and over her breasts as he pulled back and shoved again, still pulsing, each jet shooting strong and hard as though his entire supply must burst free in an instant.

Seconds later it was over. His arms shook from holding his weight. She stroked his shoulders and his elbows buckled. He eased himself on to her. He laid his head on her sticky breast. His eyes slid shut as she stroked his hair. He was easy to hold, not all that much heavier than her.

Sleep, she thought, even as she felt him fight it. She wanted him here in the morning, wanted him in her arms. Not likely, she thought, but she could pretend.

'I left your present in my pocket,' he mumbled, trying to shake off his lassitude. He couldn't stay here. To spend the night would send messages he didn't mean to send. He had rules about such things. They'd always served him well.

'Present?' she said. Her hand continued to stroke his hair.

'A bonbon I thought we might want to carry. A cream-filled devil's cake dipped in Swiss-chocolate icing.' He sensed her mouth watering. 'Of course, it's not as spectacular as your caramel-pecan crumble, but it does have the advantage of being small. Some ladies prefer their desserts small, you know, and it does pack a powerful punch.'

'You like my pecan crumble?' she said.

He ignored the way the vulnerability in her voice cinched his chest muscles. What harm could there be in pleasing her with the truth? 'I adored your crumble,' he said.

Abby sighed happily. 'That was Dad's favourite recipe.'

Surprise made him incautious. 'Your mother didn't cook?'

Her mouth puckered and twisted at the same time. 'My mother died in childbirth – having me, actually.'

He could have kicked himself. He did not want to know her personal history any more than he wanted to spend the night. He shifted slightly, letting his weight rest on his side. 'I'm sorry. I didn't know.'

'That's all right. Dad was a great father.'

Storm debated the merits of silence. Clearly, her father was dead as well. By keeping his mouth shut, he could end the conversation here. There was one fact, however, which might be useful to know. 'You father left you the inn, yes?'

'Yes, me and my sisters. When he first got sick, I came to help him in the kitchen. I was the only daughter who didn't have a family at the time. When he died, it seemed natural that I take over as manager.'

She wrinkled her nose, which forced him to ask yet another question. 'You don't enjoy managing the inn?'

Given his purpose in coming to the Cape, he would have welcomed an affirmative. But she merely shrugged, a gesture that made her breasts shift under his chest. 'I could do without the cooking, but I love talking to customers, especially when the tourists come. I like decorating, too, and doing accounts – though they've been nothing to smile about lately. Dad wasn't the most businesslike man.' She clasped her hands behind his waist and tugged him closer. 'What about you? Are your parents alive?'

'No,' he said, because that was simplest.

'Mm,' she said, her tone thoughtful.

He tensed, fearing she'd turn sentimental or expect him to supply more detail. Women often wanted a man to turn himself inside out for them, especially after a good fuck. But Abby just continued stroking his hair around his skull until the caress made him want to close his eyes and sleep in her arms.

Fighting the urge, he pushed on to his elbows. 'I should be going. I want to get an early start tomorrow. I have to make a list of supplies we'll need for the new menu.'

'All right,' she said, releasing him without protest.

She watched him in silence as he gathered his clothes and dressed. Her face was calm, even fond. Had he wanted her to be disappointed? Perhaps he had. He knew he would have stayed if she asked. He was capable of saying no to certain women, but not the really nice ones. As he backed towards the door, a funny ache bloomed in his chest. She held the flowered cover-let to her chest, modest again, her golden hair hanging in a cloud around her shoulders. The deep-pink walls cast a glow on her as she sat in the rumple of satin roses, as though she were a fairy and this was her bower. She looked so sweet and feminine – and as far removed from his life in LA as LA was from his childhood.

Had she really begged him to come on her breasts? Had she really said, 'Touch me with your cock?'

'Good night,' she said.

Good night, he tried to answer, but the words stuck in his throat. He set her bonbon on the chair and left with nothing more than a wave.

4

Marissa pedalled her bike to Wellfleet Harbor on the bay side of the Cape. This was not the wisest thing for a woman to do in the middle of the night, even during the off season, but the trip was a matter of sanity.

She'd seen Abby at the window. She'd watched tension take hold of her body at whatever she saw in the stranger's room. She'd read the hunger in her eyes, as if she wanted to leap across the space between the buildings. The shock had kept Marissa from sleep and so she'd seen him, too, in his all-black outfit, creeping across the yard and up Abby's rose trellis like some secret ninja Romeo.

She should have called the police, but she knew why she hadn't. She was afraid this particular home invasion would be welcomed – and it was.

She'd heard nothing for a while, though she strained towards the window and bit her nails. The cries came later, first hers, then his. His were louder, hers more heartbreaking. They were deep cries: groans, pleas, moans of pleasure she doubted Bill had ever inspired, the sort of sounds a woman would be embarrassed to have anyone but her lover hear. Marissa should have buried her head under the pillow, but the situation held her spellbound. She could not tear herself away until the last sigh faded. It was like watching a car accident, except she was the one bleeding her heart out in the wreckage. Worse, her own pain hadn't prevented her from becoming aroused. Too hurt to masturbate, too hot to sleep, she slunk out the back door and grabbed her rusty, no-speed Schwinn.

Though the ocean was closer to the inn, she wanted to ride to the bay side, the peaceful side. The Cape's hook-shaped peninsula wasn't wide here, three miles at most – barely far enough to raise a sweat. She covered the distance quickly and leant her rickety bike at the end of Old Man Weston's pier.

It had to be two in the morning but he was sitting at the end of the dock, his arms propped behind him, his silver hair glinting in the moonlight. She often found him here, sometimes with his camera, sometimes not. Either he never slept or he guessed when she was coming.

Marissa wouldn't put it past him. He was like a Zen master or something, the inscrutable native Cape Codder. Her ankle boots made a hollow sound as she walked down the worn planks. The old man didn't even twitch. She looked past him. The tide was in. The sandbars slept beneath the inky water. She felt as though the night were lapping at her, mocking the painful, live-wire sensitivity of her flesh. What she wouldn't have given for a good, hard fuck!

She dropped down next to Jack, close enough to rub thighs. He had good thighs for an old guy, long and solid. His head turned as she sat, not all the way, just enough to catch her in the corner of his eye. Water slurped against the pilings.

'You don't even fish,' she said.

'Don't need to.' He shifted his hands so that his shoulder brushed hers, a reassurance kind of thing – or Marissa took it that way. 'Watching the barnacles grow is entertainment enough.'

She snorted. 'Right, old man.'

'My name is Jack.'

She ruffled her hair so that the spikes stood up

straighter. 'You let other people call you "old man." Why not me?'

'You tell me.'

His voice held a strange note. She turned sideways so she could face him straight on. Their eyes met and held, her chocolate brown to his olive brown – both black in the moonlight. A zing of sensual awareness tingled in her thighs, something she'd never caught from him before.

She scrubbed her hair and shook the sensation off. 'Nah, you're not interested in me. I'm not the one you come to see every night at the inn.'

'No, you're the one I sit on the end of this dock for.'

She bumped his shoulder. 'Don't kid a kidder, old man. You've got a thing for Abby. I can tell.' But not as big a thing as I do, she added silently. Otherwise, you wouldn't sit here letting some cocky LA playboy cut you out of the picture. You're a man, after all. You've got half a chance.

Jack drew a flat stone from the pocket of his jeans and skipped it across the rippling waters of the bay. It skipped six times before disappearing with a loud plunk. 'Did that man come for her?'

Marissa shivered. He couldn't know. He'd been buried in his journal the whole time he and the stranger had shared the dining room. 'What man?' she said.

'The man with the silver-blue eyes. Did he come for Abby?'

'He came for a job.' Jack's silence said he didn't believe her. Marissa squeezed her knees to her chest. 'You may be spooky, old man, but you don't know everything.'

'I know you're wasting precious young energy hankering after something you'll probably never get.'

'Fuck you,' she said, furious, her eyes stinging with tears. She hadn't come here for this.

He caught her arm before she could get away; caught it and held. He didn't say a word, didn't move, but the hand on her wrist spoke for him. 'I'd like to fuck you,' it said. 'We could do it right here, right now.'

'I'm capable of having more than one "thing" at a time,' he said mildly.

Marissa tried to laugh. 'I guess you think I should console myself with you.'

He seemed immune to her scorn. Maybe he could feel the pulse racing in her wrist. Maybe he could see the sharp points of her nipples beneath her ragged white T-shirt. He tilted his head and looked up at her. 'Do you only like women?'

She yanked her wrist free and rubbed it. 'I like men. Sometimes.'

'Do you like me?'

'How the hell should I know?'

He inclined his head another degree. 'Why not ask your cunt?'

The word brought a flush to her face, though she'd said plenty worse herself. He had to be fifty, older than her father. He shouldn't talk to her that way. But if he felt any remorse, he didn't show it. Instead he spread his arms in invitation. He wore an old pair of Levis, velvet-soft and ripped at the knees. Helpless to stop herself, her eyes roved. Even in the moonlight, she could see his big erection. It filled the faded patches at his crotch, a strong, thick arch. Marissa's pussy went soft at the sight, more than ready to take him up on his offer.

'Here?' She looked at the tiny lights on Indian Neck, at the oyster boat bobbing within shouting distance. 'Out in the open?'

'The moon likes you,' he said. More of his crazy Zen shit.

She accepted the compliment with a toss of her head.

'I want to be on top,' she said, setting the terms up front.

He grinned. She couldn't remember seeing him do that before, not full out and flashing teeth. It made her feel good to have inspired it. Her feet seemed to move by themselves. She straddled his thighs, Valkyrie-style. The ankle boots made the pose more effective. Jack stroked their thin leather with his fingertips, travelling up the black laces and down the stretchy insets that hugged her ankle bones. Funny. Gemma had liked her in the ankle boots, too – the ankle boots and nothing else. Maybe men and women had more in common than she'd realised.

Jack called her back to the present by sliding his hands up her legs. He tested each muscle with a squeeze: ankle, calf, thigh. Her legs were kind of skinny but they were strong and long. Jack set his forehead on her thigh and breathed out softly, as if he was tired, or maybe just overwhelmed. Whatever, the warm puff of air made her pussy go hot. With sure and gentle hands he rolled her bike shorts down.

She wore no panties. He cursed and closed his eyes as his fingers found her bushy mound. He combed through her hair, tickling, grazing, spreading the little trickles of wetness that slipped past her lips.

She couldn't keep her footing while he did that. It made her feel more than she expected. Stepping out of the bike shorts, she braced on his shoulders and knelt. His hands slid down her back and cupped her bottom. He pulled her closer until her lips parted round his denim bulge. God, he was warm. She wriggled up and down, mashing her clit into his hardness.

'Are you a noisy fuck?' he asked.

Marissa stiffened.

His lips whispered down her cheek. 'Would you

rather I said "make love," Marissa? Because it's bound to be a bit of both.'

'Just make it fast,' she said, unsettled, off-balance. 'Remember, it's my butt hanging out for all to see.'

He laughed and peeled down his zip. She watched him free himself from his briefs. He had an OK-looking thing, she supposed. The shaft was long. The head was kind of pointy, though, and it veered left a little. Not that she cared. In fact, it was kind of interesting. She touched the bullet-shaped cap. It quivered under her hand. She liked that. He pulled a condom out of his pocket and showed her how to roll it on. His preparedness almost made her believe he had been waiting for her.

'You have done this before?' he asked, his voice just as hoarse as an ordinary man's would be.

'A few times.'

'Well, don't force yourself, sweetheart. Not even for a horny old man.'

She grabbed his ears and kissed him. That was nice, too. He kissed well, confident but not pushy. His lips were kind of flexible, and his tongue was . . .

He ran it to a tender spot on the side of her neck and she forgot to decide what his tongue was. His fingers slid up inside her, three strong fingers. Strong was good, she thought, as he pumped them deep into her sheath. His thumb moved up to her clit before she could remind him to do it. He was good at that, too. His expertise surprised her, but she guessed he'd had a few flings in his day.

He brought her off twice; deep, hard, shotgun orgasms. Then he poised her on top of his pointy cock. Like the Washington Monument, she thought, stifling a giggle. But, ooh, he was right there, verging on going in. She clenched her pussy, trying to draw him inside, but there wasn't enough to grab and he was too strong to force.

'Tell me something...' He swirled the glans around her gate, getting it all slippery with her juice. 'Are you thinking of Abby now?'

'Not until you mentioned it,' she said, and she laughed, actually happy.

'Sorry,' he muttered.

She was still laughing as he lowered her on to him and then he laughed, too, a low chuckle of triumph. She didn't mind. She felt kind of triumphant herself. She squirmed around him, testing the relatively unfamiliar intrusion. This was the first time she'd done this sober. She couldn't remember the other men feeling so lively inside her. When she squirmed, his cock squirmed. When she tightened, it swelled. The give and take of it intrigued her. Maybe this het stuff wasn't as dull as she'd thought.

'You're hot,' she said.

He snorted. 'No kidding, Sherlock. Watching you come is better than an week of X-rated movies.'

She gave him her best swivel, the one she practised by humping a dildo in front of her mirror. He liked it. He put his hands on her bottom so he could feel her hip action from both sides. 'I guess you have done this before,' he said, which pleased her immensely. 'Better be careful or you'll make an old man come like a young man.'

She wasn't sure what that meant, but it didn't really matter. He could come any time he wanted. She was still glowing from the two she'd had for starters. Jack, however, had other ideas. He kneaded her cheeks, a bone-deep massage that passed straight through her gluteus maximus and into her cunt. Her temperature jumped ten degrees in two seconds. She switched her angle, trying to get more stimulation for her clit.

'How about this?' he said. He took his right hand off her bottom, laid it across her belly and plastered his thumb around her mound. He bent the first knuckle and it curled into her sheath right along the top of his shaft.

'Tight,' she gasped.

'Bad tight?' He was out of breath. She knew he ran six miles every morning, but he could hardly get the words out.

'It's good,' Marissa said, and she didn't sound much better. He was holding her right where she needed to be held, stretching her right where she needed to be stretched. The good ache rose as she rode his cock and his thumb. He wriggled both from side to side, in opposite directions. Marissa's pussy fluttered like crazy, overloaded with sensation. Jack groaned and thrust his buttocks up off the pier. It was a good moan, from the belly.

'Faster,' she said, half groaning herself.

He gritted his teeth and thrust to his limit. 'Hurry, Marissa.'

She gyrated over him, keeping him deep, holding him tight. She was almost there, almost. He made this rough, animal noise and bit her shoulder through her T-shirt. That did it for her, like a switch flipping to 'on'. She gave it up with a low cry and a deep, hip-shaking shudder. He kept her going by pumping through her spasms and then he, too, went crashing through the spume.

They sagged over each other. He put his arms around her back and swayed her from side to side. The embrace made her feel peculiar. He held her like he really cared about her and it was, well, she couldn't help thinking it was how a father should hold his daughter – some other type of father than hers, that is.

But that was too, too weird to think about. She pulled away gently so she wouldn't hurt his feelings and tugged the hem of her T-shirt down. It covered her butt, just barely. The planks felt rough on her skin when she sat and leant into his side.

He looked at her, measuring her reaction; reading her mind, for all she knew.

She swallowed against the funny lump in her throat. 'Not bad for an old guy.'

He didn't smile, but his eyebrows lifted in what could have been amusement. 'Not bad for a girl who'd rather stick to her own kind.'

'Well.' She swung her feet over the water and wondered if she were losing her mind. 'I wouldn't mind another go if you find yourself in the mood again.'

That made him laugh. It was a nice laugh, but she still had a sneaking suspicion the joke was on her.

Storm woke to the sound of birdsong outside his window. He rolled out of bed, showered off a lingering sense of oddness from the night before, and headed for the kitchen. Despite the early hour, Abby and Marissa were there ahead of him, laughing uproariously over something – not him, surely; Abby wouldn't kiss and tell, or laugh about what they'd shared.

As he entered he heard Marissa say something about Abby wading knee-deep in vultures.

'They're circling,' she said, illustrating with both arms. 'Better watch your back.'

Abby caught sight of Storm and choked on her giggle. 'Storm! Good morning.'

He returned her greeting, and the less enthusiastic one he got from Marissa.

Abby had obviously been running. She sat on a stool at the work island, her hair caught back in a bright ponytail, her cheeks pleasantly pink. She wore a plain grey sports bra and running shorts. The tiniest roll of flesh swelled over their elastic waistband. He knew

Abby must hate that hint of softness, but he found it endearing. A woman as beautiful as she was shouldn't be perfect.

'What are you looking at?' Marissa said, when he continued to stare. 'Has she got spinach on her teeth?'

Abby reached over and slapped her knee. 'Marissa!'

Storm smiled at his deck shoes. 'No, but she is a pleasant sight first thing in the morning.'

'Oh, God,' Marissa groaned, 'another one.'

She left the kitchen muttering to herself. Storm didn't ask what she'd meant. He suspected he didn't want to know.

Abby was studying her neatly clipped nails. He wanted to take them in his mouth and suck each one. He wanted to slide her off the stool and on to his cock. He wanted to ask if she'd slept well, and if she'd dreamt of him. 'Hungry?' he said instead.

She gestured to her empty, crumb-filled plate. 'We ate, and I need to take a shower before I stink up the place.'

He caught her wrist before she could get away. He pulled it not to his mouth, but to his nose, sniffing his way up the tender skin to her armpit. 'You stink good,' he said.

She squirmed away. 'You are a very strange man.'

'But you like me that way.' He pulled her close like a tango dancer. The skin at the small of her back was still damp from her run, still warm. He stroked it with the tips of his fingers, up and down, down and up, the same path his cock had followed the night before.

Her breath came faster. 'I'm not sure if I like you or not.'

'Aren't you?'

'Not yet.'

He wanted to kiss her into admitting it, but it seemed

the wrong move. He settled for rubbing his hips lightly across hers. His cock stretched and lifted, thickening, elongating. A sheen of sweat broke out across her upper lip.

'Not yet,' she repeated, and he judged it best to let her go.

Too unsettled to work on anything as crucial as menu planning, Storm grabbed a picnic breakfast of red plums and French bread heels. He'd take them to the beach, he decided, watch the waves for a while and find his centre again.

But another surprise awaited him outside. In the neatly mown garden in front of the Coates Inn sat a white wrought-iron bench. Last night it had been empty, but this morning three men filled it. One was a thin, bespectacled college boy, one a fat businessman, and the last looked like a refugee from Muscle Beach. He smiled at Storm, the vacant smile of a surfer who's taken one too many spills.

'I'm afraid we don't serve breakfast in the off season,' Storm said.

'We know that,' said the fat businessman. 'We thought we'd wait a bit and say good morning to Abby.'

Storm felt his eyebrows rise.

'Yeah,' said the skinny kid with the spectacles. 'We heard about Bill and we, uh, we –'

'We thought she might need cheering up,' finished the surfer.

Then, as though their minds were working in sync, all three men looked him up and down, as if fearing he'd beat them to the punch – which, of course, he had.

Storm could have reassured them he was just the new chef. Under most circumstances he didn't mind sharing, but Abby was a special case. He didn't want anything, or anyone, distracting her from his pursuit.

For all he knew, it might take all summer to probe her hidden depths. Consequently, he left the men with a grunt and stalked towards the back of the inn.

The scenery did improve his mood. The day was bright, the grass dewy, and the light breeze free of even the slightest whiff of smog. Flowers perfumed it and brine and sandy earth. Perfection, he thought. If only they could find a way to grow palm trees here. He gazed towards Abby's pine and hemlock windbreak. Beyond that lay a field of wildflowers and beyond that, the ocean. He hungered to see it almost as much as he'd hungered for Abby when he woke this morning.

A stealthy movement near the closed north wing caught his eye. Storm squinted. A large, bearded man was peering in one of the windows. He looked vaguely familiar. Had an irate husband followed him here from LA? It was possible. If Storm expected an affair to be brief, he rarely inquired into his partner's marital status, reckoning that if she was married, her infidelity was strictly her and her husband's business.

Regardless of the reason, however, the intruder had no business poking around Abby's property. 'What are you doing?' Storm demanded, coming up behind the man.

He spun around, his face flushed, his expression guilty. He was five or six inches taller than Storm, and almost half as heavy again, but he seemed intimidated by the smaller man's confident stance.

'Whoa, there,' said the intruder, putting his hands out in a stalling motion. 'I, uh, just wanted to make sure none of the local kids have been trying to get in the windows. They do that sometimes, you know, to impress their girlfriends.'

'And why is that any of your business?' Storm asked, though he'd concluded this must be the well-hung, defunct boyfriend Bill.

Coins jingled as Bill pulled a handkerchief from his

trouser pocket and wiped his sweating face. 'Abby and I go way back a long way. She needs someone to look out for her. I keep telling her to board up those windows, but she says the customers might get nervous.'

'She's right,' Storm said, not liking the man's superior, not to mention proprietary, attitude.

'Yeah, well –' Bill scuffed his blocky brown shoes through the damp grass '– she oughta get her sisters to cough up the money to renovate then.'

'Her sisters?' Storm's attention sharpened. This man might not interest him, but the financial resources of the inn definitely did. If Abby had someone to bail her out of her hole, buying the inn out from under her might be more difficult than he'd hoped.

Unfortunately, Bill chose that moment to realise he wasn't the only man whose right to be there might be in question. He folded his arms across his barrel chest. The show of belligerence was not convincing. This man was the sort who bullied by manipulation, Storm decided, emotionally rather than physically – and never with anyone who might fight back.

'Who are you?' Bill said, his eyes betraying his nervousness.

'I'm the new chef.' Storm stared coolly until the other man blinked and dropped his gaze.

'Oh, right,' he said. 'I know Abby has been looking for one. Are you any good?'

'Better than you could imagine.'

Bill wiped his forehead again, then shoved both hands in his pockets. His trousers were polyester, his shirt an unfortunate brown and orange plaid. The thought of Abby spending two minutes in this oaf's company, much less labouring under his insensitive bulk, offended every sensibility Storm possessed.

'Yeah, well, maybe I'll come by the inn and check out your cooking,' he said.

A muscle in Storm's jaw tightened. 'Under the circumstances, it might be better to wait for an invitation.'

Bill's eyes widened, then narrowed. Storm thought the man had finally found his spine, but his next words dispelled that notion. 'I know you, don't I? I'm Bill Harris from Harris Rent-a-Car. I leased you that green Miata, the '95.'

'That's right.'

The big man smiled, his teeth white in his beard, his eyes shining with puppyish friendliness. At last, Storm understood what Abby might have seen in him.

'Rides like a beaut, don't she?' he said. 'Hugs the corners like your mother's pussy.'

Storm didn't know what to make of that analogy, so he said nothing.

Bill's smile faded. 'I guess she told you about us.'

'In passing.'

'Yeah, well.' Bill jingled the coins in his pockets. 'She's just going through a phase. This break-up won't last.'

It will if I have anything to say about it, Storm thought, deciding then and there that this would be his gift to Abby. By the time he was through with her, she'd think far too highly of herself to fall for a jerk like Bill Harris.

Storm wasn't in the kitchen when Abby returned from greeting the terrible trio out front. She smoothed her pretty green and yellow skirt down her thighs and told herself she was foolish to feel so disappointed. What did one night mean to a man like Storm? As for this morning's flirtation, he probably flirted with every woman he met. 'No obligations,' he'd said. 'Only pleasure.'

She noticed he'd cleaned up her and Marissa's breakfast things. She trailed her palm along the spotless counter top and wished she'd touched him more when she'd had the chance.

Do not chase him, she ordered herself. You'd be a fool to chase him.

Nonetheless, ten minutes later, she was tramping through the beach grass and sea rocket, just in case he'd come to see the ocean. She carried the book of samples Ivan had given her this morning. He was studying commercial art at the Rhode Island School of Design. Abby thought Storm might want to hire him to design the new menus.

Of course, she wasn't really here to discuss menu design.

She saw him before he saw her. The beach was empty except for him. He was staring at the eroded sand cliffs that overhung the Outer Beach. They were a sight. Fifty metres high in spots, the bluffs curved north and west for a good fifteen miles. Majestic and fragile, topped with spring grass, they bore the deep sandy scars of their last winter battering.

Storm was a sight, too. He'd pulled off his shoes and shirt and stood admiring the view clad only in snug black jeans. His back formed a lovely triangle from shoulders to waist, perfectly muscled and golden brown. A trio of gulls took turns diving for breadcrumbs at his feet, as bold as if he weren't present. Their fearless swoops made him seem as much a creature of nature as they were.

Abby's womb contracted with a hard stab of longing. How would she ever get enough of him?

As though her thoughts had palpable weight, he turned and waved to her. Her heart raced as her sandals sploshed across the sandy beach, trying not to hurry, trying not to look too eager. His eyes, silver bright in the sun, held steady on hers. He was smiling.

When she was a few feet away, she waved the sample book. 'I've brought some –'

He grabbed her and kissed her, a deep *From Here to*

Eternity kiss. The sample book dropped to the sand. Abby's neck went limp. Storm steadied the back of her head with his palm and coaxed her lips wider.

Abby moaned and clutched his bare back as tightly as she could.

'Here,' he said harshly, breaking free. 'Right now.'

Before she could ask if he was crazy, he kissed her again and started dragging her along – where she didn't know or care. He'd lifted her up on her toes and mashed his swollen zip into her mound. She couldn't help herself. She slid her right leg over his hip, wanting more, wanting to open herself completely.

The cliffs tipped sideways as he laid her down in the hollow between two dunes. Lips still locked to his, she heard him open his jeans – a quick snap for the button, a loud rasp for the zip. He gathered up her pretty skirt, pushing the front swiftly to her waist. Then he settled his warm cotton briefs against her damp cotton panties.

He poured his 'ah' of pleasure into her mouth and began to rock, a slow undulating grind of hard cock over soft pussy. His hands roamed her sides and she remembered that this was her chance to touch him. His back was warm brown satin under her hands, his muscles shifting, his spine rolling with his thrusts. She ventured on to his buttocks, cupping him over his jeans and wishing it was under. His tight, round cheeks tensed and released. She thought of the way he'd played with his anus the night before. Did she dare touch him there? She slid her hands into his pockets, and came before she could work up the nerve.

The swiftness of her orgasm embarrassed her. Surely he'd think she was desperate, but his mouth merely smiled against hers. He slipped his hand into her panties. She was running with cream.

Mortified, she tried to push him away.

'What's the matter?' he said, his eyes alight with

teasing fire. 'Do you think you're only allowed to come so many times in twenty-four hours?' He kissed her flaming cheek. 'It's not true, you know.' His longest finger slipped round her sopping folds, making a loud, squishy noise. 'You can come as often as you like. It won't hurt you. In fact, it's good for you.'

'But I don't need ... oh,' she groaned as he found her clit and began rubbing it from side to side exactly the way she'd shown him the night before.

He licked the shell of her ear. 'Don't need this? But you do, Abby. You need a good deal more than you believe and I, for one, think you should have it.'

He pulled back so he could see her face, his fingers working steadily, deftly, driving her swiftly to a second culmination. His eyes drank in every expression along the way – especially her expression when she came. Abby had never been so embarrassed, or so aroused.

'Now you,' she insisted, once she'd stopped quaking. With a boldness she hadn't known she possessed, she burrowed into his briefs and eased out his thick, shiny-capped erection. It was beautiful in the daylight, straight and strong and flushed like a summer sunset.

'Show me what you like,' she whispered, though she'd begun to caress him already.

They lay on their sides now, facing each other, bumping knees. He tightened her hand and slowed her pace. He lengthened her stroke until her palm swallowed the tip and her fingers rubbed the tight bulge of his balls. He made her squeeze them for a moment. She felt how firm they were inside, and how full.

Then he released her hand and resumed stroking her pussy. She couldn't believe it. As soon as he touched her, she wanted to come again. Her hips tipped towards his hand, begging silently. Storm slid one finger inside her and covered her button with his thumb.

'I want to come on you,' he said, shifting close

enough to nudge her belly with the head of his cock. 'I want to shoot my cream across your belly. I want you to rub it in and wear it all day and count the minutes until I take you again.'

Abby was amazed. He didn't ask. He didn't beg. He said what he wanted and abruptly she wanted it, too. 'Do it,' she said.

He caught his breath as though her answer surprised him.

'Do it,' she said, and intensified her stroke.

His eyes squeezed shut for a second. She knew she hadn't hurt him because he began to thrust into her grip, began to breathe faster until his stomach moved in and out like a bellows. His cock grew longer, redder. He grunted and gritted his teeth. Soon, she thought, hardly able to wait. At last, with a curse of impatience, he let go of her pussy, covered her hand and aimed himself at her belly. His shaft swelled within their clutching fingers. The muscles in his chest tightened.

'Abby,' he gasped, and shot her with a warm, thick spray of come.

She watched it spurt in ribbons of white. She felt the spasms through her fingers; heard his quick chuffs of pleasure. Beautiful, she thought. She was sorry to see it end, but glad when he rubbed his cream into her skin, massaging it over her belly and into her muff. She loved the glorious sticky feel and then the tightening as it dried. She wouldn't be able to forget it was there. She'd think about it all day long.

His fingers slipped lower, curled over her clit and made her come again, this time in a series of spangling contractions strung together like a daisy chain.

'Good,' he said when she'd settled. He withdrew his hand and stuck his longest finger in his mouth. Tongue swirling, he sucked it clean of their juices.

Abby's jaw dropped.

'Remember,' he said with a small, knowing smile, 'you must not wash it off. I have marked you. Today you are all mine.'

She should have been offended, but instead she started counting the minutes.

5

Storm could hear the hum of customers all the way in the kitchen. He'd been serving the new menus for a week now. Already the dining room was full for dinner and nearly full for lunch. Abby credited Storm's cooking skills but, given the number of single males in attendance, Storm doubted the improvement was entirely – or even mostly – due to him.

Apparently, Abigail Coates was the belle of the Cape. Her newly unattached status drew men like the roses on her cottage drew bees. Storm was amazed that Bill had managed to keep the competition at bay for so long, but perhaps their respect for Abby's sense of propriety was responsible.

In any event, the local bachelors were beginning to have to double up, since there weren't enough tables to seat them all in solitary splendour.

Of course, there would have been enough tables if the upstairs dining room hadn't been in dire need of replastering. Abby's sheepish expression when she admitted that had spoken volumes. She knew she'd misled him. The Coates Inn was hardly the 'thriving family concern' she'd claimed in her ad. That's when he realised she'd sunk everything she had into paying his salary. The move was a bold gamble, and a fortunate one for him, since he hoped to use her dependence on him as leverage for his buyout.

Giving his conscience a quieting kick, Storm threw a handful of spring onions into the clam chowder that was simmering on the stove. He'd made the soup the day before – chowder required ageing in order for its flavours to blend – but he always added something fresh on the day of serving. This evening the something fresh was onions and a dash of white wine. Crude though some of them were, the local bachelors were bound to love it. Storm vowed that, while they might have come for Abby's sake, they'd come again for the food.

In the meantime, he wavered between annoyance and amusement. One thing was certain, the last thing these bucks needed was a steady diet of his all-aphrodisiac menu. He'd be lucky if he didn't end up with a riot on his hands.

'It's a madhouse out there,' Abby said, returning with another handful of orders. Her cheeks were pink with happiness, her eyes bright with excitement. Storm wondered if she'd noticed all the cock-heads wagging as she passed. Not consciously, perhaps, but the testosterone in the air was having an effect on her. She looked radiant.

'Come here,' he said, shifting a skillet of shrimp off the burner.

'Oh, no.' She backed away, her flush deepening. 'Not again.'

She'd been helping him in the kitchen all week and he'd coaxed her into as many mutual grope sessions as he could manage. They'd traded hand jobs in the supply room, dry-humped on the workstation cutting board, and kissed each other numb in the herb garden under the moon. What they hadn't done was engage in full intercourse or oral sex. Storm wasn't sure how much longer he could wait for either. Abby made him unconscionably impatient.

'Just a kiss,' he said, puckering his mouth to prove his sincerity. 'I need a pick-me-up.'

Abby's eyes slid to his groin. Even through his apron,

the bulge of his erection was evident. His cock had been rising ever since he'd heard her light, quick footsteps advancing down the hall. The weight of her attention stiffened him up the last possible millimetre.

'You look plenty picked up to me,' she said, 'and we don't have time to, um, get you laid down again.'

He curled his tongue out and touched his upper lip. Beneath her soft cotton sweater – sherbet green tonight – Abby's nipples popped to attention.

'Oh, God.' She quickly buttoned the matching cardigan. 'You're impossible.'

'But you like me that way,' he said.

This time she didn't deny it. She sighed in surrender. 'One kiss. A quick one.'

He backed her into the counter, clasped her face in both hands, and plunged his tongue inside her mouth. Abby made a strangled kitten noise and kissed him back. She gripped his buttocks with an enthusiasm that suggested she might have a thing about his rear. Hoping this was so, Storm clenched his cheeks and savoured her anguished groan.

'It's been hours,' she said, breaking free with a gasp. Her little hand crept over his erection and gave his shaft a testing squeeze. He noticed she did that a lot. Perhaps she needed proof of her effect on him. As far as he was concerned, she was welcome to it. It was certainly easy to give. She had to be one of the most responsive women he'd ever met; a soft, squirmy, cuddly little handful. Her shyness made her all the more fun to play with.

With one eye on the stove, he ran his hands up her front and cupped her hard-tipped breasts. She moaned through closed lips. He eased his thigh between her legs. She immediately began to ride it up and down. He grinned. How delightful she was.

'I have something special planned for tonight,' he said, his voice gone smoky with pleasure.

'Please don't tell me what,' she said. 'Not when I have to go back into that dining room full of people.'

'I won't,' he promised and gave her breasts a slow, deep squeeze. 'I wouldn't want to spoil the surprise. I will tell you one thing, though.'

'What?' The word was a shallow pant. She rolled harder against him. In a minute, her skirt would be wet – and maybe his apron, too. 'What one thing can you tell me?'

'I'll be inside you,' he whispered. 'I'll shove my cock in your cunt, as deep as it can go. You'll feel the shape of me inside you, the pounding of my blood, the hardness. You'll be soft and wet. Your folds will move around me, stroking me, clutching me. We'll hold there like that, locked tight, until neither of us can stand another second without moving.'

Her hand contracted involuntarily on his shaft, a delicious death grip.

'I want that,' she said. 'You have no idea how much.'

He was about to kiss her again when the clatter of the busboy's cart broke them apart.

Later, he promised, with silent lips.

She blushed hard and quickly left the kitchen.

Still fanning herself, Abby found Francine and Richard and their two little monsters in the lobby. They had circled the beleaguered hostess like natives inspecting a nervous pilgrim. Francine was in full warpaint tonight. As short as Abby, she'd inherited her deep bosom from their father's side of the family. Her stylish, chin-length hair was red this week, a red echoed by her fluttery tunic and skirt. Her husband Richard was a tall, thin, serious man. Unlike his wife, he had no flash whatsoever, though he did look handsome in his black business suit. Francine was always after him to get fitted for contact lenses, but Abby loved his Buddy Holly-style spectacles. They were sexy, she thought, in a nerdy scientist kind of way.

'There you are,' Francine said, as if Abby were late for an appointment. 'Tell this woman there's always a table for family.'

The hostess turned pleading eyes to her employer. 'I'm sorry, Ms Coates. We've no tables for four open right now.'

Francine heaved a dramatic sigh. 'I told you, we don't want a table for four. We want a table for two.'

'And what,' Abby asked, 'do you propose to do with little Mary and Milton?' Her niece and nephew, six and four respectively, goggled up at her, both wearing their best innocent faces.

'Leave them in the kitchen with you, of course,' Francine said. 'You know they love that.'

Both kids nodded energetically.

Abby smiled, for once not feeling the least compulsion to comply. Breaking up with Bill had started a new chapter in her life, and Storm's flattering pursuit was rapidly flipping the pages. Hiring him had been one of her brighter decisions. Soon she'd be able to repair the upstairs dining room, with or without her sisters' grudging help. Of course, she still had the second mortgage on her cottage to pay off, but everything would work out. Her life was on an upswing now. She was going to think positive. I'm a new woman, she thought, or at least I'm beginning to be: a new, more sensual woman, who puts her foot down now and then and doesn't let people treat her like a doormat – not even people she loves. She ran her tongue over her lips for courage and tasted Storm.

'I'm afraid the kids will have to stay with you,' she

said, her secret places shimmering in remembrance. 'I'm not cooking tonight. The new chef is, and I sincerely doubt he'd take the same view of children in the kitchen that I do.'

'But –' Francine exchanged a look with her husband '– Richard and I were so looking forward to an evening alone.'

Richard cleared his throat and shuffled his feet. Abby suspected Francine had been looking forward to the evening alone more than he had. Her big sister had just turned forty and, from the comments she'd let slip lately, Richard was having trouble keeping up with her. Abby pinched her lower lip in indecision. She didn't necessarily believe Storm's claims about his food, but maybe a platter of oysters was just the inspiration Richard needed.

'Tell you what,' she said. Her sister's eyes brightened. 'I'll set up a table in the herb garden. You can watch the kids while they run around, but you'll still have privacy to talk.'

'Are you sure it isn't too much trouble?' Richard asked.

Francine punched his upper arm. 'Of course it isn't too much trouble. We're family.'

The statement was so typical of her and Abby was feeling so happy, she burst out laughing. The sound startled Richard into a rare, slow smile.

'Thank you,' he said, because he really was a nice man. 'That's very kind of you.'

'You'll like the new chef,' Abby promised as she sent a waiter off to find a spare table. 'His cooking is not to be missed.'

Something small and red barrelled into Storm's leg just as he was flipping a crepe.

'No, no, no!' it squealed and latched on to his calf.

Storm caught the crepe, barely, and looked down. A little boy was clinging to his leg as if the hounds of hell were after his chubby, red-corduroy tail. The boy's flight was followed by a tall man with thick, black-framed spectacles and a weary smile.

'Sorry,' he said, pushing the lenses up his nose. 'I'm Richard, Abby's brother-in-law, and Milton here is afraid of urinals. My wife always takes him to the ladies.'

'Ah,' said Storm, though the challenges of child rearing left him completely at sea. He dropped his hand uncertainly to the child's silky brown head. 'Perhaps you would like to visit the chef's private bathroom? I assure you, there is nothing scary in there.'

The boy looked up at him, thumb in mouth. 'OK,' he said around the soggy obstruction.

To both men's surprise, Milton insisted on managing his business himself.

'Kids,' said the man, in a tone most men reserved for women.

'Have an oyster,' Storm offered, nabbing one hot from the pan.

Richard accepted absently and rested his elbows on the counter as he chewed. He sighed when he was done, and not the way most people sighed over Storm's cooking. Storm poured another crepe and stirred the big pot of clam chowder. It was ready for the white wine. 'Trouble?' he asked, reaching past the man for the bottle.

Richard shifted out of his way. 'You ever try to keep up with a woman who just turned forty?'

Storm had, and enjoyed it immensely, but it would have been impolite to say so. 'You probably need more sleep,' he said. 'Or more exercise. Circulation is important, you know. And, of course, you must eat lots of Oysters à la Storm.'

The man snorted. 'At this point, I doubt a boatload of oysters could stiffen my mast.'

Storm turned out the last crepe for his order. 'Never underestimate the power of zinc. It's a testosterone building-block. Besides, these oysters are my secret recipe. Add a nice dark green salad, a glass of wine, a pecan crumble for dessert, and I guarantee you'll see things in a different light.'

'You guarantee it, huh?'

Storm laid his hand over his heart. '*Je jure de ma bonne foi.* I give you my word, or I'll pay for your meal myself.'

Richard stared at him as if wondering what his game was. Storm could almost read his mind. Was he a huckster? A lunatic? In the back of his weary brown eyes, however, a spark of belief flickered. 'Maybe,' it said. 'Just maybe.'

Storm loved moments like this. He felt like Tinkerbell being clapped back to life.

'Just promise me one thing,' said the man.

'Yes?'

'That you won't serve the oysters to my wife.'

Marissa had two fifteen-minute breaks a night. She spent the first sampling Storm's clam chowder – which even she had to admit was disgustingly good – and the second in the ladies' room, working off the thigh-clenching horniness that had been creeping up on her all evening. She didn't know if it was inspired by her frustration over Abby or her memories of what she'd done with Jack, but she literally couldn't wait to get home. She grabbed the first stall, put the lid down, thrust her new black trousers to her knees and burrowed impatiently between her legs.

Her head fell back on a sigh of relief as her middle finger found the hard, pulsing knot of her clit. God, there was nothing like frigging yourself when you were really turned on. The sensations were so intense, so deep. She cupped herself closer, kneading all the soft flesh of her mons, then slipped her other hand between the buttons of her starched white blouse so she could pinch one nipple. Her knees began to tremble. This wasn't going to take long, which was fortunate. The way the itch had been riding her lately, she'd need a few good gos before she could comfortably return to work. Even then, she might want another trip to Jack's place tonight.

The sound of someone coming in startled the grin from her face.

'Lock the door,' said a husky female voice.

A male voice muttered a protest and was silenced by a loud, wet kiss. Clothing rustled, a belt rattled, and two pepper-red heels were kicked a short distance across the grey and black tiles. A man's black jacket plopped to the floor.

Interesting, Marissa thought, and drew her feet as quietly as she could on to the seat. Just in time, too, for the man broke free and hissed a warning that there might be someone there.

'There's no one,' said the woman. 'No one but us.' Marissa heard the distinctive squeal of a zip being yanked to its lowest limit. 'Oh, sweetums, look how big you are. I can hardly hold you in my hand.' A deep, masculine groan echoed through the room. 'It's been so long. I can't wait. I've got to have your big old thing inside me now.'

'Oh, God,' said the man, a sound of mingled resignation and excitement. 'Turn around then. Turn around and lean over the counter.'

Marissa peered through the crack in the door. She could see the man's back as he pushed the woman over the green marble-topped sink. His shirt-tails hung loose, creased from being tucked inside. His hands moved beneath them and his trousers dropped to his ankles.

Marissa's eyes widened in appreciation. He had nice legs, nice, long hairy legs, and big balls. Their shadowy weight swayed between his thighs. She went over the edge at the sight, biting her lip to silence her orgasmic whimper. She needn't have worried. The couple were far too engrossed in their own little drama to hear her muffled cry.

Intent on his goal, the man took hold of the woman's hips and spread her knees with his own. He was much taller than she was. He had to dip low to position himself and, once he did, Marissa couldn't see much of his partner apart from the hands she reached back to clutch his bottom. She had long red nails, dangerous nails. Marissa shivered as they pressed into the man's hard, narrow cheeks.

'Now,' she said. 'For God's sake, now.'

The man bucked forward for a swift, deep entry. His grunt of pleasure was almost lost in the woman's moan.

'Hush,' he said, though he'd already begun to thrust. 'Someone will hear.'

'Oh,' said the woman, clearly transported. 'Oh, yes. Oh, sweetums, dig it in. Oh, yes.' Her nails made pale indentations in her partner's flesh. He grunted again and thrust so forcefully Marissa could hear his balls slap the woman's buttocks.

She came a second time, inspired by their enthusiasm.

'Touch me,' begged the woman. 'Put your big, strong hand on my pussy.'

He must have complied because she moaned even louder than before. He told her to hush again, but his heart wasn't in it. He was groaning himself, low and heavy at the end of each thrust. The intervals between his groans were growing shorter. Like a conductor beating time, his belt buckle clinked against the floor, dragged back and forth by the trousers that pooled around his ankles. The woman arched up at him, obviously welcoming his fervour.

'Oh, honey,' he said in a tone of such longing regret that Marissa's heart rose in her throat. 'Oh, honey.'

She doubted the woman heard the regret or the longing because she climaxed then, the orgasm marked by a high pulsing sigh. The man thrust faster, jackrabbit fast, his breathing harsh, his hands gripping her hips. Sweat rolled down the inside of his thighs. A sound strangled in his throat. His calf muscles tightened. His next thrust was so hard, his partner's feet left the floor.

'Now?' gasped the woman.

But he was too close to answer. His head dropped back and his hips slammed forward, then convulsed in a half dozen quick, deep spasms. Marissa joined him, timing her peak to match the final clenching of his buttocks.

'You're a maniac,' he said as the woman drew his trousers up his legs again.

'If you knew what was good for you, you'd count your blessings,' said the woman.

Marissa had to agree. Having a partner so mad to screw she'd risk discovery would have been a pleasant change. She was still contemplating that fantasy as she returned a short while later to her waitressing duties. By now, it had to be time to clear Richard and Francine's entrée. As a rule, Marissa didn't like Abby's older sister. She was rude and bossy and seemed to think being related to the boss absolved her of having to tip. Her mood, however, seemed to have undergone a sea change since the start of the evening. She was smiling and pink-cheeked and behaving as though she'd never complained about a wait in her life.

Her husband Richard looked happy, too. The marine biologist was always so serious. Marissa thought the Woods Hole Institute sounded like a cool place to work.

Imagine – getting paid to watch whales! She supposed it was a lot of pressure, trying to protect endangered species and all, but for once he seemed to have forgotten his troubles. While the kids messed about by the fish pond, he was laughing over his wine, and – unless Marissa's eyesight was failing – he and the missus were playing footsie under the table.

They were acting like newlyweds.

Now that she thought about it, she'd seen a lot of couples acting like newlyweds this week – not counting the two sex fiends who'd surprised her in the loo. Her tips had been fantastic. Soon she'd be able to afford a new bike, and maybe another tattoo. She grinned at the thought. Wouldn't that make her father flip his lid?

'Thank you for everything,' Francine gushed as she cleared the plates. 'Tonight has been wonderful.'

'You're welcome,' Marissa said, meaning it for once.

Scarcely able to credit the change, she turned at the top of the terrace for one final look. That's when she noticed Francine's heels, her pepper-red heels. Her jaw dropped in shock. They couldn't be the horny couple from the bathroom. They just couldn't. Francine might have overactive hormones but Richard would never do such a thing – not in a place where he might get caught and embarrass Abby. Besides, what woman in her right mind would call him 'sweetums'? On the other hand, the jacket that draped the back of his chair was quite rumpled, and there were suspicious sweat stains under the arms of his shirt.

Incredible. Marissa shook her head and turned away. The way people were acting around here, you'd think that Storm guy was slipping something into the food.

Abby emerged from Storm's bathroom in her panties, with her arms crossed over her breasts. She expected to find him lying on the double bed. He wasn't, but something else sure as hell was; a foot-long, plastic rod gleamed black against his ivory satin sheets. A head the size of a tennis ball topped one end of the contraption and a long electric cord trailed off the other.

Abby pressed her hand over her belly. She knew what it was, of course. Her sister Francine owned a large collection of vibrators. She insisted on showing Abby each new acquisition, a habit that robbed her of any desire to buy her own. Never in a million years, she thought. But now Storm had laid one in offering across his bed. This must be the surprise he'd mentioned. Was she supposed to demonstrate it for him? Show off her stellar masturbatory technique?

Abby swallowed hard. Never in a million years.

She jumped when Storm's arms surrounded her from behind. He was naked and warm. He sniffed the skin of her neck and rubbed his hard penis over the small of her back. The touch instantly heated her inside. She leant back into his embrace.

'You're staring at that thing like it's going to bite you,' he said, his lips to her ear, his forearms banded beneath her breasts. 'You do know what it's for, right?'

'Um, yes,' was all she managed to say. At least the vibrator didn't resemble anything. Some of Francine's toys were shaped like famous porn stars' penises. One looked like a rabbit. Never in a million years would that hop between her legs.

Storm kissed her ear. 'Do you want me to put it away, or shall we take it for a test drive?'

'We?' She craned her head around.

He pinched the tip of her nose. 'Yes, "we." It's for both of us to play with. Did you think I was going to ask you to perform for me?'

'Well . . .'

He turned her to face him. 'I wouldn't do that.

Although –' a grin flashed across his face '– if you ever wanted to perform, I'd be more than happy to watch.'

She grimaced at the thought, then met his amused blue eyes. She trailed one shy finger down the centre of his chest. 'Could I use it on you?'

His eyebrows rose. 'Of course you could. But since you apparently haven't operated one before, perhaps I should start. Then you'll know how it feels. First things first, though.' He tapped her hip. 'I see you're a bit overdressed.'

Abby blushed and touched the front of her plain white panties.

He laughed. 'That's all right, love. You have no idea what your shyness does to me. It's better than garlic shrimp frying in butter.'

That good, Abby thought, smiling as he knelt and slid her panties down her legs. As soon as she was bare, he climbed on to the bed and helped her up after him. The satin sheets – his contribution to the decor – felt cool and slippery under her knees. She immediately imagined the two of them rolling around on them.

He lifted the long wand vibrator and turned it on. A low hum filled the room. It wasn't as loud as she'd feared. 'Hold out your hand,' he said.

She held it out and he pressed the head into her palm.

'Oh,' she gasped. Tiny hairs stood up on her arms as the vibrations sang through her flesh. He ran the vibrator slowly up the inside of her arm. The effect was extremely pleasant, both relaxing and arousing. He moved it over her thighs, then her belly. He teased the head to the very edge of her labia and her clit jumped in delight at the referred vibrations. Her hips swivelled automatically to reach for more.

'Not too much,' he cautioned. 'I have a full menu

planned and I don't want to numb you out, though it can be a pleasant way to come.' He meandered up her belly and over the swell of her breasts. 'Let's see if you like this.'

She twitched away as soon as he glanced her nipple. 'Too sensitive?'

She nodded and rubbed the jangling areola.

'How about this then?' He leant forwards, nudged her hand aside with his long nose, and surrounded her nipple with his mouth.

Abby sighed with pleasure. She did love being suckled and Storm did it so well. He flicked her with his tongue and pulled with his cheeks, gentle and steady, laving first one beaded tip, then the other. Her hips began to roll and she remembered his promise to enter her tonight. She was looking forward to that. In fact, she wanted him jammed inside her right now. No, she wanted two of him, three of him, Storm shoved into every orifice she possessed. Sucking him, fucking him, completely surrounded by his hard, lean muscle.

She closed her eyes to enjoy the fantasy. Her hands floated to his head and scratched his scalp in time to his suckling. She forgot all about the vibrator until he tucked it beneath his chin. She jerked again, but this time she wasn't jerking away.

'Oh, my God, that's so . . .' She gripped his skull to hold him closer. He chuckled against her breast but she didn't care. The vibrations buzzed through his jaw and out through his tongue, into her nipple and down some hidden nerve that led, so it seemed, straight to the tip of her clit. His tongue seemed to be licking two places at once and when he took her other nipple between his fingers and pinched – oh! – she couldn't sit still. Her body shook all over. Something was happening to her. Her pussy clenched and unclenched and then clenched harder, sucking on itself, wanting him, wanting that hard driving cock. But his mouth at her breast was so nice. He suckled harder, pinched harder, and, oh, oh, heat pooled between her legs and an ache that was almost like . . .

She threw back her head and groaned as the orgasm rose in excruciating slow motion, swelling, teasing, until she thought she couldn't bear another second and then, oh, yes, it washed over the top in sweet, long waves, thick as honey and twice as slow to drain away.

'Wow,' she breathed into the afterglow.

Storm switched off the vibrator, set it down and hugged her in the breathy silence. Her head sagged on to his shoulder. 'I didn't know I could do that.'

'Neither did I,' he chuckled. 'But I thought it was worth finding out.' His touch roved her buttocks, a light, restless exploration. She knew he was still hard, still waiting for his own gratification. She trailed her hands down his spine and around his hipbones. She gathered the tight swell of his balls into her hands and squeezed. His hips rolled closer.

'You can rest if you need to,' he said, but his voice held a roughness she had come to recognise. He didn't like to admit it, but he wanted release and he wanted it soon.

The knowledge energised her. Smiling to herself, she released his testicles, scooted back a foot and grabbed the discarded vibrator. She flicked it on and pointed the humming end like a sword. 'Back!' she ordered, feinting at his chest in a move she vaguely remembered from college fencing class.

He obeyed, laughing, but she noticed his cock sprang upward another inch, twanging back and forth as if she'd slapped it. She supposed the prospect of being buzzed had set his cock a-wag. It couldn't be her mock aggression. Storm was always so much in charge; she couldn't imagine being bossed around would arouse him.

'Please lie down,' she said in a milder voice, not wanting to make a fool of herself.

'Like this?' he said, meek as a lamb. He lay flat on his back with his arms at his sides.

Abby considered the pose. 'I think I'd rather you put your arms over your head and grab the rails of the headboard.'

The headboard was an old iron arch she'd found in an antique shop and sprayed with navy enamel. Its bars were as thick and straight as the door to a jail cell. Slowly, almost reluctantly, Storm reached for the rails. As he took hold a quiver ran down his sinewed torso. His nipples stood out in sharp red points.

'Are you cold?' she asked.

He shook his head and gripped the rails tighter. His jaw was clenched and his cock, oh, his cock flamed like a summer sunset and wept slippery tears of joy. Abby shivered, her own sex heating with excitement. Something was going on here, something he didn't want her to know about.

'Is there something else you'd like me to do?' she asked, low and careful.

His eyes flicked towards the headboard. 'Not right now.'

He was lying. She knew it. But did she have the nerve to call him on it? She set down the vibrator and slid her hands up his arms. When she reached his wrists, she cuffed them with her hands and squeezed as tightly as she could. His body heaved beneath her, his cock scalding her thigh, his choked-back moan music to her ears.

'Fuck me,' he said, trying to twist his rigid penis into position. 'Abby, fuck me now.'

But he didn't release the bars and he didn't wrench free of her hands.

'I don't think so,' she said, watching his eyes for the slightest sign of anger. Instead, she found panic and, under that, an even stronger longing. 'I think you'd rather I made you wait.'

He closed his eyes. 'Abby.'

'Stay,' she said in a stern voice that made him shudder again. She leapt from the bed and rummaged through his dresser. From the top drawer, she took a pair of long black socks. She carried them back to the bed. He hadn't batted an eyelash while she was gone.

'Abby,' he said again, more miserably, as she tied his wrists to the rails.

'It's for your own good,' she said, because that's what people did say, wasn't it? In any case, he seemed to like her improvisation. His cock throbbed back against his belly, the head threatening to stretch past his navel. At the moment, he was as big as she'd ever seen Bill. Her pussy liquefied at the thought of cramming all that hot red flesh inside. First, though, first she would try out her new toy. She turned on the vibrator and waved it over his body, not touching skin, just letting him feel the humming warmth.

'You're not allowed to come,' she said, settling the head against his left hipbone. 'Not until you're inside me. We know you're good at holding back, after all.'

Their eyes met. This was the first time either had referred to the night she'd watched him masturbate. Abby felt hot blood sweep her face a second before his went dusky, too. She refused to look away. He'd wanted her to watch. She knew that now.

'I need my hands free for that game,' he said.

'You misunderstand me. I don't intend for you to have any sort of orgasm at all, not unless your cock is in my cunt.' She couldn't believe she was saying these words but she loved the effect they had on him. His heart beat so hard she could see his chest shake. 'Your job,' she said, 'is to warn me when you're about to come. Then I'll stop and let you rest.'

'Ah,' he said, but it wasn't his usual confident 'ah' and she loved that, too.

'Of course –' she swept the vibrator up his side to his underarm '– the longer you last, the better I'll like it.'

'Of course,' he agreed, then coughed as she veered sideways on to his nipple.

'Too much?'

He shook his head and trembled, his lips pressed tightly together.

She explored him slowly, lingering at the pleasure spots she'd found during previous encounters and trying to discover new ones. He was sensitive all over, really, one big erogenous zone. The first time he made her stop she was running the wand over the soles of his feet. The second time, she had his balls in her mouth and the vibrator tucked against the pucker of his anus. He'd cursed over that one, cursed and begged.

'Goddamn it, Abby, please,' he'd said. '*Arrête*. Stop.'

French was a nice language, she thought. So expressive.

She kissed his face while he recovered, soft baby kisses across his trembling lids and down his too-long jaw. His heaving chest began to settle. His mouth relaxed. When he smiled at the kiss she dropped to the tip of his nose, she knew he was ready to be teased again. She continued the trail of kisses down his chest, down his belly. She eased one finger under his high-slung erection and tilted the cap towards her mouth. His thighs tensed.

'Don't,' he warned.

She cocked one brow at him. 'Are you denying my wishes?'

He drew a ragged breath. 'I'm trying to follow your order not to come.'

She smiled. 'I have immense faith in your self-control. Besides, I'll leave the vibrator out of it . . . for now.'

Before he could protest, she tucked the big swollen cap into her mouth.

'Ah,' he sighed, hips squirming under her, up at her. 'Ah, God, Abby.'

Sighing with pleasure herself, she swirled her tongue around the hot, silky head. He tasted good, even the juice that seeped from his tiny cock slit. Knowing Storm, he probably drank some freaky semen-sweetening tea. She giggled and sank further down on him. She couldn't take all of him, so she wrapped one hand around the base and confined her gentle rise and descent to the flesh that remained.

'Abby,' he gasped, after one short, delicious minute. 'Please, slow down.'

She lifted her head. 'If I go any slower, I'll be going backwards.'

'Then stop, please. It feels wonderful, but I just can't hold on. I can't.'

She looked at him. He seemed serious. Sweat rolled down his face and his brow was knitted with effort. She'd read a few books, though. What if this was one of those situations where the person said 'stop', but really wanted to be forced to go on?

'Please,' he said again, and she couldn't bring herself to force him.

'Do you want to be inside me now?' she asked.

'God, yes.'

She smiled at that and stretched her body over his until they lay chest to chest and nose to nose. Though he'd let his arms fall to the mattress, his wrists were still tied to the railing. Abby slid her hands over his palms. He meshed their fingers together and squeezed. He did not, however, ask her to remove the bonds.

Next time, I'll tie his ankles, too, she thought, which shocked her mind blank for a moment. What was happening to her? What had he done to her? She immediately undid the knots.

He sighed and wrapped her in his arms and rolled her under him on the satin sheets.

'Go slowly,' she said as he kneed her thighs apart and shifted his hips in preparation for entry. 'I want to feel every millimetre.'

He groaned and rolled back the other way. He pushed her into a sitting position on top of him. 'If you want it slow, you'd better do it yourself. I am too, too ready to roll.'

'Really?' She smiled down at him, pleasantly surprised. 'I can be on top?'

He smiled back and gave her thighs an encouraging squeeze.

'Well, OK, then.' She lifted his cock into position, tipping the head between her wet, swollen folds. The sight of him rising from his nest of dark curls and disappearing into her fair one called a gush of cream from deep within her sex.

'Ah,' he sighed as it trickled over him. 'Look at me, Abby. Look at me.'

She looked at him, at the soft fire in his eyes, at the flush on his mouth and cheeks.

'Push,' he whispered, his hands tightening on her hips. 'Take me inside you.'

'Slowly,' she whispered back and sank until his glans was clasped inside her gate.

'More,' he said.

She leant forwards so that her forearms supported

her weight and her nipples brushed his nearly hairless chest. He slipped inside another inch.

'More,' he said. 'I want all of you.'

His hands skated over her buttocks, tickling the crease between and then lower, reaching through her legs until he touched the place they joined.

'Feel how thick I am,' he said, his eyes locked on hers, his accent deepening as his pleasure rose. His fingers slid over the stretched skin, over him and her both. 'Feel how the blood pounds inside me.'

Abby groaned and swallowed him to the halfway mark. He did indeed pound against her secret folds, warm and thick and eager.

'Deeper,' he said. 'All the way.'

Abby bit her lower lip. She wanted this. She wanted him. 'All the way,' she agreed, and thrust swiftly to his root.

It seemed he hadn't expected her to comply. He rasped out a curse and closed his eyes. His cock swelled inside her, and quivered. He cursed again and made two tight fists behind her thighs. After a few tense moments, he opened his eyes.

'*Mon Dieu.*' His laugh was hoarse. 'I can't move. If I move, I'm done.'

'That's all right,' she said. 'I don't need to –'

'Like hell you don't.' He grabbed the vibrator with a vehemence that made her start. 'Sit up again.'

She sat, then jumped when he pressed the humming end to the apex of her mound.

'Oh,' she said. 'Oh, my goodness.'

Her clit was buzzing, leaping with the ultra-quick vibrations.

'*Dieu,*' he said, and she knew he could feel it too, through her flesh, through the hungry pull of her sheath. He wagged the vibrator back and forth, not wanting to numb her, she guessed, but it made for a strange kind of torture. The vibrations felt so good, especially with him so full and hot inside her, but the rise to climax wasn't as quick as she'd expected – not like pushing a button, but more like opening a too-narrow flood gate. She wanted to come worse than she could ever remember and the vibrator just kept shoving her higher.

'I can't come,' she cried, writhing with frustration.

'You can,' he growled and rolled her under him. When they almost teetered off the bed, he yanked her to the centre of the mattress. The vibrator was trapped between them, still buzzing away. He pulled back and thrust hard.

'You can,' he repeated and thrust again.

'More,' she said, feeling the peak glimmer into reach.

'More.' He captured her hands and gripped hard. '*Pousse*, Abby. Push with me.'

She met his next downstroke with an upstroke and a whimper.

'Faster,' he said, and began to count out the rhythm. 'Now, now.' But the 'nows' soon turned to groans and the groans soon turned to cries. They rang in her ears as she struggled to meet his thrusts. Their bellies slapped together. The box spring squealed. Their hips were a flurry of movement. She hitched her knees higher, dug her heels into the satin sheets, and still they pounded together.

He manoeuvred the vibrator to the crux of their meeting. His cock buzzed inside her as he pressed it to his shaft. Her clit screamed with agonised pleasure.

'*Dépêche-toi*,' he rasped. 'Hurry. *Je viens.*' The force of his will made her climax break. She cried out, her legs stiffening with sheer, unthinking pleasure, her head thrown back, her hips shuddering hard.

He cried out as she did, a masculine echo, deep and hoarse. She knew what *je viens* meant then: I'm coming.

Shoving the toy aside, he thrust to his limit and stiffened. He pulsed inside her, then sighed with relief and sagged bonelessly on to her chest.

'Boy, oh, boy,' he said, still sounding French. His head nuzzled next to hers on the pillow. 'After that, I think we both need a little rest.'

Abby stretched and yawned and wrapped her arms around his back. She guessed that meant she was staying, at least for a while.

Hours later he woke her with his lips at her breast and his hand playing gently between her legs like a man strumming a guitar.

'Storm,' she murmured, and he rose to kiss her. Mouths coupled, they rolled to their sides. He smoothed her leg over his hip. His cock was long and hot.

'Now?' he whispered, nudging it into the split-peach softness of her mound.

'Now,' she said.

They pressed together as smoothly as sun-warmed silk. Her body parted for his as if they'd been born a matched set. This time, simplicity marked their lovemaking, simplicity and leisure. Their hands roved tenderly, here praising the curve of a muscle, there seeking the pleasure of a single nerve. Through it all they kissed, their tongues speaking a language older than words.

'Don't wait,' she said, when she read the signals of his final climb.

He shook his head, shaking sweat-dampened hair from his eyes. 'But you –'

'Don't wait.' She cupped his buttocks and added her strength to his slow, rolling thrust. 'Just let it come.'

His eyes glittered in the dark. 'Are you sure?'

'I'm sure,' she said and pressed a kiss to the cleft of his chin.

His neck released a shadow of tension. His eyes slid

shut and the angle of his thrusts changed subtly, for his pleasure, for his relief. Knowing each stroke was precisely as he wished, precisely as his cock wished, excited her. Instinct told her he didn't often let go this way. He pressed down harder, dragging his cock slowly, firmly against the back wall of her sheath. A few more strokes and his breath caught in his throat. His thighs trembled, and his hands. The first throbbing contraction tightened his cock . . .

But he didn't come alone. He pulled her down through the last of his undertow. She moaned as the sweet wash of sensation drowned her. Every time with him had been different and this was sun sparkling on a foamy wave, the ripples coursing through her strong and clear. He held her close until she finished shaking, until they both finished shaking.

'Storm,' she said when his hands fell away.

They slept.

She woke again to find herself plastered to his back like a limpet. Thighs sticky with her own juice, her sex pulsed with hunger. Her hand was wrapped around his cock – which was admirably hard – and his chuckle rumbled in her ear. She let go as if he'd burnt her.

'Oh, no,' she said. 'Not again.'

Storm laughed. 'Oh, yes, again. Very much again. You were dreaming of me, love. You were mumbling my name.'

'I wasn't,' she cried.

'You were.' He rolled free of her arms and dropped lightly to the floor. He threw the covers to the foot of the bed and grabbed her knees. '"Storm," you said. "Oh, yes, Storm."'

She had to laugh at his mimicry. She was still laughing when he dragged her hips to the side of the high bed and thrust his cock directly home. Her body offered no resistance; she was that wet, that ready. He pushed her thighs towards her chest, slowly, letting her feel each incremental change in sensation as her legs doubled back on themselves and her body changed shape inside. He slid deeper as she opened. He seemed to thicken, to harden and heat inside her.

'Again,' he said, and it wasn't a question.

Halfway to heaven he pulled out and buried his head between her sprawled thighs.

'Ah,' he said, inhaling deeply. 'You smell delicious.' He tasted her with the very tip of his tongue. *'Merveilleux.'*

His praise embarrassed her, but she didn't pull away. Her legs settled to his shoulders and she touched his long, lean cheek.

He suckled her to the brink of climax then pulled away, breathing deeply, gathering himself. She didn't protest. She knew what was coming. She opened her arms. He slid into them, and into her, with a luxurious sigh.

He brought her off first this time, then collared her wrists in his hands and drove fiercely to his finish. His forehead he pressed into the sprawl of her hair. Near the end, he turned his face back and forth among its waves and whispered something in French – *mon coeur*, she thought: my heart. She was sure he didn't mean it literally but it was sweet nonetheless. He was so close, his belly and arms and chest all pressing hers, that she felt his heart give a great pound as he came. He was silent then, every ounce of energy focused on pouring out his pleasure.

When it was over he turned her around and tucked them both back under the covers. Her pussy felt wonderfully pummelled and, though her limbs were limp with fatigue, his hard shoulder was just the pillow she wanted. His hand tangled in her hair as he shifted to find a comfortable position.

'I'll make you breakfast tomorrow,' he said in the thick, sleepy voice of a well-sated man.

'Not too early,' she said, sure she'd sleep forever.

'Not too early,' he agreed, and kissed the top of her head.

6

Abby was gone when he woke and her absence inspired such a wave of melancholy he grew alarmed.

He threw off the covers and sat up in bed, breathing hard. You're away from home, he told himself – and never mind he'd come here because LA didn't feel homey enough. He didn't know anyone here but Abby and he'd developed a small attachment. It was perfectly natural. Perfectly.

He almost tripped on the long black sock that had fallen to the floor during the night. He picked it up, rubbed it across his chest and down his belly. His cock stirred. He thought she'd found him out when she'd tied him to the bed. He still wasn't sure she hadn't. Part of him was horrified, but part of him wanted to throw himself on her mercy. 'More,' he'd said to her, and more was what he wanted now. *S'il te plaît, j'en veux encore* – until she'd bound him too tightly to move, until nothing could move but his taut, tormented cock.

She'd left a note taped to the bathroom mirror with a Band-Aid.

'Must go running,' it said. 'Thank you for last night. Will be back for breakfast if the offer's still good.'

Storm touched the swoopy letters and smiled in spite of himself. She wrote like a girl. He was surprised she didn't dot her 'i's with little hearts. He contemplated the note as he emptied his bladder and washed his hands. She wasn't sure of him; that was clear. True, he wasn't the settling-down kind, but he'd never intentionally broken a promise – not to Abby or any other woman.

He splashed water on his face and eyed his razor. He'd shaved immediately prior to last night's love-making session but a touch-up might be advisable. Perhaps Abby could be coaxed back to bed after breakfast. He pulled out his shaving brush and soap. He wouldn't want to leave whisker burns on those pretty little breasts – which put him in mind of another puzzle.

Why, he wondered as he whisked up a cedar-scented lather, was she still shy of him? Why did she treat her stream of would-be beaus like a joke Marissa had invented? And why would a woman who looked like Abby want to undress in the bathroom and emerge still wearing her underwear – and very plain underwear at that?

How could she not know how attractive she was? Had losing her mother so young impaired her self-confidence?

'Why are you obsessing about this?' he asked his soapy reflection. He knew very well that having a mother wasn't necessarily a good thing. Sometimes a person was better off without. From what he could tell, Abby had grown up in a loving family, most of whom were still alive. He couldn't think of one good reason why she shouldn't be at least as confident of her allure as he was. He dragged his razor down his left cheek, exposing a swath of smooth, tanned skin. Maybe he didn't understand women as well as he'd always believed.

Which was, he thought, a truly frightening concept.

Without warning, his mind returned to the moment he entered her for the very first time. He could see her above him, her breasts pressed close, her velvety thighs hugging his hips. Her clear green eyes had seemed huge, and as vulnerable as a child's. But they hadn't wavered. She'd opened for him without a qualm. She'd allowed his raging cock inside, inch by steaming inch.

The penetration had felt – he froze as the razor nicked his chin – it had felt like nothing that had gone before: no woman, no lover. But it had also felt very natural. Her warm, honeyed folds closing round his sex were infinitely soothing, and desperately exciting. So much so that it had been very difficult not to come at once. Even now his cock engorged at the memory. He touched the hardening shaft and left a smear of bloody shaving foam on the flushed, mobile skin.

Perhaps he would have to delay his buy-out longer than he expected. He had not got enough of her yet – not even close.

The sun rose over the Atlantic as Abby ran south along the National Seashore. Her goal was the Marconi Wireless Station where Teddy Roosevelt sent the first US transatlantic message to King Edward of England, a world-changing event that was almost forgotten today. The landscape around the site was typical Cape moorland, scrub pines and dune grass. The beach plums were in blossom, their tufted white flowers bursting – as if in surprise – from spindly black branches.

She slowed to a walk when she reached the meandering wooden paths that led to the historical site, now just a marker under an open-sided gazebo. To her relief, no one was around. Though her body was calm, and virtuously tired from her run, her mind spun with memories of the night before. She parked her bottom on a grassy hummock and gazed out at the ocean. The breeze was blowing whitecaps off the waves and solitary clouds scudded across a rich blue sky. Slowly, her thoughts began to settle.

There's nothing wrong with you, she told herself. Storm is not turning you into a sex maniac. You're simply discovering a part of yourself you didn't know before – and about time.

A familiar shadow fell slantwise across her feet.

'Hello, Jack,' she said, without turning her head.

Jack sat beside her and, as always, they fumbled for each other's hands. He pulled their twined fingers on to his knee and she leant into his side. He was warm and solid. How long had they been sharing these companionable silences? She thought back. Since she returned to help her father, she supposed. She'd needed someone sane to hang on to and neither Francine nor Sandra had fitted the bill.

Jack was her very favourite of her father's friends.

'Remember my sixteenth birthday?' she said, because he never minded a conversation that came out of nowhere.

'Yeah. You were as pretty as a new fawn.'

Abby squeezed his fingers. 'You bought me those little pearl earrings. Everyone else gave me something childish, or sensible, but you understood I wanted to pretend I was a woman.'

'Still are,' he said with a sideways glance. 'Last time I checked.'

Oh, she loved that sly dog grin of his. No wonder she'd had such a crush on him back then. He'd been recently widowed and was – or so it seemed to a Brontë-obsessed teen – terribly romantic. He'd loved his wife, she knew. They'd been horribly sweet on each other, even after ten years of marriage. They'd always hold hands when they walked. Sometimes, when they came to visit with the Coates, they'd look at each other in a certain way and Abby would think: I want that when I'm married. I want the secrets my husband and I share to shut out the rest of the world.

She remembered one day in particular, a month or so after the funeral, when she'd walked to Jack's house with a casserole – probably inedible – she'd made with her own two hands. He'd burst into tears when she gave it to him. That had been a strange moment, seeing an adult break down that way. She'd pulled him into her arms and he'd held her like he'd never let go. They didn't speak of it afterwards but they became a different sort of friends that day, not so much a girl and a grown-up, but more like equals.

'I had such an awful crush on you,' she said, without quite knowing why.

Jack's thumb stopped stroking her hand. A seagull's cry rose above the sound of the waves. 'And now?' he said.

She looked at him, blinking in confusion. 'Now?'

He turned and stroked her cheek with his other hand. To Abby's embarrassment a wave of sexual heat washed over her body. She knew her face must be turning red.

'Now,' he said, and it wasn't a question any more. He leant closer, slowly, his head tilting. Abby couldn't breathe. Her chin came up. Her lips parted – to say something, she thought – but, when his mouth brushed hers, she knew they'd parted for his kiss.

His lips whispered from side to side, teasing, tantalis-ing. Dizzy with a sudden upwelling of desire, she gripped his arms for balance. He pressed closer. His tongue flickered into her mouth, a question, an invita-tion. His kiss was gentle but he was breathing hard, almost panting against her cheek. This meant a great deal to him. She could hardly believe it, but the way he was holding her, the way he was breathing, told her so. His body heat bled through the cotton of his shirt; his muscles were rigid with tension.

Tentatively, she touched his tongue with her own, lightly, and then again. He groaned, a sound of pure, masculine lust she'd never expected to hear from him. Her initiative broke his restraint. He sucked her tongue hard, drawing it into his mouth and then pushing his deeper. His arms slipped around her back and tightened. His weight pressed her into the dune.

She didn't think. Her legs parted and wrapped themselves around his waist. She pulled his wrinkled cotton shirt from his jeans and thrust her hands up under the cloth. He jerked when she touched his skin. His back was smooth and warm. She felt the scar where she'd accidentally caught him with a fishing hook when she was twelve. Oh, how she'd cried when she saw the blood. Even then, she'd loved him. She traced the puckered tissue down, down past the fuzz at the base of his spine and on to his hard, narrow buttocks.

'Abby.' He surged into the lee of her thighs, his erection insistent beneath the denim. 'Tell me if you want this to stop.'

Almost before he'd finished speaking, he shoved her sports bra over one breast and latched on to her nipple. She couldn't have told him to stop then to save her life. She wanted. She wanted. She was one big, empty want and she needed something hard and hot to fill it.

He read the anxious movements of her hips. He fumbled between them, tore open his zip, and yanked down her running shorts. The tip of his cock touched her mons, burning silk to burning silk. The glans pushed between her lips. It nuzzled her gate. He waited one last instant. She did not refuse him. Their eyes held as he entered her, one steady, for-God's-sake-don't-try-to-stop-me push. Then he stilled, buried deep inside her. Her hands fanned out across the small of his back, restless, enthralled.

'This is so strange,' she said.

He smiled and dropped his head for a deep, wet kiss. After a minute, he broke free. 'Strange bad or strange good?'

Abby was breathing hard. 'I'm not sure.' She wriggled

against the hips that held her nearly motionless. 'But please don't stop.'

He began to stroke and it was different from either Bill or Storm. There was a discipline to it, but there was no holding back of passion. He gave and took in equal measure. The simplicity of his technique was deceptive. He knew just where to hit her. He had a way of varying his rhythm and angle that had her nails pricking his back and a groan burning her throat. He put his hand between them at the end but she scarcely needed it. She came twice, once before him and once after. From kiss to climax, the whole thing hadn't lasted more than five or six minutes.

Now I know I'm a sex maniac, she thought, as he carefully withdrew.

She rolled on to her elbow and touched his cock before he could tuck it away. He covered her hand, wrapping her fingers around his soft, spent penis. She stroked him gently, marvelling at the fact that this was Jack's penis, her teenage crush. It was long and pink now, the shape of it unique, him.

'I may not be a young man,' he said, his hand brushing hair back from her face, 'but if you keep that up, you'd better be prepared for another quickie. A man can store up a lot of unrequited lust in fifteen years.'

Abby looked up at him in surprise but his gaze had returned to her cosseting hand. Fifteen years. He'd wanted her all that time and never said a word?

'Why today?' she said.

'Guess I've been feeling lucky lately.'

'Lucky?'

'Yeah.' He scratched his chin and grinned, and she knew he wasn't going to share his other exploits. 'Besides, I wanted you to know you've got options.'

What did that mean? Her hand stilled. She barely noticed that he was thickening up again. Did he mean she shouldn't confine herself to Storm? That she couldn't trust Storm? 'Do you know something about my chef that I don't?'

He rubbed her forearm, coaxing her to continue stroking him. 'All I know is that he's a man with a hole to fill. And it's not the kind of hole anyone can fill but him.'

'So what are you saying?' she asked, but she knew. He was saying she shouldn't fall into the trap of thinking she could change his ways. Storm had seduced women like her before and he'd certainly do it again. She looked down at Jack's cock. The head was beginning to redden and lift. For the first time, she noticed his pubic hair was the same silvery grey as his head. It was thick, too.

'You're saying I should play the field,' she said.

He tucked her breast back into her bra, then brushed its budded nipple with the back of his fingers. 'I'm saying you should remember there is a field to play. They're all lined up and waiting, Abby. All you have to do is choose which ones you want.'

'I don't think I can.' But she had. She had this morning.

'That's a choice, too,' he said.

She was silent. She stroked him musingly, watching him rise bit by bit from his gaping, faded jeans. His cock was strong, not an old man's cock at all. It wasn't huge but the pointed head and the funny sideways veer had a certain quirky elegance.

'I want to suck it,' she said.

His laugh was a startled snort.

'Far be it from me to deny you,' he said. 'But for that I think we'd better move to my pick-up.'

Abby had had enough al fresco encounters for one day and so she put up no protest. Jack sat in the passenger seat with his legs splayed open, and she crouched in the space beneath the dash. She made him push his jeans down to his ankles so she could lick him all over: his cock, his balls, the sweaty crease at the top of his thighs, even the firm pad of tissue behind his scrotum. He buried his hands in her hair.

'God almighty,' he said as she tried to see how much of him she could swallow. 'I must have done something fine in another life.'

She laughed at that, even though she knew she wasn't really good at this. She'd never much wanted to practise on Bill. Poor old Bill. For his sake, she should have cut him loose long ago. Given her inexperience, she wasn't surprised that Jack pulled her off him before he came.

'Your mouth is as sweet as spring flowers,' he said as he pulled her on to his lap. 'But it's your pussy that's been giving me wet dreams for the last fifteen years, and I've just got to have another poke.'

'"Poke!",' she exclaimed, wriggling greedily down his cock. 'I'll give you a poke!'

They were tickling each other when they came, and when they came down she didn't know whether to be happy or horrified.

'I am a sex maniac,' she moaned, much to Jack's amusement.

One thing was certain. She was going to be late for breakfast.

Jack drove her back to the inn – actually, to a side road short of the inn where he pulled up beneath a shady tree and kissed her breathless. He didn't ask to see her again, but she knew he wanted to. She knew she wanted to, too.

She walked the two remaining streets to the inn and told herself she wasn't sneaking around. She and Storm didn't have a relationship: they were having a fling.

What was his motto – *no obligations, only pleasure?* She could sleep with whomever she pleased. As for not telling him about it, that was only common sense. She might be inexperienced but she knew he liked thinking of her as his creation, the woman he was awakening to the true extent of her desires.

He'd awakened her, all right, but she suspected he wouldn't like knowing she'd turned to another man for satisfaction. Men just were that way – most of them anyway. That much even Abby knew.

'We can't let you do this,' Francine said.

She and Sandra sat at the big mahogany table in the cottage dining room; the same table they'd had food fights across as children. Both her older sisters had matching prim expressions on their faces, though Sandra's was marred by the splotch of blue ink on her left cheek. She'd obviously spent the morning writing. Her long wavy hair hadn't been combed and she wore one of her ex-husband's pin-striped office shirts – a habit that disturbed Abby no end. The divorce had not been Sandra's idea, but it was more than time she let go.

She blew her breath out wearily. She'd been hoping to get this meeting over with quickly. It was almost time to prep for lunch. Since prepping for lunch involved working elbow to elbow with Storm, the responsibility seemed more pressing than usual.

Her encounter with Jack this morning had done nothing to calm her overactive libido. She'd missed breakfast altogether. Worse, images of Jack and Storm – and even Bill – had been barraging her ever since. Naked men danced across the screen of her mind, big cocks, little cocks, grunting and groaning and soft kisses, hard kisses, sand under her back and satin sheets and high-heeled shoes and that moment, that breath-stealing moment when the head of it all, the heart of it all, pushed past the tiny resistance at her gate. Damn it, she was hot and wet and grumpy and, if Storm gave her so much as a five-minute opening, she'd screw him silly.

What's more, she didn't care if the waiters did watch!

Good Lord, she thought. I'm going to have to stop eating his cooking.

Fighting for composure, she gripped the back of the tall Queen Anne chair behind which she stood and faced her sisters with a level stare. 'What do you mean, you can't "let" me do it? I'm not asking your permission. I'm informing you as a matter of courtesy and because I thought you'd be interested. Renovations on the upstairs dining room will begin next week so that we can open in time for the tourist season. I'm not asking the estate to kick in any money. I'll be paying the bills with current income.'

And what's left from my second mortgage, she added silently.

'But our investment,' Sandra protested. Though generously supported by her ex, Sandra behaved as if she were perpetually one step from the poorhouse.

'What investment?' Abby said, thoroughly exasperated. 'Neither of you have invested a dime of your money or a minute of your time at the inn. Every penny has either come from Dad's life insurance or my own pocket.'

'All the more reason to be careful.' Sandra folded her hands on the tabletop. 'You don't want to impoverish yourself.'

'Jesus H. Christ.' Abby pressed the heels of her palms to her forehead and ignored her sisters' gasps. 'Don't you get it? I can't make the profit I need to turn the inn around unless I have both dining rooms open this summer. Look.' She let her breath out slowly and loosened her grip on the chair. 'You know Daddy intended that money as a capital reserve to support the inn.'

'And he wanted the inn to provide support for us,' Sandra interjected.

'Yes, he did.' Abby pushed a lock of hair off her forehead. 'But there won't be any income unless I get the inn back on its feet and I can't do that unless I put more money into it. We will make a profit, Sandra, if you just give me time to undo Dad's — well, his oversights. I do have a business degree, remember. I'm not making this up. And by rights I could demand the estate pay me a salary, no matter what the inn's profit or loss. I really don't see how you can object to my plans.'

'He left you the cottage,' Sandra said, as though that explained everything.

'Daddy left me the cottage because I set aside a promising career to help him when he got sick. He didn't leave it to me because he loved me better than you.'

Finally shamed to silence, Sandra stared down at her ink-stained hands.

Francine cleared her throat. 'Maybe we should consider paying you a salary, instead of just your share of the profit.'

Sandra's head came up sharply. She cheeped in distress.

'Well, we don't have to decide right now,' Francine soothed her. 'We can take it under advisement. There is one other thing that concerns me, however.' She turned back to Abby with her sister-knows-best face. 'You seem to be putting a lot of faith in this new chef of yours. I know he's increased business a gazillion per cent, but how do you know he won't pack up one day and leave you in the lurch?'

'He won't do that,' Abby said firmly, as sure of that as she was of her own name. 'Storm Dupré is a man of integrity.'

He might break my heart, she thought, but he'd never harm my business.

7

Marissa was combing Abby's pale blonde hair with long, slow strokes that had Abby purring and Marissa creaming in her snug white shorts. The object of her fantasies slouched before her dressing table in a worn wicker chair. Her eyes were closed, her arms limp on the low, curved rests. It was Monday – the inn's off day. Storm had driven to Provincetown to meet one of their suppliers and Marissa had Abby all to herself.

The only thing that would have made her happier was actually having Abby.

Stroking another thick blonde sheaf down Abby's back, Marissa watched her boss in the mirror. Her breathing was regular, her cheeks pink. One strap of a baby-blue tank top fell off her shoulder. The top was tucked into a pair of khaki walking shorts. The combination was more revealing than her usual twin sets and skirts, especially considering the bareness of her breasts. Beneath the ribbed cotton her nipples rose almost as sharply as Marissa's own.

Marissa knew Abby must be daydreaming. The flush on her neck told her so; the way she squirmed in the chair and curled and uncurled her toes. She was probably fantasising about Storm, but at the moment Marissa didn't care. She'd never been in the same room with Abby when she was aroused. The scent of her secret heat made her tremble. Someday, maybe, someday . . .

'Your hair is so pretty,' she said, brushing it up into the sunlight and letting it fall. A hundred golden strands danced in the air. 'It's as fine as a baby's. Just like silk. I could brush it all day.'

'And I could let you,' Abby said, her sweet voice husky. 'When I was little, Francine used to do this. It's funny –' she shifted in the chair and stretched her beautiful bare legs under the table '– Sandra was the eldest, but Francine always played mother.'

'Still does,' said Marissa.

Abby's lashes shadowed her sun-kissed cheeks. She looked so relaxed. She looked like she'd just been fucked. Her heart in her throat, Marissa set down the brush and stroked Abby's hair with her bare hands.

'Mm.' Abby squirmed deeper into the chair's cushion. 'You'll put me to sleep.'

'You deserve it,' she said, venturing cautiously on to Abby's arms. 'You've been working hard.' But she didn't look as if she'd been working hard. She looked as if she were getting eight solid hours of sleep a night. Her skin glowed. Her hair gleamed. Her eyes sparkled like a woman with a secret, or a woman in love.

Marissa shook off the thought. Even Abby wasn't stupid enough to fall for that playboy. Still, Marissa couldn't deny that Storm had been good for her.

'How are your folks?' Abby asked as Marissa's fingers trailed lightly back to her shoulders. 'Is your dad still trying to get you to return to Boston?'

'He never stops.' Marissa moved her hands to Abby's forehead and stroked them down her hairline. Her skin was soft as butter. She stared at the shadow between her breasts and wished she dared explore that curving darkness. She forced herself to breathe evenly. 'He doesn't understand why I'd leave a perfectly good teaching position to wait at tables. "Stifled-schmifled," he says. "Harvard is a great university." Mom thinks I'm dissatisfied because I only earned a sociology degree. "What use is that except for teaching?" she says. She thinks I should go back to school so I can be a psychiatrist like her and Dad, and no doubt grow up to raise kids who are just as fucked up as me.'

Abby's eyes fluttered open. A crease appeared between her brows. Marissa could have kicked herself for spoiling the mood.

'You are not fucked up,' she said. 'Lots of people your age don't know what they want to do.'

But I do know, Marissa thought. I want to lock us in this room and not come out for a month. She picked up the brush and started braiding Abby's hair.

Abby closed her eyes again. 'Maybe your purpose in life has nothing to do with a regular career. As long as you're happy with what you're doing, that's all that matters.'

'You should have been the therapist,' Marissa said, 'instead of my batty parents.'

Abby smiled and reached up to press her hand. The gesture was friendly, even motherly, but it brought a quick rush of moisture from her core. A hot flash prickled across her chest and she had to squeeze her thighs together to contain a sharp stab of lust.

Even if Abby had guessed that she liked women, she couldn't have known what this simple touch did to her. Marissa had to bite the inside of her cheek to keep from crying out. She sagged in relief when Abby let go. 'Old man Weston has been asking me to pose for him again,' she said, more as a distraction than because she wanted advice.

Abby sat up and turned sideways in the chair. 'Jack Weston?'

Marissa secured the end of Abby's braid before she could pull it loose. 'Yeah, and he wants me to pose nude. Can you imagine me baring my scrawny self for that dirty old man?'

Abby propped her chin on the back of the wicker

chair. She looked Marissa thoughtfully up and down. 'I'm sure any pictures he took would be beautiful. Besides, Marissa, he's not that old.' A blush stained Abby's cheeks at her own words, a new blush.

My God, Marissa thought, horror spreading through her chest like cold, dark water. The old man had done her. It had to have happened recently, too, because Abby never would have two-timed Bill.

The bastard. The lousy, rutting bastard. He knew how Marissa felt about Abby and he still slipped her the salami. Just wait till she gave him a piece of her mind. He'd wish he'd kept his cock locked up tighter than his precious Hasselblad.

Like a lot of old-timers, Jack didn't lock his doors. Marissa let herself into his fifties-style rancher and slammed into his darkroom without bothering to knock. The regular light was on and he was examining a stack of proofs. He looked up at her entrance, surprised but not furious. She was disappointed. In her current mood, she would have been happy to ruin a week's worth of work.

Make that a month's.

'You fucked her,' she said, her voice breaking with emotion. 'You knew how I felt and you fucked her anyway.'

He set the photographs down. 'I take it you mean Abby.'

'Yes, I mean Abby.' She lashed at him with her fist.

'Hey,' he said, catching it.

She was quicker with the next blow. It struck the centre of his chest. 'Bastard!'

He caught that fist, too, and trapped both behind her back. Screaming with fury, she kicked his shins and butted him with her head. Chemicals sloshed as she jostled an open bath. Cursing, he lifted her off her feet.

She was so intent on injuring him she didn't notice straight off that he was carrying her somewhere, out of the darkroom, through the living room of his L-shaped house, down the hall and –

The fucker was taking her to his bedroom!

'Bastard,' she said, and took a nip at his ear.

He threw her off him so hard she landed on her bottom and slid five feet down the narrow hall. The impact stunned her speechless.

'Do that again and I'll slap you into next week,' he said. 'I'm not too proud to hit a woman who's biting me. Now –' he stood over her with his hands on his hips, barely even breathing hard '– if I offer you a beer, will you drink it or smash it over my head?'

He made her feel so childish. She hated that worse than anything. She knew Abby didn't belong to her; knew she'd never belong to her – never, never, never.

She started to cry.

'Oh, baby.' Jack knelt down on the floor and pulled her into his arms. He rubbed her back like a man who'd comforted a lot of sobbing women. She cried harder.

'My butt hurts,' she wailed, freeing a hand to rub her tailbone. 'And I love her.'

'Oh, honey.' Jack rocked her from side to side, laughing through his sympathy. 'I know. I know you love her and it hurts just awful. But we can never own the people we love, not even when they love us back.'

Marissa's sobs diminished to a hiccuping snuffle. 'It's not fair.'

He hugged her tighter. 'No, it isn't.'

'I can't even fall in love with anyone else.'

This time his laugh was all amusement. 'Don't count on that, honey. The heart is a marvellously flexible organ.' He stood and held out his hand to her. 'Come. Pose for me. I want to catch you with the fire in your eyes.'

She sniffed. 'How about the snot dripping from my nose?'

He winked. 'I'll loan you my hanky.'

His expression was soft and kind. She knew he pitied her. At the moment, however, she could do with a dose of pity. She took his hand and let him pull her to his studio.

He'd added this room to the house with the proceeds from his first book, *The Cape in Moonlight*. Along with the stunning photographs, his offbeat, philosophical prose had made it a surprise bestseller. He followed up that success with *Nantucket Rhapsody* and his latest photo essay, *The Art of Winter*.

Appropriately, nothing obscured the studio's picture-perfect view of Cape Cod Bay. The space was glassed-in like a greenhouse and Jack's land extended down a long grassy slope to the water's edge. The shore birds that nested among the reeds were so used to his antics he could lie within feet of their hiding places and they wouldn't stir a feather.

'Back in a minute,' he said, leaving Marissa to look around.

Though he didn't take many indoor shots, Jack kept equipment in the studio – light meters and tripods and special screens to make the most of whatever light he found outside. He also did his writing there. His desk and computer sat at one end, turned so he could stare at the bay while he composed his deathless prose. That was his term for it. Marissa thought his prose probably was deathless. The shops in Boston carried his books. They were always on the shelves; even the old editions.

Must be nice, she thought, wishing she could do something deathless.

Pressing her nose to the window, she watched a tall white heron stalk an unsuspecting fish and wondered why the hell the famous Jack Weston wanted to photograph a screwed-up nobody like her. She heard his footsteps approach from behind and then he slid an ice-cold bottle of Sam Adams Boston Lager down the centre of her chest. A wisp of vapour curled from the open mouth. Marissa watched it for a moment before taking a melancholy swig.

'The camera will love you,' he said.

She closed her eyes and relaxed into his embrace. The moon loved her. The camera loved her. She wondered if a human being ever would.

Jack undid the fastenings of her snug white shorts and slid his hands down inside her panties. His palms were warm, slightly callused and surprisingly arousing. 'This is new for me, too,' he said. 'I haven't photographed many people.'

'I've got a tattoo,' she warned, clutching the bottle tighter.

His lips curved against the side of her neck. 'I'm sure I'll love your tattoo.'

He helped her finish the beer, then stripped her off. He began by posing her naked against the glass with the bay sparkling in the background and a small spotlight beaming up at her from the floor so the outside light wouldn't black her out. He shot half a roll that way, crouching, then standing, his face entirely absorbed in the vagaries of light and composition.

'Good,' he said, after long minutes of silence. He handed her a white terry-cloth robe, grabbed a different camera and led her outside. Except for a few tiny fishing boats bobbing on the bay, their solitude was complete. He sat her cross-legged on the pier with her back to the water and the robe pooled around her hips. As though she were no more than another prop, he draped a thick hawser rope across her lap and up between her breasts. His impersonal attentions dissolved her last shreds of self-consciousness.

Weary from her earlier outburst, she rested her head against a piling and wondered how the pictures would turn out. Would he make her as beautiful as a snow-covered dune? She smiled and touched the blue Chinese lion that reared on the outer curve of her right breast. Jack's arm shot out. She thought he was going to move her hand away from the tattoo, but he touched her nipple instead, very lightly, brushing it back and forth and then moving to its partner until they both stood out like tiny raspberries.

When he finally withdrew his hand, it was shaking – a fact that astonished her. She'd never seen anything ruffle Jack. She looked at the zip of his tan cotton trousers. It bulged like he'd stuffed a pair of socks in there.

'You like this,' she marvelled. 'This turns you on.'

He scratched the side of his chin in apparent bemusement. 'I'm afraid you've caught me out. This is a long-standing fantasy of mine.'

'Do you want to –?' She gestured towards her naked pubis.

He shook his head. 'No. Not yet.' He snapped another half-dozen shots in quick succession. 'Lord, you're a beautiful girl, Marissa. Don't let anyone tell you different.' He turned her on to her belly then and had her reach over the edge of the pier to dabble her fingers in the water. Kneeling over her buttocks, he shot her gazing at her wavery reflection.

'So.' She looked back at him over her shoulder while he changed film rolls. 'Are my pictures going to end up out on the coffee table or hidden under the bed?'

He grinned at her. 'Definitely coffee table. Although –' he sank down far enough to brush her buttocks with his erection '– I may want to keep them to myself for a while.'

For a moment, she imagined him wanking off over

her pictures. The thought was both amusing and arousing. She turned over between his spread legs and, after a quick glance to check the position of the fishing boats, kneaded his muscular thighs. 'If you turn me into a book, will you write about me, too?'

He covered her hands, edging them closer to his balls. 'No.' He inhaled sharply as she swept her thumbs over their warm, bulging curve. 'I'd hold forth about the mysteries of women in general.'

'Know a bit about that, do you?' She shifted her hands and began scratching his whole swollen package.

'A bit.' His hips pressed closer, and wagged a bit to direct the scratch where he wanted it most. 'Marissa, you're distracting me. I want to shoot another roll.'

She ran her nails backwards and tickled the seam that covered his anus. 'You can shoot another roll later.' She arched her back, putting her breasts on offer to his avid eyes. 'Just think how nice I'll look when I'm afterglowing.'

'Fine,' he surrendered. 'Put on the robe and we'll go back inside.'

'No. Here.'

'Marissa, it's broad daylight.'

'I like the look of your rowboat,' she said, and popped his trouser button. The head of his cock immediately poked through the opening, rosy and moist with arousal.

They clambered in carefully.

'I'm too old for this,' he muttered, but she knew he wasn't. He was too eager to be too old.

The tide was low enough that they could shove the boat into the shadows under the pier. Like an echo chamber, the shelter magnified every excited breath, every slap of the dark-green water on the fibreglass hull. Fortunately, it wasn't too dark to see. The waves threw thread-like ripples of sun on to the weathered underside of the dock, on to her arms, on to Jack's face. Marissa smelt fish, wet reeds, waterlogged wood, and the faint, intoxicating scent of sex about to happen.

'Take your clothes off,' she said. 'I want to see you naked this time.'

He complied without a word, struggling to get everything off quickly. He had a good body, really good. He was tall and firm and his chest and thighs bore a satisfying silver fuzz. Marissa couldn't wait to scratch her way all over it.

He reached past her to knock one of the seats off its supports so she could lay back. With the robe spread out beneath her, Marissa lounged back on her elbows and watched his eyes run over her body, from her high, pointy breasts to her concave belly and down her long, wiry legs. She was all bones and angles. Even her breasts thrust from her ribs like little cones, nothing like Abby's beautiful, rounded handfuls. But Jack seemed to like her looks. He was breathing hard when he finished the survey. His cock was veering even further left than it had the first time they made love. She realised this must be his personal flag of high excitement.

She beckoned him closer with one curled finger. He dropped over her on to his arms. 'I'll be on top,' he warned, as if offering her the chance to change that.

She laughed and scratched his cloud of chest hair. 'I think you need to be on top today.'

He did. Oh, he did. He took her after a single kiss and a brief two-fingered probe of her dripping pussy. He slid in easily and they both sighed with pleasure. He was wonderfully long and hot. He seemed to reach so, so far inside her. He held there, ten seconds, twenty, and then he began to surge and withdraw, surge and withdraw, like the tide sucking at the sand.

The boat rocked with them, its rebound sharper than a water bed, alternately jarring them closer, then apart.

They fought the apart; they revelled in the closer. The water slapped the hull with the rhythm of their fucking, an exaggerated, sexual noise. Listening to it drove Marissa high and fast. She wrapped her legs around his waist.

'Fuck me,' she said, using her legs to strengthen her thrusts. 'Fuck me, Jack.'

He drove harder. 'I am fucking you. God love you, I am.'

He kept up the pace, driving left, then right, then up against the sweet spot behind her pubic bone. He could tell she liked that from the way she clutched his back and gasped. He kept pumping her there with firm, steady strokes. His balls slapped against her cheeks, the sensation changing as they drew up higher with excitement. They were close, both of them. Marissa's breath began to whine in her throat. Ooh, it was going to be a good one. She could tell. It was going to be sweet and hard and . . .

He dropped his head to kiss her, once, hard. Then he sat up, still lodged deep but no longer thrusting. Marissa swallowed back a cry, wondering what was coming now. Her pussy fluttered crazily around his cock, whimpering 'don't stop, don't stop'. But she trusted him; she did.

He reached into his pile of discarded clothes and pulled out his camera, not the Hasselblad – he wouldn't risk that so near the water – but his second best, a Nikon. He removed the lens cap and pointed it at her with trembling hands. He advanced the film. His cock throbbed inside her, measurably harder than it had been a moment earlier. He pointed the camera at her face.

'Touch yourself,' he said, his belly moving in rapid, shallow jerks. 'Bring yourself off. I want to catch your expression when you come.'

His excitement was infectious. Marissa touched her breasts, drawing out the nipples in long, pulling strokes. Jack licked his lips and snapped a shot. She ran her hands down her belly, circled her navel, then combed through her thick, black pubic hair. She parted her lips to bare the sharp pink triangle of her clit. The shutter snapped twice.

'Touch yourself,' Jack rasped. He shifted his thighs so that his knees slid under her bottom, tipping her higher. The root of his cock slid into view, cranberry red and roped with vigorous, pulsing veins. His skin gleamed with her juices. His lens was pointed at her cunt.

'This isn't for the book,' she said, hesitating a moment longer.

He shook his head, his eyes hidden by the camera, his jaw tight. 'This is just for me.'

'Then take a picture of that.' She touched the swath of glistening cock. 'Just for me.'

He took two shots of his half-buried cock, then three, and then she touched herself. She closed her eyes, both forgetting he was there and thrilled that he watched. She brought herself up as slowly as she could but she was so excited she couldn't draw it out very long. She rubbed her clit from side to side over her slippery flesh. She slid her fingers around the column of his sex. She groaned for him. She twitched for him. She pinched her nipples and said *soon, soon* and then finally she shattered to the music of the shutter going wild.

She opened her eyes, stretching languorously around his rigid cock. Sweat shone on his lean, wind-roughened cheeks. The knuckles that held his camera were white. He screwed the lens cap back on and set it back in its nest of clothes. He rolled forward over her, driving himself to the bone. His body shook like a beech in a storm.

Marissa grabbed the back of his neck and brought

her lips to his ear. 'Don't come right away,' she whispered. He groaned and she dug her fingers into the knotted muscles of his shoulders – half threat, half caress. 'I want to feel you suffer.'

'I'm about to blow, Marissa, no matter what I do.'

'Go slowly,' she insisted. 'I want to feel you come.'

He pulled back, slowly, slowly, with a strangled grunt of effort.

'Fuck,' he said, pausing on trembling arms to catch his breath. Then he pushed back. Marissa hummed with pleasure, feeling her flesh give way for his cock, feeling her sheath twitch in little tremors of after-orgasm. He felt them, too.

'Yes, suck me,' he said, reaching the limit of his thrust. 'Suck me with your cunt. Bring me off, Marissa. Bring me off like that.'

She pulled at him, trying to roll the contraction from root to tip. She was strong inside. She'd felt the pull on her own fingers. She knew he must like it. His cock pressed the walls of her vagina, swelling, stiffening.

'Yes,' he said. His head went back. His eyes drifted shut. 'Again.'

She rippled over him one more time. The tension left his face, years falling away in a surge of intense, sexual pleasure. Waves lapped the boat. His mouth fell open. He drew a deep, deep breath.

Then he came. It was a slow pulse, sleepy heartbeats of orgasm from which all the violence had been removed. He sighed and it almost sounded like he was singing. Marissa smiled, her eyes stinging with unexpected tears. As they spilt from the corners, he sank down on her and kissed them away.

'That was good,' he said, rolling them both on to their sides. 'That was very, very good.'

Yes, she thought, but not good enough to erase the dream of Abby.

8

Abby was waiting in his sitting room when he returned from Provincetown. She sat in one of the big plaid chairs with her feet tucked under her rump. Her outfit consisted of a baby-blue tank top and the virginal white panties he was beginning to develop a fetish for. The shutters were closed.

'Well, hello.' He smiled as he set down his packages. 'I didn't expect to find you here.'

She immediately sprang to her feet. 'I'm sorry. I shouldn't have assumed –'

'Hush.' He crossed to her and took her by the shoulders. 'You're welcome here anytime.' He kissed her. 'Very welcome.'

'Oh, I thought –' she tilted her head for another kiss, endearingly distracted '– I thought I might make up for missing breakfast yesterday.'

'Really? What did you have in mind?'

His question took her aback. She crossed her arms over her breasts as if that were where her secret wishes lived. 'I thought you might have something you wanted to do,' she said.

'I think it's your turn to decide, don't you? Although –' he gestured to the brown-paper parcel he'd set on the lamp table '– I do have a little present that might put you in the mood.'

'You bought me a present?' Her eyes alight, she crawled back into the chair and held out her hands.

His mouth turned up on one side as he handed it to

her. 'I guess this means I won't have to bully you into accepting it.'

'Certainly not.' She burrowed through the tissue paper. 'I love presents. Oh!' She'd found the first of his gifts, a sugar-pink chemise and panty set. She held the top to her chest and stroked the silk over the swell of her breast.

He crouched in front of the chair. 'That's for everyday wear.' He pulled another tissue-wrapped bundle from beneath the first. 'And this is for special.'

She was quieter now, her eyes big. From the second package she lifted out an emerald-green cami-knicker cut high in the legs and decorated with exquisite Belgian lace.

'Ooh,' was all she said.

'And this –' he tapped the last, largest package '– is for fun. But only if you think it's fun.'

Her lashes slid down to her cheeks. She folded her hands on top of the tissue. 'You said this was a "little" present.'

He laid his hands over the cool, smooth skin of her knees. 'I hope it's a present for both of us. But, if you don't like it, I can return it to the shop.'

He couldn't actually, since he'd had everything custom-made to her measurements, but she didn't have to know that.

She took a breath for courage and opened the last package. The sheer white paper parted to reveal a midnight-blue basque with lacy push-up cups and a light, mostly ornamental boning. A matching thong panty completed the ensemble.

'Oh,' she said, and this 'oh' was different – shocked, but the sort of shock that sends heat flooding to a person's groin. She squirmed in the chair and pressed her hand over her belly. 'It's ... it's beautiful.'

Storm cleared everything off her lap except for the

basque. Then he slid his hands up her thighs. Abby looked at him. He ran his fingers around the legs of her pristine white panties. 'I want you to know I'm very fond of these. But I thought you might enjoy seeing yourself in something fancy.'

A brief silence fell. When she spoke, her voice was thick with emotion. 'I never wanted to dress up for, well, before. But you –' she cradled the basque against her chest '– you make me feel differently about everything. I don't know if it's because you're the one who's asking, or because you've changed me.'

'You've changed you,' he said, pleased by the compliment in spite of his demur. But perhaps 'pleased' was too pale a word. She was giving him a kind of virginity, the virginity of adventure. Gratification coursed through his veins like brandy. A woman never forgot the man who introduced her to herself.

She trailed her finger down a line of boning. 'May I wear it now?'

In an instant, his gratification turned carnal. His cock rose so swiftly his clothes could scarcely make way fast enough. 'You don't need my permission,' he said, his voice as heavy as his sex.

Still clutching the basque, Abby climbed sideways out of the chair and headed for the bathroom. Storm had to shake his head at her continued reserve. To his surprise, she stopped at the entrance to the bedroom. She turned to face him and set the lingerie on the floor, then grasped the hem of her tank top in both hands. She bit her lip.

'Go ahead,' he said as reassuringly as he could. He still crouched before the chair. He didn't dare move. His cock was pounding in his shorts like a twelve-piece band.

Just as he was about to lose hope, she peeled the shirt over her head and shimmied out of her panties, quickly, as if she feared losing her nerve. Her breasts jiggled with the energy of her movements. God, she was beautiful. He almost told her to leave the basque alone, but this was her moment of courage. He had to let her finish.

She pulled the thong on first, then the top. It took a bit of wriggling but she soon had everything straight. The boning cinched her waist and the push-up cups did indeed make the most of her pretty breasts. She pressed both hands to the unaccustomed swell and gaped at her cleavage.

'Goodness,' she said.

He smiled and rose to take her hands in his. He held them out from her sides. 'You look very pretty. Do you feel sexy?'

'I felt sexy the minute you walked in the door,' she blurted, then blushed bright pink.

He laughed and kissed her. 'I'm glad.' He kissed her again, with his tongue this time, and began backing her through the door.

'Wait.' She put her little hand in the centre of his chest. 'I thought it was my turn to decide what we do.'

Stopping was harder than he expected. 'It is.'

She looked back over her shoulder towards the bed. His thumbs rested at the base of her throat and he registered a sudden jump in her pulse. 'I was wondering if you had any more toys?' she asked.

Storm closed his eyes, his own heart beginning to thunder. He hadn't expected her to be so adventurous so soon. 'They're in the bedside table.'

She pulled gently away from him. He heard her open the door to the cabinet and kneel down. He wished he'd known she was going to do this. He'd have moved his bondage paraphernalia somewhere else. Those toys were in the bottom, though, in the back and bagged. She might not find them.

Or did he secretly want her to?

'I think I need to take everything out,' she said. 'There's too much stuff in here.'

'Fine,' he said. Too nervous to watch, he turned his back and began removing the clothes in which he'd met the inn's supplier. He pulled his tie off first, then his crisp white shirt, draping both carefully over the bentwood chair. He heard her removing objects from the cabinet. His belt buckle fought his shaky hands and against his will he remembered all the uses a long strip of leather could serve. He pulled the belt free with a muffled curse. Abby was too engrossed to hear.

'My goodness,' she said over something – one of the dildos, most likely.

Storm heard the ben wa balls clank in their velvet box as he shoved his trousers and briefs down his legs. He'd forgotten his shoes. He almost tripped getting them off. But his anxiety hadn't done his erection any harm. It thrust from his body in a long upwards slope, bobbing ecstatically in anticipation. He squeezed his hands into fists as tightly as he could, then ordered himself to relax.

When he turned, he saw she'd laid his toys in three neat rows across his mattress, including the bondage accessories, which she'd taken from their black velvet sacks. One bag contained leather cuffs for binding wrists and ankles. The leather was worn and soft, like an old saddle, though the Velcro fastenings were fresh. The contents of the second bag were more unusual, but equally suitable for solo use, consisting of a dozen long black latex straps. An inch or so wide, the latex was stretchy and tended to cling to the skin, especially damp skin. Abby had coiled the straps together on top of the bag like a nest of shiny snakes. It was hard to look away from them, but he forced himself. She was waiting.

'Do you have any questions?' he asked, praying she wouldn't ask about the straps.

She pointed to a small ivory-coloured dildo, his favourite, though she couldn't have known that. The silicone cock had a smooth, velvety surface, a slender diameter, and just enough flex to make it ideal for anal play. Unfortunately, the dildo was almost as big a threat to his self-control as the latex ties. He noticed Abby's blush had spread all the way down her chest.

'Um,' she said. 'I was wondering. Is that too big to use on you?'

'No.' Struggling for his usual paternal amusement, he unconsciously clenched his bottom cheeks. 'But you'll need some lubricant.'

'Oh.' She pressed one knuckle to her lips and said in a very small voice, 'Do you have any?'

His anus quivered violently. He could hardly get the words out to answer her. 'There should be some in the drawer.'

Abby reached for the knob, then paused. 'Do you mind my doing this?'

Her question restored his sense of humour. 'What do you think?'

Her eyes travelled down his body, stopping at the bold outward jut of his cock. Her breasts rose and fell with her quickened breath, pressing against the navy lace in delightful pink and white swells. 'I think you like the idea,' she said. 'I think it arouses you.' She squared her shoulders. 'All right. I know what I want to do now. Go into the sitting room and wait for me.'

Did she know – could she know – what her order did to him? To wait, to wonder, to feel as if he might explode with the force of his lust while she remained in the bedroom, deciding his erotic fate? He could scarcely bear the suspense.

She returned with the dildo *and* the cuffs *and* the shiny latex straps. With that triple threat, he'd be lucky if he didn't come before she started. Oh, God, he thought, don't let me humiliate myself.

She set her booty down in the overstuffed chair, then took him by the wrist and led him to stand before it, facing the seat. A homey braided rug covered the wide floorboards here, soft under his bare feet. She knelt down behind him. Without a word, she nudged his feet farther apart and used the leather cuffs to attach his ankles to the chair's front legs. Her silence intensified his response more than any amount of play-acting could. Tonight, they would not pretend to be anyone but themselves. Each sigh would be true, each cry sincere. His knees trembled. He stiffened them and set his jaw.

She ran her hands down his arms and pulled them gently behind his back. Removing a single black tie from the tangle on the chair, she lashed his wrists together. She had good instincts for this. The binding was neither too tight nor too loose. Another wave of lust pooled in his groin. The tip of his cock felt strangely cool, as though its inner heat caused the air to chill in comparison.

She put her hand on the centre of his spine and slid it upward, exerting a slight forward pressure as she did so. When she reached the nape of his neck, he understood the message. He bent at the waist and braced his head on the back of the chair. A single drop of sweat rolled off the tip of his nose. It plopped on to the cushion, darkening a single navy check. She slid her hand the other way, stroking it over the curve of his buttock.

'*Mon Dieu*,' he said, because he couldn't help himself. She had defeated his strength with the force of his own desire. He wanted what she was doing so badly he could not resist. But he had never been more aware of his own power than when she wrapped the whole of it round her delicate finger.

She lifted the dildo from the chair, then the lubricant. He felt her go to her knees behind him, between his spread legs. She blew lightly on the back of his scrotum, stirring the silky hairs, cooling the heated skin. He shivered violently, and then she did as well, as if the involuntary response were communicable. She took one cheek in each hand and spread them. He braced for the entry of the dildo, but instead she kissed him.

At first he thought he'd imagined it, but she did it again and this time her tongue drew a circle round the pucker of his anus. He couldn't believe it. She was too shy, too inexperienced, but – ah – there it was again, the sweep of hot-cool wetness.

Then it was gone, as if he had dreamt it.

He heard her open the lubricant and oil the dildo. She stood to press it into him, bit by bit, kneading his hip as she did it and dropping soft kisses to his sweating back. His body opened and he knew she must be thinking of the way her body had opened for him. When she kissed his shoulder blade, her heartbeat thudded through her breasts, through the prickly lace of the bra cups. Her breath was hot and uneven. He was glad she liked doing this, so glad.

A sound escaped the back of his throat as the bulbous head of the dildo brushed his prostate. She stopped.

'No,' he said, the word squeezed between ragged breaths. 'I'm all right. It feels good.'

She hesitated a moment, then continued pushing until the flared base of the dildo snugged up against his anus. The silicone quickly soaked up his body heat and, as it did, its velvet-smooth surface began to feel like human flesh. Would he like that? he wondered. Would he like having a man take him back there? Would he like having her watch?

The hard throb of his cock said 'maybe'. If she were watching, maybe yes. He clenched tight inside, loving the hard intrusion, moving himself subtly around it. She patted his cheek, in encouragement or satisfaction; which, he didn't know or care, especially when she took hold of the base and rocked it.

Sensation exploded through his bowels, hot, tingling sparks. His breath huffed out in a rush. His bound hands clenched into fists in the small of his back. The quick little rocking motion knocked the firm, velvety head against his sweet spot. He was so sensitive there, too sensitive. The skin of his cock tightened to the point of pain. No, he tried to say, but all that came out was a moan. He was going to come. He couldn't stop it.

She saved him from immediate ignominy by drawing the dildo halfway out. Then she pushed it in again, rocking it all the way. He grunted as she repeated the trick. How could she know how incredible that felt? How could she guess? He locked his knees. It was so good. He had to last a little longer, just a little.

She pulled and rocked. She pushed and rocked. She lingered at the deepest point of entry and jiggled the dildo even faster. Ah, God, he couldn't. He rolled his forehead against the back of the chair. His balls drew upward. He gulped for air. She pulled and rocked. He thrust his hips back at her. She pushed to meet them. She kissed his shoulder blade.

'Yes,' she whispered. 'Come.'

Her permission stung like a whip. Feeling seethed in his loins, vinegar sharp, cayenne hot. He was going to come. She began to pull. *Merde*.

'No,' he gasped. 'Push.'

She shoved deep again, rocking wildly, right there, right there, on his joy spot. The pressure spiked. He felt the first contraction and then he overflowed. His seed oozed from him, slow and thick, as if the pleasure were being squeezed from the marrow of his bones. His hip joint popped with the tensing of his muscles. He groaned, still coming, still squeezing and then the orgasm rolled past the knot of tightness and into the land of milk and honey.

'Are you all right?' she asked, after a moment of watching him shake in reaction.

He nodded, his head still supported by the back of the chair. He forced his hands to relax again, trying to work the cramps from his fingers. She pulled the dildo carefully from his body.

'I can loosen these cuffs,' she said, touching his wrists. But they weren't too tight. He could feel the circulation returning as he relaxed. She seemed to sense it, too. She bent and kissed one palm. 'Do you want more?'

He groaned, not because he didn't, but because the question inspired an aching resurgence in his cock: not a recovery, but a definite wag of interest.

'I hope you can wait just a bit,' she said, with a shadow of humour, 'because I have a problem I need your help with.'

'Problem?'

She curled her arm beneath his chest to help him stand.

'Yes,' she said, and climbed into the chair to sit on its back. Since it touched the wall, her weight did not overbalance it. She was smiling and he thought he caught a spark of mischief in her downcast eyes. Still not looking at him, she spread her legs and drew her hands up her inner thighs. The thong's front triangle covered her plump little pubis, but around the edges he saw the damp gloss of arousal in her curls. The gusset was damp as well, the navy silk gone black.

'I see what you mean.' He licked his lips and his cock gave another wag. 'If you were to remove those panties, I believe I could help you.'

She stood on the cushion and slid them down her curvy legs. The show was up close and personal, but she didn't rush it. By the time she'd kicked them away, his cock was flying at least half-mast. She perched on the top of the chair again, thighs agape. She made quite a picture, wearing nothing but the bust-lifting, waist-narrowing basque.

'You'll have to hold yourself open for me,' he said. He didn't suggest she untie his hands. He didn't want her to. Half the pleasure of bondage was all the pleasures he had to do without. They sharpened his appreciation of the pleasures that remained.

With a shiver of self-consciousness, or anticipation – or both – she drew her labia back with the fingers of one hand. He stared at her pretty fruit, at the glistening folds, at the quivering entrance to her sheath and the sharp protrusion of her clit from its encircling hood. Her colouring ranged from salmon pink to raspberry red at the tip of her clit – a true feast for the eyes. Her scent, a light, spicy sea smell, stirred his appetite to taste.

He leant forwards, carefully, so as not to lose his balance. The chair supported his knees and Abby steadied his shoulder. Then he was there, his nose buried in her curls, his tongue probing her folds. Was there ever a more fascinating landscape than a woman's sex? If there was, he hadn't seen it. He explored her slowly, learning her dips and swells before centring on her secret jewel. She sighed musically, pressing closer.

He knew he ought to tease her but he couldn't bring himself to do it. He hungered for her climax every bit as much as she did. He sucked her hood and shaft firmly into his mouth, tapping the sensitive bead with the tip of his tongue, a quick, steady rhythm that made the nails of her left hand dig into his shoulder and the fingers of her right spear through his hair.

'Oh, yes,' she said, holding him close. 'Oh, yes. Oh!'

Her hips shuddered strongly and her sheath quivered just beneath his mouth. Her scent rose in his nostrils like a drug and he thought: one more, one more. He backed off for a moment, drinking in her sigh of relief, then pushed her quickly up the slope again. No mercy this time; he rasped his tongue hard against her tiny stiffened shaft, pressing it to the smooth shelf behind his front teeth.

His ruthlessness took her by surprise. She cried out. Her hips thrust closer. The muscles of her thighs tightened around his ears. She cried out again, a growl of effort this time. Then she shook, harder and longer than the first time, her knees jerking uncontrollably, her cream flowing over his face. He kissed her as she settled.

Her fingers played through the long, damp strands of his hair before pushing him upward again. 'Thank you,' she said. 'I feel much better.'

They smiled at each other. She wiped his cheek with her hand, but he turned his head and licked her fingers clean before she could pull them away. 'You're outrageous,' she said, her blush utterly fetching.

He ran his tongue around his lips. 'I like the way you taste. All that chocolate you eat must keep you sweet.'

She covered her face, then peeked at him through her fingers. Her gaze fell to his groin. She reached out, curled one finger under his resurrected cock and gave it a slow upward stroke. His flesh barely gave. Bringing her off had restored his former glory.

'That's looking much better,' she said. 'But I think it could still use some encouragement.' The words alone lifted him another fraction, and the way she snapped a black latex tie between her hands made him even harder. The remaining ties draped the arm of the chair, all within easy reach. 'Let's see.' She tilted her head to the side. 'Where would this look best?'

He could not answer her, but she did not need his advice. She wrapped the tie around his chest, twice, so that his nipples were pinched between the two rubbery edges. She kissed each button lightly and grabbed another strap. With this, she bound his elbows to his torso. She made an X with another pair, passing the straps between his legs to either side of his scrotum and tucking the ends under the other straps. The arrangement felt extremely secure and looked brutal, like a strange gladiator costume. The straps of the X thrust his balls into greater prominence – not that they needed it. Though his testicles still hummed with remembered pleasure, they were as swollen as if he hadn't come for days.

'Now.' She tapped her cheek in thought. 'What's the best way to do this?'

If he couldn't answer before, he certainly couldn't now. He could only stand, his skin pulsing from head to toe, no more sure of his ability to control himself than he'd been the first time.

'You leave everything to me,' she said, as if she sensed his worry. 'I'm in charge and whatever happens is my responsibility.'

He groaned and she kissed his helpless mouth, goading him with the probe and retreat of her tongue. Then she turned in the chair and got down on her knees. 'Take me,' she said, and wiggled her bare white bottom at his cock.

For a moment he froze, unable to believe it could be this easy. His hips moved before his brain did, knowing what he needed, knowing what he wanted. He slid into her sheath with a silent shudder of relief. She was hot, hot and dripping wet. But with his hands tied behind his back his balance was unmanageable. Every motion threatened to topple him over.

'Lean on me,' she said.

He bent over her, blanketing her back with his chest. She was such a little thing he surrounded her completely. Her position could not have been more vulnerable and yet all the power was hers. The latex straps simmered against his skin as if they were extensions of her flesh, her will. He had the sense of being entirely enslaved, and more grateful than he could ever recall being to a woman. The feeling frightened him, but at the moment he was in no state to resist its allure.

'Fuck me,' she whispered.

He closed his eyes and began to thrust. She came almost at once and he thanked God for that because he was veering out of control. His thrusts were choppy, ragged. He couldn't slow down. He couldn't get deep enough. He dragged his face across the tender skin of her back. He groaned and bit the nape of her neck, the way a horse will, or a cat. She arched her back and let him in deeper. She reached between her legs and massaged his balls.

He cried out in the language of his childhood.

'*Ouu, c'est si bon*,' he moaned. It's so good, so good.

Her sheath quivered at his words, and grew hotter, and wetter. She tilted her hips higher still and gripped him with her hidden muscles. Her fingers moved on his balls. She squeezed the straps that pressed the two swollen eggs together.

Words spilt beyond his control, words he thought he'd forgotten. '*Aie pitié de moi!*'

She laughed, guessing at his plea for mercy, and sucked him irresistibly deeper. It was heaven. She was the sweetest – the dearest.

'*Fourre moi,*' he crooned, thrusting like a madman through her delicious contraction. '*Fuck me, mon cœur. Fourre moi.*' It felt so good to let the words out, as good as the slick, hot friction of her pussy on his cock. He grew delirious with the unbearable pleasure of feeling, speaking, fucking so deeply all at one go, like a child tearing off his clothes to race in the sunlight. When she began to come again, with a ripple of shudders that trilled down the length of his cock, his head seemed quite literally to spin.

'*Je t'aime,*' he groaned as if he truly were dying. '*Mon Dieu, je t'aime.*' His passion exploded with the force of a star going nova. He poured it into her, sobbing with pleasure, sweet, *mignonne*, sweet . . .

Then he heard the echo of his own words. A chill washed over him. *Mon Dieu*, what had he said?

Neither of them spoke once the last of his spasms trailed away. He sensed she didn't wish to comment on his lapse any more than he did. They were both breathing hard. His cheek lay on her back and he hadn't the will to lift it. An involuntary protest broke in his throat as she disengaged their bodies and eased him away.

When she turned to face him, her eyes were strangely quiet. She must have known what he'd said. The most ignorant American could translate *je t'aime*. But her expression gave nothing away. She ran her hands over the spaces between the shiny black straps that criss-crossed his chest. The contact was both welcome and nerve-wracking. He felt like a lathered horse, spooked and grateful for the touch of its master.

'Abby,' he said, to break the silence, but after that words failed him.

Apparently, she preferred to ignore the issue altogether.

'You aren't soft yet,' she said, cradling his diminished but not quite vanquished cock. Her lashes rose and for the first time he knew what men meant when they spoke of drowning in a woman's eyes. A ring of Caribbean green surrounded the huge glossy circles of her pupils. She had the gentlest gaze he'd ever seen and, though it did not seem guarded, he could not read the mysteries behind it.

'Do you want more?' she asked. 'Shall we take you to your limit?'

He would have given his right hand to have his arms free then, to touch her face, to pull her into a long, wet kiss. 'Yes,' he said, despite the further loss of control he might be risking. 'Take me to my limit.'

He knew he might never find another partner he trusted so completely.

Abby let her eyes fall from his, still shaking and not wanting to dwell on why. She couldn't afford to indulge in wishful thinking – not with this man who could reduce her to jelly with both hands tied behind his back. He had placed himself at her mercy. He had offered his body as her personal playground. That was all she needed to know for now.

She drew another strap from the tangle on the chair and trailed it thoughtfully across her palm. His body stiffened and his dangling cock flushed a deeper red, though it did not lift. She was reasonably certain she could remedy that.

He enjoyed this bondage business. The more she restrained him, the better he seemed to like it. But what about her? she wondered. Did she like binding him for its own sake, or did she like it because he liked it?

She wound the strap around his narrow waist and contemplated the question. Both, she thought. If he hadn't enjoyed it so much, the thrill would have been empty. But she did like the look and feel of the straps, and the sense of power they gave her. This kink in her nature was not as hard to face as it would have been a week, or even a day, ago. She'd faced more sexual firsts in the past few days than she had in her entire adult life – not the least of which had been making love to her father's closest friend.

The secret sent a pleasant frisson through her sex. She tucked the ends of the narrow strap together, then made a little opening to bare his navel. Storm jumped when she stuck her tongue into the curving shadow. He was ticklish. That was good to know – almost as good as knowing how easily this play made his cock rise. Determined to give him the full treatment, she covered his thighs in the stretchy ties, then his shins. Finally a single strap remained. She knew just what she wanted to do with that.

She licked her lips and eyed his now proud cock. It stood red and tall again, its plum-like cap flaring to full prominence. If her preference were all she had to take into account, she wouldn't have covered one inch of that gorgeous rod. But she knew how much he'd enjoy it and so, taking her time, she looped the last tie round the base of his cock and evened up the ends.

Storm muttered something in French, a curse from the sound of it. Then he clenched his jaw as if determined to say no more. But that was all right. She liked watching him hold back as much as she liked watching him lose control.

She wrapped his shaft, turn by turn, all the way to the flange. She did not tie the ends for fear of doing him damage, but let them trail loose. As his erection bobbed, the two tails clicked together.

They clicked faster when she bent over the naked head and licked him.

'Mm,' he said, his hips dancing closer.

He vibrated for a moment against her lips and then she let him press himself between – just the head, no more. She licked him slowly, swirling her tongue around the hot satiny skin. This was good. This she could handle – not a whole cock shoved down her throat but this one bursting mouthful. She dug the tip of her tongue into the tiny hole and he sighed. She sucked him between the softness of her cheeks and he moaned. She tugged the ties that trailed off his shaft and he shivered like a wet dog.

'This is my limit,' he said, his voice gruff. 'You won't bring me up again after this.'

She looked up from his crotch. His face was dark with blood, its muscles taut. She understood what he was saying. If she brought him off in her mouth, he'd have nothing left for her.

She stroked a bare triangle of skin at his hip. 'Do you want to come between my legs?' His breath came a little faster and he nodded. 'Shall I unwrap you?'

He hesitated. 'Free my ankles and arms. And take off the basque. I want to hold you.'

As soon as she accomplished these tasks he bore her beneath him on to the circle of the braided rug. The feel of his body pressed full-length to hers was a pleasant shock. She could feel not only the naked skin, but the straps – that was interesting, too.

He reached out and grabbed the forgotten lubricant, then rolled to the side and squirted it down his cock. With three long, squeezing strokes, he'd coated both head and straps.

'Storm,' she said, suddenly doubtful, but he'd already rolled into position to enter her. She gasped at the strange sensation of his wrapped cock parting the folds of her body.

'Good?' he asked, chuffing a little as he pressed to his root.

Abby nodded and clutched his back. His thickness was exaggerated, his texture foreign, but the difference was arousing. The loop at the base of his shaft had rucked up a bit. With every thrust it hit her swollen clit dead on. Despite her pleasure, she noticed almost at once that something wasn't working for him. Each stroke was marked by a grimace of frustration, by a small dissatisfied realignment of his hips. His lack of satisfaction ruined Abby's.

She cupped his perspiring face. 'What's wrong?'

'It's nothing.'

'It is. I can tell.'

He thrust once more and gave up. 'Hell. I can't feel you through all this wrapping. I don't think I can come.'

'Then we'll take it off.'

'No.' He smoothed her hair back from her face. It must be a terrible tangle by now, but he seemed to like it because he smiled tenderly and kissed her brow. 'There's something else you could do for me, if you would.'

'Name it,' she said, drunk with her own fearlessness.

He kissed her again. 'I'll show you.'

He slipped his hand beneath her buttocks. His fingers were still slippery from lubing his own cock and he easily pressed one past the muscle that guarded her anus. She caught her breath at the strange burning tickle. When he pushed his finger to the second knuckle, he stopped and moved it in a slow, blood-heating circle.

'Fingers are the best,' he said through her startled groan of pleasure. 'Warm, slippery fingers that can move and stroke just the right spots.'

With that clear a demonstration, she had no qualms about letting him coach her into doing the same for him. His passage was smoother than she expected, and more responsive. She could see why he liked this even better than the dildo. Fingers were so intimate. She could feel every twitch, every ripple of reaction.

'A little deeper,' he said.

Then she felt it, the little swollen gland she'd only read about till now. He groaned when she rubbed it, so loudly she had to grin.

'Now rock with me,' he said, his voice hoarse with pleasure, his hips putting his request into action. They rocked, close and tight, more rubbing than thrusting, kissing each other until they had to break free to gasp for air.

'Now,' she said. She struggled to remember the words he'd said the first time they made love. '*Je viens*, Storm. *Je viens.*'

He laughed until his own orgasm broke the sound. He came as hard as she did, a quaking shudder that passed from groin to groin like a fault line slipping. Afterwards, though, she suspected she'd said the wrong thing. She shouldn't have reminded him of his habit of babbling in French *in extremis*.

He lifted her before she was ready to move and set her on her feet beside his bed. To both their dismays, it was still covered with toys. 'I'll put them away,' she said, knowing what a neat freak he was.

'To hell with it.' He gathered up the bedspread with the toys still in it and dumped the whole mess in a corner. Then he ripped off his remaining bonds and threw them in the corner, too.

He's angry, she thought, angry with himself.

He controlled it well, though. He turned down the sheets and gestured her into his bed with a gentlemanly flourish.

'Ladies first,' he said, but she didn't know whether it would be better to stay or go. Should she give him time alone to digest what they'd done tonight, or would that make tomorrow more awkward? In the end fatigue decided her, and the lack of a diplomatic reason to refuse.

He slept almost as soon as his head hit the pillow.

He'd curled on his side with his back to her. She knew he must be exhausted. Perhaps later she would remember his instinctive turning away and be hurt, but for now she was grateful for a moment to think.

She lay on her back in the double bed, her side touching his spine, her thoughts and emotions in turmoil. What had she done? How had she dared? The fact that he'd enjoyed it – immensely from all indications – hardly mattered. She'd tied him like a Maypole. She'd practically ordered him to eat her out. She'd licked his bum, for goodness sake. And wrapping up his cock that way – was she insane?

What must he think of her?

Most of all, why did the memory of what she'd done bring a heat to her breast that had nothing to do with embarrassment?

She pulled Storm's cool satin sheets further up her chest and turned her head on the pillow to gaze at him. He'd pushed the covers to his waist. He was so beautiful he made her throat ache. Every muscle in his back was perfect, every line and curve. Nothing she'd done had degraded him. His innate dignity had shone through it all. Even when emotion had caught him up and he cried out 'I love you' in French, there was something noble in his abandon. Here was a man whose passions were larger than life. To her mind, there was no shame in that.

She stroked a single lock of his hair across his pillow.

She knew he'd hated losing control that way. He probably feared she'd take the avowal seriously. But even she realised men said things in the heat of the moment that they didn't really mean. Bill had once shouted out 'Mommy' when he reached his peak, which had thoroughly mortified both of them. So she knew Storm didn't really mean 'I love you'. He meant 'I love what you're doing to me right this second. I love how you're making me feel' – which was a fine compliment all by itself.

She wished there were some way to tell him she understood without embarrassing them both.

I won't try to own you, she promised silently as she spooned herself around his back. You're like a beautiful wild stallion. You can't be tamed and you shouldn't be corralled.

He mumbled in his sleep and caught her hand closer to his chest.

Touched, she rested her cheek against his warm, silky skin. No obligations, only pleasure, she reminded herself. But he was awfully good to hold.

Just after dawn, it began to rain: a steady grey patter that dragged him from a muddled dream.

Abby slept on, her head snuggled to his chest, her arm draped loosely around his waist. Her hair was a mess, a bright, spider-silk cloud that tickled him under the chin. The numbness in his shoulder told him he'd been holding her a long time.

I don't want to let her go, he realised. The thought inspired the same shiver of fear he'd experienced the night before.

He didn't love her. He couldn't. She was a symbol to him. She typified the sweet, salt-of-the-earth woman men dreamt of when they dreamt of home and hearth, of slippers by the fire and all that old-fashioned claptrap. So he loved what she represented, not her. Even if he had the blasted slippers by the fire, he'd be bored within a week. Owning the inn would be enough to satisfy his need to put down real roots, as opposed to crazy, plastic LA roots. He didn't need her.

He blew a sheaf of fine blonde hair away from his face. He knew what he felt for her was ruled by the child in him, the child who wanted to come first with someone, anyone, who didn't want to be left behind like a broken sofa his mother didn't want anymore.

He closed his eyes against the image of himself at sixteen, pounding on the mud-brown door of their crappy flat, pounding and pounding and hearing the hollow echo inside: nobody home.

It had been raining that day, too – raining and cold. Mr Kozlakis had stuck his head out of his own door and told him his mother was gone. 'Gone with her fancy man' was how he'd put it. Storm had possessions in the flat, not much, but things he could have sold if his key had fitted the lock any more. He'd cursed and cried hot tears of fury. Though he'd never liked Storm much, Mr Kozlakis came back and pressed some money into his hand. The missus was at work, he'd said, but she'd want him to have it.

Storm knew very well they couldn't spare it, but he also knew he couldn't afford to turn it down.

He'd never seen either of them again. Years later, he'd tried to pay them back, but they were gone beyond finding – moved on. Moved up, he hoped. Still, he wished it had been Mrs Kozlakis who'd opened that door. At least he could have said goodbye. And thank you. The skills she'd taught him had saved not only his self-respect, but very probably his life.

The memory lodged in his throat. He eased Abby's head off his shoulder and slipped from the bed. He padded naked to the window, cracked the shutters and stared out. Her little cottage looked lonely in the rain, as lonely as he felt.

Stop it, he thought. Just stop it. In real life people didn't love each other unconditionally. If he wanted that, he'd have to buy a dog.

'Storm?' Her voice came from the bed, drowsy and perhaps a bit wistful.

'Go back to sleep,' he said.

She rose up on her elbow and shoved her hair from her eyes. 'Are you OK?'

'I don't like the rain.'

'It will clear up. The weatherman said the showers would only last the morning.'

See, he told himself. If you stayed with her you'd have to learn to talk about the weather. He watched the drops trickle down the window, and swallowed a comment about clouds massing in the east.

'Storm?' The sheets rustled as she sat up. 'About last night. I know you didn't mean what you said. I know you were just caught up in the moment.'

He looked at her wide green eyes and found he couldn't say a word of what he should, which was 'Yes, you're right. I didn't mean it. Thank you for understanding'. She stared back at him, clearly waiting for a response. Her little brow began to furrow as his silence lengthened. She looked so innocent he could scarcely believe she was the same woman who'd pushed a dildo between his cheeks and trussed him like the Christmas goose.

He closed the shutters with a snap. 'I'm going to take a shower now. I have a lot to do today.'

She blinked as if he'd slapped her. He knew she'd be gone when he came out.

9

Abby returned to her room and crawled into her own bed. To her surprise, she fell asleep and – according to the clock on her bedside table – remained that way for two hours. Feeling unexpectedly refreshed, she sat up and pushed her hair out of her eyes. Maybe she was finally growing up, finally learning not to make one man the focus of her life.

Of course, it was also possible that Storm simply wore her out too well to stay awake a moment longer.

But the reason didn't matter. She padded across the hall and stepped into the claw-footed tub for her shower. If Storm was going to break her heart, well, *c'est la vie*. At least it would break because, for once, she was taking an honest-to-God, push-the-envelope risk. Who said she was in love with him anyway? Maybe she was just in lust.

She turned her face into the spray. A picture of Storm formed behind her closed lids: his face lowering over hers as he entered her. Clear as day, she saw the warmth in his eyes, the half-smile that made their corners crinkle. Sometimes she'd watch him when he wasn't aware of it. Though his expression was often melancholy, during the moments he pressed his body into hers, she'd never seen anything but joy and anticipation of goodness to come.

Arousal swelled between her legs and longing tightened her throat. When she soaped her face, she felt his fingertips tracing her features between long, deep kisses. She moaned softly at the vivid tactile memory and at what it probably meant. Maybe she ought to admit she wasn't just in lust. Maybe she liked him as well. That didn't mean she was or ever would be in love with Storm Dupré. After all, if she were in love, would she have slept with Jack?

Maybe, she thought, running her soapy hands over her breasts. She grimaced. Maybe, maybe, maybe. She sounded like a broken record. Maybe could wait for tomorrow, and maybe might never come to pass.

All morning Abby sensed Storm's restlessness. He grumbled over the size of the shrimp their supplier delivered, sent a waiter home for a cleaner shirt, and told Marissa he didn't want to see her nose ring at the inn again.

'Then don't look at it,' the waitress said. 'Because I think you're forgetting who's the real boss here.'

Abby pretended to be engrossed in the contents of the silverware cart. Storm's glare was a pinging weight in the centre of her forehead, but she wasn't going to back him up on this. The uniforms, yes. Marissa's nose ring, no. It was a tiny fourteen-carat gold hoop. Abby liked it and, as far as she could tell, none of the customers minded, either.

'What flew up his butt?' Marissa asked as they set the tables for lunch.

'I did,' Abby almost said, then gave in to a giggle. Let him have his stupid male morning-after mood. She didn't have to share it. She was her own woman now, her own, independent, commanding woman. She put her shoulders back. She liked the way that sounded: commanding. Much better than sweet or biddable.

Her new attitude must have communicated itself to her admirers. Up until then, she'd got friendly smiles and 'how's it going's. This particular afternoon, however, three different gentlemen asked her out: two for a film, and one for a weekend in Boston. None interested her enough to accept, but it was good to know Jack had told the truth. She did have options, lots of them.

She was in her office after the lunch rush, humming a happy tune, when Ivan Lederov dropped by. The artist was his usual low-key self. He tossed the final batch of hand-lettered menus on to her credenza and sat on the corner of her desk.

Her office was small, a converted butler's pantry with a window overlooking the rain-freshened herb garden. The ship captain's wife would have stored her dishes here. Now the room had just enough space for her bookshelf, three filing cabinets, her desk, and Ivan, of course. His leg swinging, he watched her tot up the previous day's receipts.

'Looks like business is booming,' he said.

Abby smiled. 'Booming like a big brass band.'

Ivan wagged his slender foot, then tossed a square white envelope on to her blotter. Her name was lettered on the front in his beautiful copperplate.

'That's from the boys and me,' he said. 'Read it when you get a minute and cash it in whenever you like.' He covered her hand before she could open it in front of him. His wire-rimmed spectacles glinted in the cloudy light as he bent closer. 'Read it later, Abby. When you're alone.'

As soon as he left, she ripped the envelope's flap. She found a coupon inside, another of Ivan's hand-drawn creations. 'Good for your heart's desire,' it said. 'Whatever is in our power to give, we'll happily supply.'

It was signed, 'Ivan, Horace and Peter.'

Abby laughed. Apparently, the three musketeers believed in teamwork. She had to admit this was the most unusual proposition she'd received. Three men at once, and two of them reasonably good-looking. Not that Horace was ugly. He was just heavy, and somewhat pompous, as befitted his position as President of the Picker's Hollow Chamber of Commerce. Under the posturing, he was a nice man, the first to take up a collection for any needy soul whose roof blew off in a gale. His friendship with Ivan and Peter certainly spoke well for him. From what she could tell, Horace never tried to lord it over the younger, less affluent men.

For goodness sake, she scolded herself, you'd think you were seriously considering their invitation.

But maybe she was. She fingered the crisp white edge of the coupon. She'd occasionally wondered how Ivan would look in nothing but his spectacles. Big, shy Peter was a stunning male specimen – like someone off the cover of a romance novel – and she did like Horace. He had a good sense of humour and plenty of energy. It might be fun to try him out in bed.

She swivelled her chair back and forth as she let the idea play through her mind. She was curious to see them interact in a sexual situation. Despite the differences in age, temperament and personality, the three men were so in sync they could finish each other's sentences. Was there a sexual element to that connection and, if so, did the men realise it? Had they done this before or would this be a first for them, too?

She propped her elbows on the blotter and rested her chin on her hands. All three men were her friends. None was the sort to brag about their conquest, except to each other and, since they'd all be there, what did that matter?

I could do this, she thought as a little muscle quivered between her legs. She read the coupon again. My heart's desire, and three healthy men to see that I get it. What sort of woman would turn down an offer like that?

Before she could lose her nerve, she dialled Horace's number at the Chamber of Commerce. She turned her chair backwards to face the window. 'I received your invitation,' she said as soon as his secretary put her through.

'Did you?' She heard his chair creak, and the smile in his voice. 'I trust you understand we make this offer with the utmost respect for your person and your privacy.'

Abby smiled at a lone ray of sun breaking through the clouds. 'I appreciate that. And I was wondering how I'd go about setting up an appointment.'

'The boys and I could be ready at any moment. In fact, it's safe to say we've been ready for quite some time.'

Abby leant back and tapped her pen on her knee. 'Thought you'd pool your resources, did you?'

'Well, we have noticed the stiffness of the competition, which is not to say we couldn't promise to be equally stiff, if not stiffer. We simply wished to set ourselves apart, as it were, by the originality if not the supreme selflessness of our approach.'

'Selflessness!' Abby couldn't contain a snort. 'Come on, Horace, this is me you're talking to.'

'Your pleasure is our pleasure,' he insisted, sounding aggrieved. 'If you should deign to perform some small act for our benefit, we would receive it with all due gratitude. However, we expect nothing from you, only that you allow yourself to enjoy the experience to the full.'

Abby scratched her knee with the end of the pen. A pleasant mixture of arousal and amusement swirled in her belly. 'I want to know one thing first. Have the three of you done this before?'

'We have not,' Horace said. 'However, we have subjected this matter to an exhaustive planning process. We have discussed and rehearsed and – dare I say – visualised this happy event many times. I assure you, you will not find us amateurish.'

'I believe you,' Abby said, thinking: rehearsals? They had rehearsals? Boy, would she have liked to be a fly on that wall. Her sex heated at the thought. 'So. How about tonight, then? Is that too short notice?'

'Absolutely not,' Horace said in the same tone he used to assure visitors they wouldn't be bored in Picker's Hollow. 'If you would be kind enough to arrive at the Chamber Ballroom around midnight tonight, we will have everything in readiness.'

Abby was chuckling to herself as she dropped the phone into its cradle. She couldn't quite believe she was doing this but, if nothing else, she knew the adventure would be good for a few laughs.

The rest of the day passed slowly. The construction crew arrived to begin repairs on the upstairs dining room but, aside from a few questions about colours and time frames, they had no need of her. Besides which, she couldn't help noticing how cute the foreman looked in his paint-splattered jeans – hardly the sort of distraction she needed.

Storm left directly after the dinner clean-up, muttering something about finding a 'decent gym in this puny town'. His continued surliness hurt, but at least she didn't have to invent an excuse to avoid him tonight. His mood also convinced her she was doing the right thing. Clearly, he wanted no commitments between them and, the way he was acting, he certainly wasn't going to get one!

Shortly before midnight, she drove her ten-year-old Toyota to the Chamber of Commerce. The building wasn't much, just a square of tan brick with a columned portico tarting up the door. Small garden lights lit the landscaped paths, but even so there wasn't much chance of Abby being spotted. Most of the citizens of Picker's Hollow were snug in their beds right now.

She followed a pebbled path to the ballroom's back entrance. The knob turned when she tried it, so she went inside. The room was dark except for a distant EXIT sign.

'Hello,' she called, hoping she hadn't been stood up.

At her call, the footlights for the ballroom's stage came on. The sudden blare of light made her eyes water. Someone – Horace, most likely – had borrowed a set from one of the local theatre companies. Ancient Rome sprang to life on the platform, complete with columns, a working fountain and an assortment of cushioned benches. A moment later, music began to play: Middle Eastern music with sitars and chinging bells. The exotic sounds made Abby think of belly dancers and harems.

Apparently, her hosts weren't going to show themselves just yet, so she crossed the long ballroom and climbed a set of stairs on to the stage. She decided Horace must have friends in one of the good theatre companies. Even up close, the set looked swank. The fountain tinkled actual water, the backdrop painting was exquisite, and the furniture could have graced a real Roman house, or so it seemed to her untutored eyes. A large Persian rug demarcated the area on which the furniture sat. It was easy to pretend that the spotlights warming her shoulders were sunbeams pouring through the windows of an ancient salon. She turned in a leisurely circle, drinking in the atmosphere, imagining herself in that time of sophisticated decadence.

A simple white gown with a gold border lay across the sapphire velvet of a chaise. Her neck prickled. A card sat atop the gown's bodice – a blood-red card with delicate black lettering. PUT ME ON, it said.

Right here? she thought, feeling like Alice down the rabbit hole. The chances seemed good that the musketeers were watching. It was a test, she supposed. Her response would tell them how open she was willing to be and, consequently, how open they could risk being. If she wanted to see all, she'd have to bare all.

Blowing her breath out to steady her nerves, she shrugged out of her peach lambswool cardigan, then stripped off the matching sweater and shoved her skirt over her hips. She stepped out of the puddle of cloth wearing the pink camisole and panties Storm had given her the night before. Despite the tension between them, she hadn't been able to resist slipping into the silky little nothing.

A muffled cough from the shadows of the wings told her she was indeed being watched.

She kicked off her low-heeled shoes and closed her eyes. She let her hands slither over the pale-pink silk, over her breasts and down her belly. Cupping her silk-covered mound, she imagined what her show must be doing to her audience, how they'd swell inside their trousers and shift from foot to foot, how they'd cup themselves as she was doing, or rearrange their rising cocks into more commodious positions.

Her panties dampened under her fingers. She gave her sex an encouraging squeeze and felt a rush of elation at her own bravado. She'd been promised her heart's desire. In that moment, it seemed possible she might get it.

With a smile she couldn't suppress, she pulled the camisole over her head. Her nipples puckered in the open air, rosy and ruched and sensitive to the tiniest draught. Now she wore only the panties. She debated whether to take them off. They were very pretty, high cut and lacy, but she'd already decided she'd demand every bit of courage the men possessed. She couldn't offer any less.

She wriggled the panties down her legs.

'I could use some help with this,' she said, gesturing towards the long white gown.

Heavy footsteps sounded on the stage behind her. She turned and saw Peter approaching. He wore a Roman toga, suspiciously tented, and a shy smile. A genuine laurel wreath crowned his head. His hair was sun-streaked gold and brown. Normally he wore it in a tidy ponytail, but tonight it hung past his shoulders in a thick, gleaming mane. With his muscular build, he resembled a hearty young Olympian.

He stopped a foot away from her, his breathing light and quick. His smile widened to a grin as his eyes travelled up and down her naked body. Something about that grin spoke to her more persuasively than an hour's worth of eloquence. She felt more attractive than she could ever remember feeling before.

She handed him the one-shouldered gown.

'Step in,' he said, holding it for her with the confidence of a man who'd dressed a few female siblings. His body brushed hers as he slid the silky tube of cloth up her body. First his head, then his shoulders, and finally his full front pressed lightly against her back. He was tall. The tip of his erection caught the middle of her spine. Even through two layers of cloth it felt hot and strong.

He adjusted the single sleeve over her shoulder. Abby looked down at herself. Elastic cinched the smooth cloth beneath her breasts. The gown flowed past her ankles and on to the tops of her feet. Other than the length, it fitted perfectly. Heavier than silk, the material felt lovely against her bare skin – lovely and sensual.

Peter kissed her bare shoulder a little 'hello' with light, tender lips. When Abby sighed with pleasure he wrapped his arms around her ribs and hugged her. His hips moved, a restless side-to-side swish. She pressed backwards so he could meet his need for more forceful friction. At once, he took the invitation, bending his knees and rubbing the thick, hard swelling over the curves of her bottom.

'Shall I take you now?' he murmured against the side of her neck. 'Just for starters?'

'Can the others see?'

'Yes.' He mouthed her earlobe, flicking it with his tongue. 'But I can send them away, if you prefer.'

'No,' she said. 'I want them to see.'

He shuddered and she knew she wasn't the only one with an unsuspected exhibitionist streak. His arms tightened and he lifted her off her feet. 'Pull up the gown,' he said, still holding her off the ground.

She gathered it up until the stiff gold hem reached her waist, then helped him raise his own skirt with her other hand. His erection found a home between her dangling thighs. Enchanted by the unfamiliar feel of her new toy, she reached down to touch the head. A drop of warm silky moisture beaded its tip. She spread it slowly across his tautened skin. A second drop joined the first.

Groaning, he shifted so that one arm ran lengthwise up her chest. His forearm filled the valley between her breasts. 'Lean forward,' he said in a tight, husky voice.

She did and immediately felt as if she were flying. She remembered hearing a rumour that Peter came from a family of acrobats. She'd thought it nonsense at the time, but the easy way he supported her weight told her it might be true. With a quick laugh of pleasure, she hooked her ankles behind his thighs.

'Good,' he said, and cupped his second hand around her mons.

They both sighed as he shifted her slightly and pressed his cock inside her. Oh, he felt so good – not long, but thick and solid, as if he could support her on the stiffness of his cock alone.

He took one careful step, then another, turning her

to face the back of the stage. The flying sensation increased, especially when the backdrop painting of a seaside temple came into view. She could almost hear the sparkling Mediterranean waves breaking on the shore.

'Fast or slow?' he asked. His longest finger wriggled between the top of her labia, catching her just where she needed catching.

'Fast,' she groaned, aroused beyond waiting.

He began to move her because she could not move herself, merely swoop out and back, out and back. He held her so securely she had no fear of falling and yet the inherent precariousness of her position was exciting – a true leap of faith.

'Ooh,' she said when he shifted to a particularly effective angle and 'oh, yes' when he increased the speed of his rubbing finger.

Wanting to participate somehow, she reached down and covered his hand. He began to tremble, not from fatigue, she didn't think, but because her touch excited him. Perhaps that was why he'd devised this strange lovemaking position. Perhaps, if his partner couldn't touch him, he had better control. She stroked her fingers between his knuckles to test her theory.

'Oh, God,' he said, and thrust faster.

Her climax rose quickly but she wouldn't have cared if it hadn't. She loved feeling this young Hercules going wild with lust. He lifted her to the very tip of his cock and shoved her back to his root. He whimpered when she caressed the arm that supported her front, and moaned when she licked the thumb that crooked her left shoulder.

'Don't,' he pleaded, but he had little cause for worry. She was almost there. Her breasts swung back and forth with each swoop of her body, their slight weight stimulating her sensitive nipples. She clamped her hand over his and ground his finger into her clit. She shattered with a harsh cry.

Her response pushed him past some crucial edge. He began slinging her back and forth so quickly she had to clench her teeth. He grunted with each thrust, his fingers like iron, his muscles rigid. His cock swelled inside her, and swelled, and swelled. His grunts ran together into a moan. He thrust one last time and held her, hanging in the air, her body thrumming in sympathy with his. Then he burst, a long violent shudder that made his knee give way for one heart-stopping second. With a gasp she echoed, he locked the knee straight and finished squeezing out his climax.

'Wow,' he said, carefully righting her and setting her on her feet.

Before his toga could flutter back to his knees, Abby turned and embraced him. Rising up on tiptoe, she plastered a big, wet kiss on his startled mouth. With a strange awkwardness, considering his grace of a moment before, he put his arms around her. His mouth opened over hers, shy at first but growing bolder. He licked her tongue with his, then sucked it hard when she returned the favour. Judging his distraction sufficient, she began to explore his body with her hands. She started with his muscled back and moved to his mile-wide shoulders, then to the hard, flat slabs of his bum.

Her touch had precisely the effect she expected. His cock jerked against her belly and grew. By the time she broke the kiss, Peter's peter was flying so high the skirt of his toga hung in folds behind its upward slope.

'Nice,' she said, giving his cock a friendly one-fingered twang.

Peter grinned and ran his tongue around his rosy, kiss-stung lips. 'Come on,' he said, taking her arm and leading her stage left. 'The others are waiting.'

The others, Ivan and Horace, walked out from the

wings with matching red faces – and matching bulges pushing out the front of their togas. Horace's was just visible beneath the high, round swell of his belly. He had much better legs than she expected. Thin, rangy Ivan proved to be quite long in the tool department. Abby was no judge of inches, but he certainly extended beyond the average. She couldn't help staring a bit.

'Care to hop up here?' Horace said, patting a massage table she'd been too distracted to notice. It sat close to the wing, away from the Roman props.

Peter frowned at Horace and lifted her on to the table himself. Abby shivered with anticipation. Peter made his living as a professional masseur. She'd never felt self-indulgent enough to patronise him, but this was bound to be good.

'Shall I take my gown off?' she asked.

The three men exchanged glances and nodded in unison. Abby concluded the massage was going to be a group effort. With Peter's assistance, she removed the gown and lay face down on the table. He had her choose an oil that she liked the scent of, then poured some into each of the men's hands.

Their first touch had her purring with pleasure. Three pairs of hands slowly rubbing oil over her naked skin. Surely this had to be heaven. Peter and Ivan stroked the sides of her torso while Horace massaged her legs. Peter had coached them well. Each one's touch was sure and soothing and very, very sensual. Horace would be in for a surprise when he reached the top of her thighs. She was sopping. Fortunately, she was also too relaxed to be embarrassed by it.

'Oh, look,' Horace said as his fingers found her overflowing well. 'She's enjoying this.'

Two more hands joined his at her pussy. They pushed her thighs apart and explored her with a forest of warm, curious fingers. Someone gently pinched the hood of her clit and drew it back to reveal the bud within. Its swollen state provoked a trio of approving hums.

Abby was beyond humming. She moaned with need and – as if they shared a single brain – the three men each slid one finger into her dripping sheath.

'My goodness,' she gasped at the extraordinary feelings this inspired. Each finger moved with the others, but massaged its own separate spot inside her. The fingers were as hard as a penis, but much more agile. The ache of wanting intensified inside her. Her clit was throbbing, and her sheath. But, as good as this felt, they'd never bring her to climax like this.

Ivan must have read her mind because he worked a hand under her hips and began to massage her pulsing bud. His touch was very focused, very precise, as if the satisfaction of her desire were his personal design project.

She squirmed and sighed, knowing her climax was close. The three joined fingers moved inside her, a steady, tantalising rhythm. She wanted more, though. She pumped her hips to take them deeper. Their breath hitched in unison. They were all watching, waiting for her to come. Their eyes were burning weights on her sex. They could see everything, every twitch, every trickle of fluid, and it made them breathe as hard and fast as she.

She turned her head to one side and saw Ivan's cock throbbing beneath his toga. She reached out, but couldn't quite touch.

'Give it to me,' she pleaded.

Ivan started and stepped closer, close enough for her to fumble beneath his skirt and grab hold of him. Oh, he was hot. She wrapped her fingers around his shaft and squeezed him in time to their thrusting fingers. She wasn't trying to bring him off. She just wanted to feel what she'd done to him, how hard he was, how hot.

She pushed her hand down to his root then pulled it up to the crown, stretching him slightly away from his body. He made a sound, soft and yearning. His knees jiggled but he pressed no closer. Such a good boy he was. She swept her thumb across the moist curve of the head, and measured him again. He grew in her hand, lengthening, stiffening. Yes, his heat was all hers, his iron-hardness, his dewy skin. She was the reason for all of it.

Knowing this drove her past the point of no return.

'Now,' she said. Ivan's cock jumped in her hand. Her pre-orgasmic tension coiled tighter, making her pull hard at their fingers, making her buttocks tighten, making them work more frantically to please her until – yes, yes – the tension twanged open in a bright brass arc of feeling. Her hips shook uncontrollably as they worked her, coming, coming, until the last drop of sensation had been wrung from her sex.

Ivan touched her wrist. She must have been holding him too tightly but, oh, he felt too lovely to regret it. She stroked him once before letting go, then sighed and closed her eyes. Hands turned her on to her back. More oil was rubbed into her front in long, slow strokes that never once lifted from her skin. If the process hadn't been so arousing, she'd have fallen asleep. They stroked her legs, her arms, her breasts. For a while, Ivan massaged her face and neck – a wonderful treat – but then he disappeared.

It didn't matter. Peter and Horace were each suckling one of her breasts as they stroked the rest of her with sleek, warm hands. They said nothing, but their admiration for her body was clear. They wanted to touch everything, every fold and curve.

Abby opened her eyes to watch their heads jostling together over her chest, one blond and leonine, one dark and beginning to bald. How strange it was, and how strangely appealing. Peter was making the loveliest crooning noises, primitive little sounds he probably couldn't have held back if he tried. Horace was nearly silent, but she'd definitely discovered his particular talent.

She'd thought Storm had a clever mouth. Horace, however, was an oral maestro. His mouth made love to her breast; his lips cajoled her areola; his tongue whispered sweet, dirty nothings to her nipples. Everything he did suggested something that might be done elsewhere, doubling and tripling the pleasure of every lick and pull.

Her sex clenched with hidden ripples of ecstasy. She could have lain there all night.

But then the sitar music rose in volume, signalling the arrival of the next entertainment. With gratifying sighs of reluctance, the two men released her breasts and helped her into a sitting position. Peter climbed on to the table behind her to support her back. His chest was hard as a board, but he was warm and reassuring. It was easy to relax into his arms. As she did, Horace slipped away on some errand of his own. A minute later, the stage lights dimmed to a single golden spot.

The music swelled still further, wailing, seducing. She imagined a marketplace brimming with foreign spices, a glaring sun and then shadows, cool, enticing shadows, and women whose great liquid eyes were rimmed in kohl. She imagined pleasure without end, pleasure that thought of nothing but its own continuation.

Peter's cock was hard against her back, an echo of her thoughts. He drew his hands down her breasts and cupped her nipples in his palms.

Melting, she thought of male slaves, naked in the Mediterranean heat, mute and anguished with desire as they attended to her bath. They could wash her. They could watch the perfumed water sluice down her golden body. They could even kiss her soft, clean skin. But they were only allowed to bring her pleasure, never to take their own – unless she, their mistress, deigned to take them between her legs, or in her mouth, or . . .

A figure draped in black danced out from the shadows: Ivan. She knew him despite the veiling, despite his unexpected grace. His dance was dignified, seductive, androgynous. One moment she thought she was watching a proud desert chieftain dancing for his fellows, the next a haughty woman, the queen of the houris.

His feet were bare, his trousers sheer and full. The veil covered his upper body until he pulled it from his head and began teasing it like a snake charmer around his torso. His chest was lean and lithe, muscled but without much bulk.

His spectacles were gone. He had painted his face, lightly, just the eyes and mouth. Those two touches brought out the beauty of his features, transforming him into a mysterious, exotic stranger. Abby literally could not look away. His burning, kohl-rimmed eyes said he knew she loved the way he looked. He knew she loved the fan of muscle over his ribs as he moved in sinuous, weaving curves; he knew she loved the narrowness of his waist, the wiry strength of his arms.

He spun closer, his head snapping for each turn the way a ballet dancer's will. The spotlight followed him and she realised then what errand had stolen Horace away.

Leaping to a standstill before her, Ivan looped the long veil around Abby's neck. She gasped, nerves glittering as he slowly pulled it free. 'Does the slave's humble dance please the mistress?' he asked with sly, downcast eyes.

'Yes,' she said. 'Very much.'

'Good!' Before she could protest, he pulled her off the table and into his arms.

The music changed as soon as her feet hit the floor. It became a sultry saxophone piece, perfect for slow dancing. Ivan was a wonderful partner. He practically carried her through the steps, their bodies pressed close by the hand he'd clamped beneath her buttocks. That hand grew tighter and tighter the longer they danced, urging her groin to his until her softness rode the thrust of his desire. His erection burnt through the sheer cloth of his black harem trousers. With each movement of the dance he rubbed the ridge against her naked flesh, bending his knees now and then to drag it through the generous wetness between her legs.

Oh, she was dizzy with lust, a wonderful, sweet hunger. Finally, she had to throw back her head and laugh. 'This is so much fun,' she said.

Ivan didn't smile. Instead he lowered his head and kissed her, a teasing, twisting kiss that quickly became a part of the dance. Each turn earned her a lick, each dip a probe, each sway a stinging nibble on her lower lip. She learnt the steps, began to anticipate the next and beat him to it. Then he opened his reddened mouth and went deep, deep inside. He tasted smoky and sweet. He smelt of sweat and young male musk. Abby stumbled over his foot. He lifted her and set her feet on his own. Now this was flying.

They kissed; they kissed. Ivan's arms twined round her, alternately roving and squeezing, supporting and exploring.

Ten minutes later, Horace broke them apart by clearing his throat. Ivan hugged her close a moment longer. 'I'm mad for you,' he whispered, hot and fierce. 'I've dreamt of dancing with you since the day we met.'

Abby stroked the back of his short, ash-brown hair.

'Right now I'm mad for men in general.' He released her and nodded, understanding her warning. The dignity of his bearing inspired a quick decision. 'I want this slave,' she announced in what she hoped was a ringing tone. She pointed at Horace. 'You will prepare me for him with your mouth.'

Horace bowed. 'It would be my pleasure, mistress.'

She strode to the centre of the Persian carpet, then lowered herself on to the soft, plush wool. She lolled back on her elbows, her thighs gaping, her breasts high. The men looked at each other, then at her. They were shocked by her imperious pose, but hardly put off. Their eyes were avid, their erections pulsing beneath their robes.

'All of you strip off,' she ordered.

The men hesitated a moment, then complied. She noticed they snuck glances at each other, their eyes catching on cocks and balls before veering away. Ivan was by far the hardest and the highest slung. He was the youngest of the trio and, unlike Peter, had not had any release this night. His shaft was a bright, rosy pink. His balls – a plump, joggling handful beneath his cock – had the interesting distinction of being hairless. Abby noticed the other two looked most often at him.

The interplay sent heat rushing to her belly. They were curious about each other, but it seemed to her they hadn't indulged that curiosity. She wondered if she might be able to change that. Shivering with a pleasant frisson of anticipation, she watched Horace lumber into position between her thighs.

'You.' She snapped her fingers at Peter. 'Kneel over me. I wish to suck you while I'm being sucked.'

Peter's eyes widened but he quickly obeyed.

'And me?' Ivan said quietly.

'They are preparing me for you. But if you wish, you may hold my hand.'

She was glad he accepted because she soon needed something to hold on to. Horace's assault on her pussy was nothing short of devastating. He used his lips, his tongue, the flat of his teeth. He opened her with his thumbs. He blew on her. He nuzzled her flesh with the delicacy of a snake.

'My goodness,' she said, clutching hard at Ivan's hand.

Peter took her exclamation as a signal to press his thick, red cock into her mouth. She writhed with pleasure, scarcely able to encompass all the wonderful sensations. He was just the right size for this, a solid, satiny mouthful. Sucking this hot, wet, living flesh stirred such a primitive satisfaction. She bore down farther then pulled back, tugging him with the pressure of her mouth. He groaned with enjoyment and a burst of pride warmed her chest.

She could grow to like this, she decided, especially with Horace's spectacular ministrations to reward her for her efforts.

He had pushed back the hood of her pearl and now his tongue fluttered over the tiny rod. The tip of his tongue was stiff, its rhythm marvellously quick. A sharp spangle of feeling sparked through her sex: not an orgasm, but something like it. Almost painfully pleasurable, it made her open her mouth and gasp for air.

Peter's hands tangled in her hair to keep her sucking. Yes, remember Peter, she told her addled brain. As she returned to the task, Ivan kissed the palm of her hand, then the inside of her wrist. His moist, nibbling lips crept up her arm, making her tongue quiver in reaction against the neck of Peter's cock. He sighed and thrust carefully deeper and – oh! – Ivan nipped the back of her neck.

She could not scold him for leaving his designated post. Delicious sensations swamped her, soaking through her from the mouth that stroked her pussy, from the cock that stroked her mouth, from the warm chest that swept from side to side across her back. The pleasure was too much. She would come. She couldn't stop it. She cried out as she started to slide. 'Oh, no. Oh, stop. Stop!'

The men ceased what they were doing, Peter last of all. He rubbed his swollen glans round her lips one last time before pulling away.

'I am ready for the slave,' she said shakily, knowing she'd have to compensate for this interruption later.

Ivan came round her and knelt between her legs. He stared at her pussy, breathing hard. With both hands he stroked his already hard cock. His eyes were glassy with arousal. He looked like a man possessed. Abby was glad she'd saved her orgasm for him.

Horace offered him a condom from a marble dish on one of the tables.

'You put it on,' she said.

Horace hesitated a moment before ripping the package open and seating the condom on the head of Ivan's cock. Horace squeezed the air out of the tip with two thick fingers.

'Just do it,' Ivan snapped, but she noticed the other man's performance of the intimate task had not discouraged his erection, or Horace's. For his part, Peter spread a squirt of latex-friendly lubricant over the sheath. His initiative pleased her, though she didn't let it show.

'Balls, too,' she said.

Already on his knees beside his friend, Peter bit his lip and shuffled closer to do it. Ivan's eyes screwed shut. He moaned through gritted teeth as Peter's big, strong fingers worked the lube over his balls. From the sound of the moan, they were tender from his long, unassuaged arousal. Peter was not intimidated. He made a thorough job of it, coating every inch of pink, hairless skin, and even working back behind his scrotum to the sensitive pad of his perineum. Ivan's hips jigged up and down through the entire process, telling Abby just how intensely he was enjoying this even if it wasn't his idea.

'I love watching his hands on you,' she said, low and husky. 'It really makes me hot. In fact, I'm dripping with honey right now. It's trickling out of me right this second. And there'll be more when you come inside me. Lots more.'

'Jesus,' Ivan said, going pale then red at her words.

The sight of his torment almost sent her through the roof. She made a sound. Ivan's eyes snapped to hers. His gaze heated at what he found, then narrowed. Abby knew he wouldn't last much longer.

'Now,' she said, just as he shoved Peter's hand away and dipped forwards on his knees.

'Now,' he agreed. His hands hit the carpet above her head. He probed her mons with his penis, uttering a small pained cry at the first instant of contact, his aim true, his crown pressed inside her tender mouth – and stopped. He drew a small circle just within her. His eyes slid nearly shut. 'Oh, yes,' he sighed and pressed inside. His entry was easy, so easy, but it seemed to last a long, long time. There was more of him, and more and then, yes, the give of his abdomen met the give of her mons.

'I'm about to come,' she whispered.

He shivered and kissed the arch of her neck. He drew back slowly and thrust, another long drive and another long pull. Again she marvelled at the difference between her lovers. How lucky she was to be able to sample this feast. How very . . .

He pushed again.

'Oh!' The first quivers of orgasm caught her and shook her. Ivan doubled his speed, intensifying her orgasm and then, abruptly, driving her up the rich, red incline to the next. Ooh, she wanted it, another good hard one. Her pussy clenched. She held her breath and pulled at his cock with all her strength.

The contraction destroyed the last of Ivan's control. He muttered a curse, his taut little buttocks churning, his cock going this way, that way, some primitive body sense all that kept him from pulling loose. His strokes were as long as they were crazed, down to the root, back to the tip. His pubis banged her clit. His balls slapped her buttocks. Her orgasm hovered, started to break. He fumbled for her hands and gripped hard. His head snapped back, dripping sweat. He gulped for air and stiffened and swelled and thrust incredibly deep and – oh, yes! – came through her second volley of achy-sweet spasms.

'Mm,' she said, totally replete.

But Ivan was still hard. His thrusting slowed but did not stop.

'Enough,' Peter said, dropping a brotherly hand to Ivan's shoulder. 'You'll make her sore if you keep at her like that.'

With a wistful sigh, Ivan disengaged.

'Don't worry.' She dropped a conciliatory kiss to the tip of his cock. 'The night's not over yet.'

10

Storm drove to Provincetown to a gym he'd spotted the day he'd met Abby's supplier. Judging from the number of people inside, it was a local hot spot. It even had a message board for singles. A cursory glance told him most of the customers were interested in same-sex unions, but that was just as well. He was here to work out – period.

He bumped into the woman as she left an aerobics class. She was small and blonde and head-to-toe muscle. She wiped the sweat from her face with a neon orange towel, complimented him on his upper-body definition and invited him to meet her after her shower.

What the hell, he thought, with the fatalistic feeling he used to get ordering the one last beer that would guarantee him a hangover. What the hell.

Within the hour they were in her apartment and he was in her, pumping slow and deep just the way he liked. A cunt was a cunt, right? They were all warm. They all got wet and slurpy if you treated them right.

He used all three of the condoms he'd had the foresight to keep in his holdall. He didn't experience the urge to blurt out French endearments, and he made each engagement last. He took her from behind first, with her leaning over a Lucite chair that looked more like modern art than furniture. She had a beautiful arse, as high and round as a long-distance runner's. Her body was still hot from her workout – inside and out. His cock felt pleasantly steamed as it probed her intimate folds.

Next he took her in her bed. She had a canopy of gauzy white mosquito netting – quite atmospheric. She was also very flexible. At the end, she locked her ankles behind his neck and came with a funny gasp, almost a sneeze. The position and the depth he achieved as she quivered in climax almost made him spill. He controlled himself with an effort and pulled carefully free. They moved to the shower. They kissed some more and played games with her sandalwood soap. When he judged his arousal had abated to a manageable level, he took her standing up against the tiles with the water pounding over their bodies in lukewarm needles of spray.

Only then did he allow himself to come. There was nothing wrong with his orgasm. It was as deep and intense as he knew how to make it.

'When can I see you again?' she asked as he sat in the strange transparent chair pulling on his shoes.

His usual diplomacy deserted him. He shook his head.

'I get it,' she said. 'You're a one-night-stand kind of guy.'

He grimaced and pushed his left heel into the trainer. 'I'm sorry.'

'No, no.' She smoothed her platinum hair – dyed, he now had reason to know. 'Better you should tell me the truth than promise to call. Anyway –' she flashed a too-bright grin '– that was pretty stupendous for a one-night stand. You can really cook.'

Storm sighed to himself. She didn't even know he was a chef.

He got home late. The cottage was dark. He stood in the cool grass and stared up at Abby's window. His throat hurt and a strange pressure burnt behind his eyes. Pictures of her rolled through his mind: the curve of her breast; the way it swayed when she bent to pick up her clothes; the little smile she wore when she palmed his groin and found him hard, as if she'd discovered something sweeter than chocolate but didn't want to let on.

He didn't think. He didn't hesitate. He grabbed the trellis and pulled himself up between the thorny branches. Twice the roses pricked him to the point of bleeding, but it was worth it, or so he thought until he peered through the window and saw her empty bed.

He climbed down in a huff. Where the hell was she? He glanced towards Marissa's room, but that was dark, too. Come to think of it, he didn't remember seeing Abby's car when he drove in.

He would have gone straight to bed and brooded if he hadn't spotted the note taped to Marissa's door. Without a qualm, he ripped it off and opened it. 'Just so you know,' it said. 'I'm meeting some friends at the Chamber of Commerce. I shouldn't be late, but if I am, please help Storm do the inventory tomorrow morning. Thanks. Abby.'

Storm looked at his watch. Who would she be meeting at the Chamber of Commerce at this hour, and what could they be doing that would last through till morning? Knowing Abby, she'd probably got suckered into volunteering for some charity board. Or a quilting circle for vampires, he thought with a doubtful snort. Whatever the reason, who knew how careful she was being?

It couldn't hurt to make sure she had an escort home.

He found a map to the Chamber of Commerce in the minuscule Picker's Hollow Business Directory. He broke a few speed limits getting there, but didn't actually peel the rubber from his tyres. When he arrived, he found Abby's car parked outside along with a BMW, a van and a dusty black racing bike. That struck him as odd. What sort of group met in the middle of the night with so few people?

No lights shone behind the porticoed front door and no one answered his knock, so he followed a pebbled path to the back. There he found a door marked BALL-ROOM. The knob turned when he tried it. Shrugging to himself, he stepped inside.

His end of the cavernous room was dark, but the opposite end blazed with light. A stage set of some sort had been erected. A painting of a Greco-Roman temple decorated the backdrop. Music played. It sounded Indian. A low male laugh cut through its ululating melody. That's when he realised there were people on the stage, naked people. His legs moved in a state of nerveless shock across the bare wood floor. One of the naked people had a familiar mass of sunny blonde hair. Abby. He walked faster. He stopped just out of reach of the footlights and stared until his eyes hurt.

She was down on her hands and knees, in profile, on the carpet that covered centre stage. A man with a big belly was taking her from behind. At first Storm thought he was taking her in the arse, which inspired a flash of anger since he had yet to take her that way himself. But the penetration was vaginal. The man had merely picked the best position for keeping his stomach out of the way.

At the moment, he was reaching forwards over Abby's back, hastily braiding her hair.

The only explanation Storm could imagine for this was that the man wanted to see what she was doing. Another man lay on his back in front of her, perpendicular to the line of her body, his feet towards the front of the stage. Storm watched the man's toes curl and uncurl with pleasure. Abby was lapping the very tip of his erection, which was one of the longest he'd ever seen. It was so brightly pink it glowed – and no wonder. He'd called her kittenish, but in truth her tongue moved like a cat's, now teasing the head with the point, now dragging across with the soft wet flat.

Storm's own groin tightened in sympathy. His cock moved inside his jeans, still soft but lengthening.

A third man crossed the stage, a tall, sturdy blond. He ripped a condom open with his teeth, knelt, and rolled it over the supine man's cock. He looked familiar. Yes, it was the beach-boy-muscleman he'd met in front of the inn his first morning here, and these must be the friends he'd been sitting with.

Muscleman's hands slid down Tallboy's cock and squeezed his balls. Tallboy groaned. Big Belly laughed. Abby's breasts jiggled with her quickened breaths.

She likes this, Storm thought, unconsciously cupping himself through the worn denim of his jeans. She likes watching them touch each other. Knowing this made him harden more fully, and made him aware that he was groping himself. If he were caught, he'd look twice the fool. But he didn't want to stop. The room smelt of sex, of male sweat and female honey. The blood pounded in his groin, urging him on. He was not one to turn away from an unusual arousal, whatever the cause. He squeezed his balls, much the way Muscleman had squeezed Tallboy's, then scratched one nail in a circle around his glans.

The touch made him twitch. His skin was as sensitive as if it had an electric current running through it.

'I'm starting,' Big Belly announced. He drew back and made his first thrust. He sucked in a breath. 'Everyone synchronise your watches.'

Abby laughed and put her hand over Muscleman's. Now they both massaged Tallboy's scrotum. Tallboy's feet twitched. Muscleman leant towards Abby. He nipped her pouty lower lip, then the upper, and then settled in for a deep conversation of tongues. Tallboy's cock bobbed an inch beneath their chins, straining upwards as if it, too, wanted kissing. The rhythm of their mouths was unmistakably sexual, and intensified by Big Belly's slow push-pull at Abby's back.

After a minute of the hypnotising ebb and flow, Abby broke free.

'I need some help, Peter,' she said, nodding at the supine man's cock. 'I'm no Deep Throat and Ivan here is no shrimp cocktail.'

The man named Peter grinned and licked his lips. 'You take the head. I'll see what I can do with the rest.'

Storm was interested to see how they managed – more than interested, actually; his buttocks had been clenching in time to their rhythm, pushing his now rigid penis tighter to his palm. He held his breath and leant closer. Peter lay down on his side and pillowed his head on Ivan's hip, extending his throat until he could reach the long, rosy shaft. He touched the skin tentatively with his tongue, then his lips. Then he swallowed hard and wriggled closer, taking to the task in earnest as he alternated between lapping and sucking the swollen rod. Ivan's groans of pleasure sounded as though they were wrenched unwillingly from his gut. Storm realised these men weren't used to interacting this way. They were doing it to please Abby and discovering they liked it more than they expected, perhaps more than they wanted.

Apparently, Peter was aroused by Ivan's dilemma as well. He wrapped one hand around his own cock and began to masturbate in tight, get-down-to-business pulls.

'Curl up towards me,' Abby said, her voice jolted by Big Belly's continuing thrusts. 'I'll help you.'

When Peter drew his legs up, she twined her fingers with his and joined his strokes. As soon as she touched him, he began to quiver as though her caresses were his personal Spanish fly. A flush spread from one of his nipples to the next, each a stiff, ruddy point. Storm experienced a strange urge to crawl up on the stage and suck them himself. Instead, he thrust one hand beneath his sweaty workout shirt and pinched his own nipple. The twang of sensation shot straight to his cock. He was going to come like a train wreck before this was over. He only hoped he wouldn't make too much noise.

'Oh, God,' said the big, blond man. 'Your hand is so little. Your skin is so soft. Go slow, Abby. Go slower.'

'Lick him,' Abby ordered in an imperious voice that made Storm flush. 'I want to see your tongue on his cock.'

Peter's skin shivered as he moved his head back to Ivan's waiting shaft. Abby's sigh oozed from her throat like honey. Her eyelids drifted downward, lowering but not closing at the sight of the big male tongue lapping back and forth, back and forth. With a dreamy smile, she captured Ivan's hot pink glans between her lips.

Storm took an involuntary step forward just as Ivan moaned. No one heard his footfall. No one had the least idea he was there. He was cloaked by the darkness beyond the footlights: the perfect voyeur.

He watched her swallow one inch, then two. Peter opened wide and licked her lips at the same time as he licked Ivan's shaft. Ivan cursed, his knees jerking so wide the dark pucker of his anus was exposed to view. His plump pink balls joggled between his legs and again Storm imagined himself joining in.

Crazy images flashed through his mind. He would kiss Ivan as they kissed Ivan. Their tongues would duel up and down that long, rigid cock, fighting for room. He would tickle the dark, secret entrance between Ivan's legs. He would make Peter suck his own cock until it glistened. Abby would watch. Abby would run wet and silky with admiration. She would take him in her soft little hand and press his bursting glans against the tiny pucker of Ivan's arse. He would guide their heads up and down Ivan's cock. He would roll his hips forward and press –

'Abby,' Ivan moaned. 'Suck me deeper. Suck me hard.'

She took him deeper, then sucked back towards the head. Peter's tongue followed her withdrawal, lashing the other man just under his crown where the sensitive little wrinkles drew together.

'Ooh.' The man's hips heaved upwards in an ecstatic quest for more. 'Ooh, Peter, let her do it. Let her do it right there.'

Peter chuckled but he let Abby reclaim her territory.

Meanwhile, Big Belly was claiming his own territory. His upstage hand roved back and forth between Abby's swaying breasts and his downstage hand burrowed through the golden hair of her mound.

She cried out sharply as he pinched her clit and began tugging it outwards from her body. Gripping her between forefinger and thumb, he pulled and let it slip free, pulled and let it slip free, a steady motion timed to match his thrusts. It was a nice little trick, one that Abby seemed to like. Storm wondered if he dared try it himself.

'Mm,' she moaned around her shared mouthful of cock. She arched her back, opening herself to the big man's increasingly forceful drives. She wriggled the globes of her arse against him. He began to pant – as did she, a breathy, moaning expulsion of breath.

Storm knew what those sounds meant. She would come soon, and come hard. Unable to bear the pressure behind his zip, he ripped the tab down and shoved his hand into his briefs. His glans was lodged down over his balls but he didn't pull himself free. He wanted the constriction, the feeling of being tightly surrounded. Widening his stance, he worked three fingers over the head and rubbed it hard. The sensation was sharp, almost too sharp, but by this time his urgent need to come overrode such concerns.

Abby was still moaning as she bobbed further down Ivan's shaft. Her arousal had relaxed her. Her mouth joined Peter's in a kiss low on the base. Her throat worked. Her cheeks drew in as she sucked back upwards. Ivan began to kick a little, his feet scrabbling on the rug.

'Oh, man,' he said in pre-orgasmic panic. 'Oh, man.'

His arm swung down. He caught the back of Peter's head with his hand and started in surprise. Clearly, he'd meant to catch Abby but was too far gone to care. With a moan of surrender, he shoved his friend up tight against the root of his cock. His fingers kneaded the thick gold waves in clear, feline enjoyment. Then he brought his other hand to Abby's head and pressed her closer, too.

Abby and Peter both sucked fervently, working harder, faster. Ivan's moan rose to a wail. His legs shot straight out. He stiffened. His back bowed sharply as he came, as if he were trying to throw them off. A second later Peter blew, spurting four quick jets between his and Abby's braided fingers.

The fat man groaned like a beached whale. 'Help me finish her,' he panted. 'I can't hang on much longer.'

With no more than a gasp for breath, the two younger men scrambled to their knees and pushed Abby upright. This forced the fat man to lean back or forego his nice, deep penetration. Abby laughed, then moaned as Peter took one of her breasts into his mouth and the other into his palm. Ivan crouched between her thighs and buried his face in her pussy.

'Oh, yes,' she said as the slender man found a sweet spot and latched on. 'Right there.'

She cupped the back of his head and closed her eyes. The fat man thrust harder. Her neck sagged. The muscles in her thighs tightened. She was almost there.

Storm rubbed faster. This was what he was waiting for: her orgasm. He pressed one finger over his slit, feeling a preliminary flutter, a pressure at the base of his cock. He swept his thumb down his upper shaft, rubbing as much of the velvety skin as he could reach. His cock was swelling to its final limit. He could hardly move his fingers past the constriction of his crotch seam, but he pressed their pads into the swollen crown, pressed hard and vibrated them back and forth.

Come, Abby, come, he thought, pained by the need to let go.

Then she cried out and shuddered. He let the orgasm rise, let it swell up from his balls and belly. It hurt, oh, it hurt so good. A brief spurt of seed flamed up his urethra, a warning shot, an agonising tease. His shaft pulsed hard, contracted, stiffened and then his seed spurted free in deep, aching throbs like a laser pulsing through the pleasure centres in his groin.

Unable to restrain himself, he groaned with relief. Luckily, Abby was moaning, too, and his cry was lost in hers.

His chest heaved as he pulled his hand free, his sticky, trembling hand. Abby had sagged forwards into Ivan and Peter's arms. Along with the fat man they were petting her, praising her. Storm had to leave. They'd quieten soon. They'd hear him. He didn't want to be caught here like some idiotic possessive boyfriend. Some idiotic voyeuristic boyfriend, he amended, drying his sticky fingers on his shirt.

He slipped off his trainers, picked them up and padded to the door. A childhood of tiptoeing ensured that his exit was soundless.

While he watched them he'd been caught up in the fascination of the tableau, in his own swift arousal and release. Now, however, driving down this narrow back road with the top down and the shore breeze cooling his skin, he felt a sick tightening in his stomach and a pain that brought one fist to the centre of his chest.

He'd made a terrible mistake – not in awakening Abby to her sensuality, but in failing to make it clear he wanted to keep her to himself for a while.

Fuck 'a while', he snarled in the silence of his mind. You want to keep her period. You've fallen in love with her.

Merde alors! If he hadn't been negotiating a turn, he'd have banged his head against the steering wheel. He'd fallen in love with her, with the monster he'd created. Well, maybe she wasn't a monster. What she'd done was daring, yes, but hardly monstrous. The four of them had reminded him of puppies rolling on the floor, tongues hanging out, yipping with excitement. It was a rare woman who could keep three men amused at once.

He parked the car behind the inn and switched off the engine. His ears rang in the sudden quiet. In the distance, the ocean dashed its foamy self against the sand. Up close, his heart dashed itself against his ribs.

'*Espèce d'idiot*,' he muttered, disgusted with his own stupidity. He couldn't even claim she'd betrayed him. He'd made his distaste for commitment clear. If his heart felt betrayed, that was his problem; his problem twice over, considering he'd spent the first part of the evening fucking a woman whose name he didn't know. Abby, at least, had confined herself to friends.

He let his head fall back and stared at the diamond pinpoints of the stars. The sky was so clear on the Cape, so velvety black and huge. No city lights, no smog obscured his vision of wave upon wave of stellar fairy dust. Other worlds. Other dreams. The perspective should have shrunk his problems. Instead it made him feel horribly alone.

But he refused to sit and suffer. Action was called for,

swift, decisive action. He tapped the steering wheel with both index fingers. He'd have to seduce her all over again – her heart this time, not her body. Everything considered, he'd feel ridiculous demanding fidelity. He'd have to make her want to volunteer it and, if she strayed in the meantime, he'd simply have to grit his teeth and bear it.

Which didn't mean he couldn't do everything in his power to ensure she was too well pleasured to think of another man, much less three.

He grinned in the darkness, his nervous tapping turning into a cocky jazz riff. That challenge, at least, he knew he'd enjoy. Then another thought struck him with the force of a gut punch. That it hadn't occurred to him already was a testimony to the depth of his agitation.

He'd have to abandon his plan to strong-arm her out of the inn. He'd never been entirely comfortable with the idea but, now that he'd fallen in love with her, he simply couldn't do it. *Merde* and *merde* again. Why couldn't Abby have been a man – a nasty, cigar-smoking *cochon* who deserved to get the short end of a deal?

He couldn't even look for an alternate site for his own restaurant until she got securely on to her feet. With all the debt she'd taken on, if he left her before she recouped she'd go under within a week. Of course, that had been his plan from the beginning: wait until she had a taste of the success he could bring her, then threaten to walk unless she sold out.

He shuddered with disgust. He was the *cochon*, the pig, to have devised such a plan. His only excuse was that he'd fallen in love with the inn before he'd fallen in love with her.

With a weary sigh, he climbed from the car and slammed the door.

* * *

'You don't want to do this again, do you?' Horace asked.

Peter and Ivan had already left, with Ivan's bike stowed in the back of the van with the massage table. Abby and Horace stood in the empty parking space between his car and hers. He bounced his presidential key ring in the palm of his hand.

'I don't think so,' Abby said, her eyes following the shine and jingle of the keys.

'Was it Ivan? I have to admit he was more serious than I expected. I could speak to him.'

'I doubt that speaking to him would change his feelings, but that's not really the problem.' Abby pushed her tousled hair behind her ears. 'I had a wonderful time tonight, but I don't think it would be fair for me to always be in charge.'

'We could take turns,' Horace suggested in a tone so careful it seemed utterly out of character.

Abby smiled at the pebble she was scuffing across the tarmac, then looked up. Horace's face was as carefully non-eager as his voice. 'I like you,' she said, 'all of you. I don't think I could take orders from you, though. Maybe I shouldn't talk about Bill, but one thing I learnt from being with him was that, unless I feel more than affection for a person, I really resent having to bend my will to someone else's.'

'And that Storm fellow doesn't make you do that?'

Abby's eyes widened. She hadn't realised people knew she and Storm were intimate. 'No,' she said, her shoulders hunching in discomfort. 'We . . . we take turns and . . . I enjoy it both ways.'

'I see.' Horace buttoned his suit jacket and shook it straight. 'All I can say is, if that's the case, I'm surprised he doesn't keep a closer eye on you.'

Abby put her hand on his arm. 'He doesn't know about this, Horace. I hope you don't plan to tell him.'

'Of course not.' Horace puffed up his chest. 'I wouldn't discuss this with anyone.'

'Good, because my personal life is none of his business.' Abby heard the falseness in the words as soon as they left her mouth. Horace cocked a doubtful brow at her. She winced and suddenly wondered if her personal life might be Storm's business, after all.

'I'd like you to have dinner with me,' he said.

They sat at the work table in the kitchen, dining on peach and honey crepes. Guilt had goosed Abby out of bed in time for the weekly stocktaking, but when she reached the kitchen she found Storm preparing a beautiful three-course breakfast for two. He'd carved a honeydew melon into stars and roses, sliced a small salmon filet to mouth-watering transparency, and his presentation of the peach-laden crepes could easily have graced the pages of *Gourmet Magazine*.

She wondered if he were one of those people who worked their stress out in the kitchen. He certainly appeared stressed. His face was stony, all the muscles in it clenched with tension. She rubbed her hands down the grey bike shorts she intended to run in later. Surely he wasn't still upset about that *je t'aime* business.

'Um, well, sure we could have dinner together,' she said, 'as soon as we clean up tonight.'

Storm slid his fork an inch higher beside his plate, then moved the knife to match it. He wore a snug black T-shirt with his jeans. It clung so loyally to his chest muscles that Abby could see the tiny points of his nipples. They rose with a deep inhalation. 'I meant I want us to have dinner out, like a date.'

'A date.'

'A date,' he said, and set his jaw.

Abby shifted on her stool. 'But I thought you just wanted to have fun.'

'Dating is fun.'

You'd never know it to look at you, she thought, rubbing the skin over her left eyebrow where a headache was beginning to bloom. Was he trying to confuse her? Or was she simply too tired to follow this conversation?

'I'd like to get to know you better,' he said in that same grim tone. 'We haven't had much chance to talk.'

'But why?'

The plaintive note in her question made him smile. With the smile, the grimness left his face. His lips and his eyes tilted up at the corners. He was so beautiful. Abby's insides heaved an involuntary sigh. He drew one of her hands across the table and cradled it between his own. 'I like you, Abby.'

'You like me.'

The pad of his thumb stroked a tickling arc across her palm. Her toes curled inside her trainers. 'Is that so hard to believe?' he asked.

'I suppose not.'

His thumb slid over the bend of her wrist and covered her pulse point. 'You seem uncomfortable with the idea. Would you rather I didn't like you?'

'No.' Flustered, she pulled her hand away and rubbed the tingling skin. 'I just don't think affection has much to do with what's happening between us.'

He flinched and dropped his eyes, then dragged his thumb across his lower lip. Abby felt her own mouth tremble and clenched her teeth to still it. She'd spoken the truth, hadn't she? She did like him, yes, but that wasn't why they were sleeping together. She had no reason to feel as if she'd just kicked the family dog. He was the Casanova, the *homme fatal*. She was the one whose heart was made of mush.

'Affection has always had something to do with what's happening between us,' he said, his voice deeper than normal. 'In any case, there's nothing wrong with being friends.'

'So it's a friendly date,' she said, struggling to get her feet back on solid ground.

His lashes rose. The gleam in his grey-blue eyes made her breath catch. He did not acknowledge her statement, just tucked the tip of his thumb into his mouth and sucked it slowly, lasciviously clean. The look, the gesture, sent spears of heat to the tender harbour between her legs. With arousal, however, came a spark of anger. What sort of game was he playing, pretending he wanted to get to know her? Or was it a game? She clenched her fork. Was he beginning to feel more for her than Pygmalion's thrill of conquest?

No. She speared a bite of golden-brown crepe. She couldn't afford to think that way. He was a dyed-in-the-wool playboy, a heartbreaker of the first water. He'd been honest up till now, but that didn't mean he was incapable of deception.

'If you don't want to have dinner with me . . .' he said, beginning to eat again himself.

She studied his lowered face and her resolution wavered. He did look hurt, lonely even. Maybe he needed a friend. Maybe it was as simple as that. 'I'd be happy to go on a date with you,' she said, swallowing against the lump in her throat. 'Maybe next Monday when we're closed.'

'Good,' he said. He looked up and smiled, baring straight, white teeth. He looked ten years younger. The pleasure in his eyes warmed her down to her toes, reminding her just how dangerous Storm could be.

11

Marissa spent the night at Jack's house – the first time she'd spent the night with anyone since she and Gemma had split up. Staying in his home was strange but less awkward than she'd expected. They ate take-away from the inn, watched an old Ingrid Bergman flick, then got ready for bed.

Jack's casual attitude reminded her he'd once been married, but it was just about the only thing that did. Abby had said he'd been widowed fifteen years – more than half Marissa's life. There weren't many wifely touches left in the house: matching dinnerware, a set of bridelike lace curtains in the bedroom, a few painted lampshades she knew Jack never would have chosen for himself. His taste was cleaner, simpler.

But he still knew how to act like a man who'd lived elbow to elbow with a woman.

He waltzed into the bathroom while she was wash-ing her face, whipped out his dick and started peeing. Marissa's jaw dropped so fast he laughed and almost missed his aim. With a small frown of discomfort, he squeezed off the stream.

'You want to hold it?' he offered.

She felt like a kid doing it, but it was fun. By the time she shook off the last drop he'd thickened up a bit. He had one prominent vein running along the upper side of his cock that begged to have a thumb run down it. She entertained herself, and Jack, by pressing it down and watching it spring back even fuller than before.

She hadn't imagined a man's body could fascinate

her this way. She'd known she was a lesbian the first time she'd heard the word, as if a flashbulb had gone off above her head: oh, that's what I am, a lesbian! She'd never bothered playing doctor with the boys when she was little, and when she was older it seemed politically incorrect to express any interest. Hell, sometimes she felt as if she were letting the sisterhood down because she liked playing with dildoes.

One of the reasons she and Gemma had hit it off was because Abby's old room-mate didn't make those kind of judgments. Neither did Jack, it seemed.

They made love with aching slowness before they fell asleep. Jack went down on her afterwards and he was almost as good as Gemma. She could tell he liked doing it, that he wasn't just being nice. He paid attention to her responses and he didn't rush her; he let her take her time and enjoy it.

'Sleep,' he said, when she made a half-hearted attempt to return the favour.

The best part was the way he cuddled her while they slept. She hadn't expected him to. Gemma had always slept like the dead, lost in her own space. But Jack curled himself around her, his soft cock snuggling against her rear, his arm draping her belly – not so much possessive as protective.

His embrace did make her feel safe, and cherished in an old-fashioned way. She wished, for a few seconds at least, that she could fall in love with him and stop beating her head against the wall over Abby. But she knew no man would ever satisfy her completely, and anyway he showed no signs of wanting to start up anything exclusive. Why should he when Abby might drop into his lap again at any moment?

He woke her with his hard-on, a nice, hot, stiff one that pulsed insistently between her bottom cheeks. His cock felt slippery and she realised he'd already sheathed and lubed it. He must have been waiting for her to wake up. 'So it's true about men in the morning,' she said, stretching her back and wriggling her arse against his randy prick.

'It's true for me.' He slid his hand down her belly and cupped her mound. 'I love a good morning fuck. Gets the blood going, I think. But some men would rather roll out of bed and take a piss.'

Marissa turned her head back over her shoulder and squinted at him. 'Should I wonder how you know that?'

His eyes twinkled, their brown irises brightening towards green in the morning sun. He caught her earlobe between his teeth. 'Want to do something else I love this morning?'

The sheets rustled as he shifted his hips. The tip of his cock pressed between her cheeks, over the jealous pucker of her anus. The suggestion couldn't have been clearer. Luckily, Marissa had always liked backdoor play and, unlike some women, she was fine with sex in the a.m.

'Oh, yes,' she said, and reached back to open herself to him.

He pushed in carefully, giving her time to relax and himself time to find the natural curve of her body. She didn't experience even a twinge of discomfort, just the intrigued pleasure of being penetrated in a new way. She'd never had a living cock inside her there. The knowledge that his nerves were sharing in the experience created a wonderful sense of connection. She liked the way his warm, lubricated flesh moved, the way his blood pounded. The tight constriction of her passage emphasised the looseness of his velvety outer skin. It and the condom dragged slightly behind the push and pull of his solid inner core.

Cool, she thought. Very cool.

She also liked how much buggering her excited him.

A few minutes' worth nearly toppled him. With a curse that made even her blush, he stopped mid-thrust and breathed hard against her shoulder. His cock twitched hungrily inside her as if just resting there in that dark, forbidden place was enough to get him off. While he tried to calm, he played with her pussy and breasts. He was sweaty and hot and that made her sweaty and hot, too.

'Don't move so much,' he grumbled when she couldn't help squirming under his hands. 'I'd like this to last a while.'

The insight came to her like a flash of sunlight through a tree. 'You've done this with men, haven't you?' she said.

Jack groaned and cleaved her with another slow push. 'Once –' he pulled halfway out and pushed again '– or twice.'

Marissa grinned and squeezed the skinny knee he'd shoved up between her thighs. 'So what do you think of Storm's butt? It looks pretty firm. Think you'd like to take a crack at him?'

Jack's cock pulsed harder inside her, as though her words had pumped an extra measure of blood through the expansive tissues. 'Leave it alone,' he growled, even as he thrust with a little more force, a little more speed. 'My fucking Storm wouldn't get you into Abby's bed and, even if it did, you wouldn't find the answer to your dreams there.'

Well, screw you, Marissa thought, angered by how easily he'd read her mind. He might be right, but she deserved a chance to find out for herself.

Jack read her anger as easily as he'd read her ploy. 'Some other woman might live up to your fantasy,' he said. 'But it won't be Abby.'

'Fine.' She slapped his groin with her bottom, her happy mood ruined. Her lust, however, ran as strongly as ever. She clapped her hand over the hand he'd laid over her pussy and pushed it where she wanted it to go. 'Finish it,' she said. She moved his longest finger back and forth across her clit. 'Finish it, damn you.'

He wouldn't, though. He became gentler and slowed again, kissing her shoulders and rolling against her back like the billows in the bay. He slipped two fingers inside her so that his cock massaged one wall of her pussy and his fingers massaged the other. Her clit he covered with his thumb, rubbing and rolling until a cloud of steam seemed to expand through her body, hot and dark and wet. The combined movements of his cock and fingers felt better than anything she'd ever done for herself. His thumb was performing some unsuspected magic on the stiff red button of her sex. She was afraid to touch him, afraid to move for fear of breaking the spell.

Enraptured, helpless, she released his hand and gripped his knee again, squeezing fiercely as he swept her up to the edge and held her there. He gripped one breast with his other hand and pinched her nipple in time to his thrusts.

Waves of sensation throbbed through her body until it seemed her very skin was poised to come. 'Oh, please,' she moaned, both loving the torture and dying for it to end. 'Please finish me.'

Jack was almost beyond speech.

'Don't tighten up,' he gasped, trembling behind her as he pushed. 'Bear down.'

Marissa bore down and, to her surprise, his cock slipped deeper. The feeling of steam suffusing through her body intensified. She was hanging, dangling. Sweat rolled between her breasts – his or hers, she couldn't tell. He felt thick inside her, burning hot. He jerked his hips forwards, jamming deeper still. He was down to his root, his balls flattened against her cheeks, every muscle straining to hold his prick where it was. Her bowels quivered in reaction, contracting around the fiery intrusion.

The tiny increase in stimulation was more than Jack could take. He groaned like a dying man. The head of his cock swelled, then pulsed sharply.

'Je-sus,' he gasped as his climax overtook him.

His thumb stiffened on her clit, mashing it hard against her pubis. His fingers shook inside her cunt. The steam expanded inside her, thickening like storm clouds, dark, darker, darkest – and then she came, too, a rich, diffuse throb, strongest in her groin and arse but reaching outwards in warm flowing rushes that tingled deliciously from the tips of her toes to the hot, crawling crown of her scalp.

'Oh, my,' she sighed when the last wave faded, her eyes too heavy to hold open.

The bed dipped a moment later as he eased out. She was dimly aware of him pulling the sheet back over her and pressing a soft, fatherly kiss to her brow. 'Oh, Lizzie,' she heard him murmur with the last of her consciousness, 'what can I do for this little lamb?'

She knew without having to ask that Lizzie had been his wife.

The official letter from Abby's loan officer lay on the dining-room table. The dark polished wood reflected its turned-up ends, along with the blurred edges of her face. Her head propped in trembling hands, she squeezed her temples and closed her eyes. Unfortunately, the notice didn't disappear.

Damn. How could she have forgotten the balloon payment on her mortgage? She'd been so careful, reckoning every expense to the penny – and now this. She bit her lip hard, fighting back tears. She couldn't pay it. Half of it, maybe, if she sold her car and stopped repairs on the upstairs dining room – which would make it that much harder to settle her accounts in the future. She shoved the letter to the other side of the table and stood. It wasn't fair. She'd come so close to turning everything around.

'Damn,' she said again, then pushed her hair out of her face. With a heavy exhalation, she forced her frustration away. She'd have to swallow her pride and ask her sisters for the money. She hated the idea, but there was nothing else for it.

She'd simply make it clear they couldn't refuse her this time.

'Oh, God,' she moaned just as the doorbell rang.

Jack was waiting outside with a black portfolio tucked under one arm. 'Good,' he said, bending to kiss her cheek. 'I was hoping I'd catch you. I need your opinion on something.'

Abby stepped back to let him in, her brain barely functioning. It took a moment before she realised he was spreading a collection of eight-by-ten, black and white photographs across the dining-room table. He encountered the loan notice midway through the process. He began to set it aside, then straightened as the words caught his eye. He read it through, his lips moving slightly, then looked at her.

Abby shrugged, knowing her worry and humiliation must be blazoned on her face.

'Oh, honey,' he said, but his concern was quickly replaced by a look of determination. He folded the letter and pointed it at her. 'I'll talk to you about this later. I think I can help. But first I want your opinion on these – as a woman.'

Abby stepped closer to the photographs. 'Oh,' she said, instantly enchanted by the sinuous lines, by the velvet-soft shades of grey. The pictures were nudes, or pieces of nudes, but they had the same feeling as his landscapes: that somehow every inch was monolithic and profound. They were all of the same woman, she thought, though in none of the pictures could she make out a face. Snippets of background flowed behind the closely viewed body parts. She could just make out sparkling water, barnacles on a piling, beach grass, sand.

Jack put his arm around her back as she traced the dune-like curve of a hip. 'You don't think they're pornographic?'

'Hardly,' she said, her troubles forgotten in her awe at Jack's talent. She pulled one photo closer. A thick length of rope snaked between two firm, high breasts. The nipples were sharp, beaded with water or sweat. 'They are erotic, but I don't see anything offensive here. It's Marissa, isn't it? I wouldn't have recognised her unless I knew you'd asked her to pose. Is this your next book?'

'Part of it.' Still holding her, he rubbed her upper arm. 'I'm hoping to find another subject, someone whose body type will contrast with Marissa's.'

'Well, I'm sure you'll have no trouble. Most of the artist's models around here would jump at the chance to work with you.'

Jack stroked her hair behind her ear. 'I was hoping you'd jump at the chance.'

'Me? You must be –'

'Shh.' He pressed two fingers over her lips. 'Don't say "no" until you hear me out. I'll pay you enough to cover your mortgage payment, plus a small percentage of the royalties if the book makes a profit. I'll make the same arrangement with Marissa.'

'You can't do that.'

He winked at her. 'Sure I can. I'm a rich old coot. Besides, I have a feeling my publisher may go into shock over this book. I'm going to produce it myself. That way I can make sure everything goes out the way I want.'

Abby pressed one hand over her mouth and the other over her stomach. 'I do need the money.'

'Don't do it for the money,' he said, his voice both seductive and kind. 'Do it because you want to help me create something special. Do it because Marissa wouldn't feel comfortable posing with anyone else.'

Abby blinked and turned to face him. 'You want us to pose together?'

Jack cocked his head inquisitively. 'Does that bother you?'

'I suppose not,' she said slowly, wondering if it would. Showering at the gym was one thing, but this?

'Does what bother you?' Storm asked.

Jack and Abby turned as one. Storm stood under the dining-room arch with a covered platter in his hand. As they stared, he grinned and whipped off the silver dome. 'I'm trying to develop a new *hors d'oeuvre* assortment. I've got black-bean fritters, Parmesan-cheese oysters and bite-sized pieces of grilled red snapper with avocado sauce. I'm afraid the combination is too heavy, though. Here –' he waved the platter closer to Jack, bringing with it a heavenly mixture of scents '– you can try some, too.'

'Why did you bring this over here?' Abby asked, before she could think better of it.

Storm appeared genuinely confused. 'I wanted your opinion while they were still hot. Is there a problem?' He looked from Abby to Jack. 'Am I interrupting something?'

'No, no,' Jack assured him. He bent forwards to examine the platter, nabbed what looked like the red snapper and avocado, and popped it into his mouth. He sighed happily as he chewed. 'Fantastic.' He brushed his hand on his jeans and offered it to Storm. 'I'm Jack Weston.'

'Oh, sure.' Storm shook it with a blazing smile. 'I've

seen your pictures hanging at the inn. It took me about ten seconds to become a fan. I've been meaning to ask Abby to introduce us.'

Abby scratched her scalp and wondered what Miss Manners would recommend in a situation like this. The men's friendly grins could not disguise the tension that crackled between them – like rival wolves squaring off. She couldn't help thinking they both knew more about each other than they ought. Despite Storm's outward innocence, she got the distinct impression he had walked in before the tail-end of the conversation.

'I've been meaning to ask Abby to introduce us, too,' Jack said. 'She and I go back a long way. I'm glad she's decided to broaden her horizons. Bill, her old boyfriend, kept her in a bit of a stranglehold.'

'Is that so?' Storm's grin tightened to the point where he was gritting his teeth.

Abby judged it time to step between them. 'Jack was showing me the pictures for his next book.'

Storm set his platter on the sideboard and lifted the nearest photo. His face was stiffly unreadable. 'Very nice. I can see why you'd agree to pose for him.'

So he *had* heard that part. Abby opened her mouth to say something, anything, when Jack moved next to Storm and put his hand on the other side of the proof, as if to help him hold it. Storm's head came up, a short jerk of surprise. Jack was taller than him by four or five inches. That took Abby aback. She'd always thought of Storm as being larger than life. He was younger than Jack, and more powerfully built – and certainly more skilled in the arcane mechanics of lovemaking. But somehow Jack's charisma outshone his, as though the older man's confidence had deeper roots, as though it depended less on anyone's opinion but his own. Perversely, the fact that Jack could intimidate him, if only minimally, made Abby feel more drawn to Storm.

'You could help,' Jack said, his thumb sliding up the side of the photo in a gesture that was oddly suggestive. He did it again and she shivered. No. She had to be imagining it. Except Jack's shoulder and thighs were crowding Storm's and he was breathing slow and deep, next to Storm's ear, the way a man will when he's thinking of kissing someone.

Watching the interplay, Abby felt as if a rug were being slowly but firmly pulled from beneath her feet. Never in a million years would she have guessed that Jack would be attracted to another man – or that he'd come on to one in front of her. He'd only eaten one *hors d'oeuvre*. As potent as Storm's cooking was, it couldn't account for a shift in sexual inclination. Jack must have been with men before.

The revelation brought juice and heat and movement to her sex. The walls of her sheath swelled and sensitised. What wouldn't she give to see the two of them together, to watch Jack initiating Storm? Last night's adventure had merely whetted her appetite for that peculiar thrill.

Meanwhile, Storm's eyes followed the motion of Jack's thumb. His lips parted slightly and a faint wash of colour climbed his neck. He must have realised what Jack was doing. He didn't move away, though; didn't in fact betray any reaction except for those two small signs.

'You'd like me to pose with the women,' he said, and it was not quite a question.

'Very much.' Jack's voice was low but steady. He sounded just as he had when he asked Abby if she still had a crush on him – hopeful but feeling his way. He moved his thumb upwards again, this time stopping with the pad resting over Marissa's dewy nipple. 'The play of disparate bodies moving together is a wonderful photographic challenge.'

Storm broke the current between them by raising one sardonic brow and letting go of the picture. He took a step back. 'I'm sure it is. And I'd be honoured to help. You needn't pay me, though. I'd do it for the pleasure of watching an artist at work.'

They made small talk for a few minutes longer and then Jack gathered up his pictures and left. Storm watched the door until it shut, then turned to stare at Abby as if she'd grown a second head. Either that, or he wanted to grab her by the hair and fuck her senseless.

Wondering just how much he'd guessed about their relationship, and wishing she didn't feel so uncomfortable about him knowing, Abby smoothed the front of her skirt. 'Don't look at me like that. He's a world-renowned photographer. It's not as if he's trying to lure us into an orgy.'

Storm snorted and shook his head. 'You may believe that, love, but I wouldn't bet the farm.'

That night Storm told Abby he could handle clean-up himself, and sent her off with a curt goodnight as he put his shoulder behind the mop. He should have left this chore for the busboy; should have smiled into her eyes and whisked her to bed. But anger and pride wouldn't let him do what he knew was wise.

Now he shoved the mop back in the cupboard and stalked through the east wing to his room. The silence mocked him. It was one thing to say he'd grit his teeth and bear whatever she did until he managed to make her fall in love with him, and quite another to put the strategy into practice.

How many men had she slept with since he'd started sleeping with her?

Tearing off his clothes as though they were strangling him, he threw himself into the navy-and-plaid-checked chair, the very same chair to which Abby had bound him the other night. Not satisfied with his position, he pushed it out from the wall and turned it to face Jack Weston's portrait of herons flying over a marsh. He glared at its heart-stopping perfection until his eyes grew hot from not blinking.

He crossed his legs on the cushion and rubbed his hands down his bare thighs. His cock was rising. Without a thought for why this might be so, he wrapped his hand round its centre and squeezed. The pressure was pleasurable, hot with anger and lust. He shifted his index finger and rubbed its tip over the sensitive folds of the frenum. His cock stiffened further. His blood pounded. He stared at the photograph and clenched his jaw.

He had a subtle mind, this Jack. Storm knew he would prove a more formidable rival than big ole Bill and the three puppies from the Chamber of Commerce.

'Abby and I go back a long way,' Jack had said. Storm didn't go back a long way with anyone. He'd had friends in LA, but none deep enough to leave a hole when they were gone. He'd always considered a lack of attachments to be an advantage. Now he wondered if that might not always be the case. Again he saw how Jack had slung his arm around Abby's back. His fingers had stroked a tender circle on her hipbone. Only a lover would take such a familiarity. Abby hadn't returned the caress, but she hadn't pulled away, either. Storm sensed that, while their friendship might be old, their sexual relationship was new. Jack had probably given Abby this photograph as a spontaneous gesture of affection, a gift between friends.

Storm's grip on his cock tightened and the fingers of his free hand curled into the arm of the chair. To his mind, the fact that Abby and Jack were friends made the situation that much more unpalatable. He wanted to rip the picture off the wall and smash it, but his throat hurt to even think of it. The photograph was so beautiful, one pure moment captured for ever with the snap of a shutter. The birds hung in the air, stretching for home.

The man had a poetic soul. The man liked women as much as Storm did. He radiated sexual energy, the sort that could flow in more than one direction. Storm could almost admire his anything-goes attitude.

But how could Abby believe this modelling job was anything but a set-up for a lesbian encounter? Storm had seen how Marissa looked at her and no doubt this Jack fellow had, too. Hell, he'd probably slept with the waitress himself. What red-blooded male wouldn't want to see two women exploring each other for his benefit, especially two women who wouldn't shy at letting him join in?

Which left the question of why he'd invited Storm along.

Storm's cock gave a vigorous pound. His mouth twisted even as his finger swept soothingly over his glans. He knew the answer to that question. He'd have to be blind to have missed the vibrations the man was giving off. He'd been the recipient of that sort of interest before, though he'd never returned it. The question was: did the man know Abby liked to watch men together? Had she divulged more of her activities to Jack than she had to Storm? They were friends, he'd said. Long-time friends.

Storm's frustration erupted in a low, self-disgusted growl. *C'est de la folie, la jalousie!* This jealousy would make him crazy. But perhaps it seemed worse than it was because it was a new emotion for him. He'd never cared enough about anyone to be jealous of their friends. It was a disgusting emotion, useless, degrading – but he didn't know how to purge it from his system. The only thing he knew for certain was that he was missing some crucial piece of the puzzle. Jack Weston had a secret agenda, one neither he nor Abby fully understood.

He looked down at his cock, which was red now and angling upwards towards his belly. He could use a good, cleansing release, maybe a few. He looked at the window. Abby's light was out. Did that mean she was asleep, or that she was out trawling for more partners?

Only one way to find out, he thought, with a grim, determined thrill. He pulled on a pair of dark-grey pyjama bottoms, silk: all he slept in when he slept in anything. He'd grown adept at climbing the side of Rapunzel's cottage. He only pricked himself once this time, and managed to slide up the screen without a single squeak.

She lay in her bed, half on her side, half on her front, with her butt sticking up a little like a child's. The urge to leap on her and fuck her senseless was nearly overwhelming. Until the urge passed, he stood at the foot of the bed breathing hard through his open mouth. He'd fuck her all right, but first he'd enjoy the anticipation.

Delicately, inch by inch, he pulled the sheet down her sleeping body. She stirred once but did not wake. He had to bite his lip when he saw she wore only her snug white cotton panties. Oh, what those panties did to him! His cock was abruptly so hard it hurt. But he wasn't ready to take her, not quite yet.

He drew four grey velvet ties from the pockets of his pyjama bottoms.

She had a high tester bed with carved mahogany posts marking the corners. Gently, patiently, he coaxed her hands and feet towards the poles and tied them securely. When her last ankle was bound, he nuzzled it with his nose, then licked her instep. Her bottom wriggled as though she were thinking of humping the mattress.

'Storm,' she murmured, still asleep.

That made him smile. At least she was dreaming of him; at least he ruled supreme in her subconscious. He licked her second foot until her plump little toes curled, then he clambered on to the mattress. When she still didn't wake, he flicked on the bedside lamp.

Her body jerked. Her head came up and she yanked at her bonds. 'What? Jesus, Storm.'

He let his body settle over hers, his limbs following the X that hers had formed, his cock prodding her vulva through complementary layers of silk and cotton.

'Ohh,' she groaned, and a sudden flare of heat warmed the crux of her thighs.

He rolled into her, a slow, sliding curve that pulled another groan from her. 'I'm sorry,' he said, because he knew women liked hearing men say that.

She didn't ask what he was sorry for, just tipped back her head and rubbed it against his cheek. 'Storm,' she said. 'Storm.'

It sounded like an invitation to him.

At first he remained as he was, letting her take in the feel of his body through all her skin. Her flesh was soft and warm beneath him – the curve of her back, the cushion of her buttocks. She smelt of nothing but herself and the mild chamomile shampoo she favoured. He dragged his face through the silky waves of hair and closed his eyes in an ecstasy of sensual bliss.

'I have dreams about your hair,' he whispered. 'I dream that you're sweeping it down my body and winding it around my cock.' She squirmed beneath him, a restless undulation of her hips. Encouraged, he went on. 'You put your hands around it and stroke me through the coils, soft and slow, over and over until I think I'll die if you don't let me come. You bring your mouth closer and breathe on me, warm and moist, right over the head. It brings me close. I push my hips at you but you won't touch me, not yet. You bare the head with feather-light touches. You stare at me. You see how I tremble and swell. My fingers curl like claws into the sheets. You purse your lips and blow into the little hole. Oh, it feels incredible. I grit my teeth. I'm ready to scream. Then your tongue curls out and laps me, soft and wet. It makes me come, Abby, so hard.'

Abby gasped for air at the same time he did.

'Would you do that for me tonight?' he asked, low and dark. 'Would you?'

'If you like,' she whispered back.

He smiled to feel the blush that heated her cheek. He kissed the warm, butter-soft skin and trailed his hands down her arms. 'Good,' he said, fighting to steady his own temperature. 'I may need help recovering when I'm done with you.'

He stroked her hair aside and kissed the back of her neck. She shivered when he licked it, but he was already moving on, tickling her underarms, the side swell of her breasts, her spine. With lips and hands and the light brush of his torso he woke her skin to tingling awareness. He teased her with the silk of his pyjama bottoms, then slid them off and grazed her with the stiff, vibrating shaft of his cock. When he brushed it over her calves, she moaned out a wordless plea. Taking pity on both of them, he swept back up to the taut white cloth of her panties.

'I need to remove these,' he said. 'They're in my way.'

'Fine,' she panted. 'Do it.'

He grabbed the side seam between his teeth and fists and ripped it, slowly, so she had time to take in the sound. She shuddered as he pulled the cloth away. He lifted the damp gusset to his face and inhaled. The scent of her hardened him beyond bearing. He grabbed a big pillow from the wicker chair that sat beside her bed. She was so eager she lifted her hips herself so he could shove it under them.

He paused to admire the uplifted swell of her arse. Her legs were splayed wide by the ties. The position revealed her sex to him, the dark pink furrows and the bright gold curls, the red tip of her clitoris, the damp flickering mouth of her sheath. She had a gorgeous quim. If he hadn't been so ready, he would have stared at her all night.

But the pounding in his cock pulled him onwards and upwards. He settled his knees and positioned himself.

'Oh, yes,' she said as his cock parted her lips. 'Oh, yes.'

She tilted back and the crown slipped inside. He grunted at the feel of her, not a romantic sound but one he couldn't hold back. She was wet and hot. She gripped him with her folds. The sensitive cushion behind her pubic bone was swollen already, even though she hadn't come. He prodded it with the head of his cock and her breath burst from her in a rush. His angle of entry was perfect for this, just perfect.

He slipped a hand beneath her to steady her and to give her slippery little clit the pressure it needed. He circled it lightly with two conjoined fingers, loving the stiffness that hid within her tender folds – women's magic, women's secret.

'Storm,' she said, jerking back at him. 'For goodness sake, come all the way in.'

With a sigh of pleasure, he pushed deep and then shallow, deep and then shallow. He caught her cervix with the deep and her G-spot with the shallow. Her sheath rippled around him, tightened and tugged, loosened and wept warm trickles of cream. He changed his stroke, thrusting once deep and twice shallow. She moaned and called his name. He stroked twice deep and twice shallow and pressed harder with his cock, massaging the juicy cushion until her body went limp beneath him.

'Oh, God,' she said, turning her head back and forth beneath his roving kisses. 'Don't stop. Don't stop.'

He had found the magic combination and he kept at it, steady, relentless, holding his own climax at bay through force of will.

'Don't rush,' he whispered, when she began to tighten around him. The ties were there to free her of the need to work, to make her trust to him alone. 'Ride the wave.' He caught her ear long enough to lick the ticklish shell. 'Just relax. I'll carry you home.'

'I can't bear it,' she gasped, but her grip loosened. She breathed more deeply. She gave in to him.

'Ride it,' he crooned, twining his free hand with hers, stroking his thumb over the grey velvet tie that held her prisoner. 'Ride it, love.' He stroked her deep and then shallow and then shallow again and then deep, reaching for her centre with his cock. His own agony was sweet, a gift to her, a poem of praise.

'Oh,' she said, her neck arching in preparation.

He stroked shallow, shallow, shallow, telling himself deep would wait, could wait a few seconds longer for her. She began to quiver inside, to pull at him with her hot, seductive flesh. He wanted to come, needed to shove so badly he ached.

Stay, he told himself, working her shallows, rubbing her with the head, the neck. His balls were pulling up, the pressure at their base bringing tears to his eyes. She cried out and came, and came, gushing over him in a hot, quick flood. But he held steady, he held –

Without warning, her hips swung up at him, slapping his belly and driving him to her core. Sweat popped out on his brow and he froze, lodged deep, deep inside her.

'Fuck me,' she rasped, in a voice that brooked no disobedience.

Mon Dieu, he thought, but all that came out was a groan and then the groan was his thought, a long, anguished mental rumble as he thrust fully in and out a half-dozen times, hard, deep, fast until his climax burst ecstatically from his belly and shot through the hot, tight passage of his cock.

'*Mon Dieu*,' he said, aloud this time, and collapsed on top of her, his cock still twitching in her sheath.

'Gosh,' she said, breathing hard beneath him. 'That was good.'

A chuckle warmed his chest, as nice in its way as the orgasm. No wonder he'd fallen in love with her. Any woman who could say 'fuck me' and 'gosh' in the space of a minute was a prize worth holding on to.

12

Abby dressed carefully for their evening out. Never mind that she'd convinced herself it was only a friendly date; she still retrieved a stretchy, sleeveless, electric-blue dress from the back of her closet. She'd bought it while dating Bill, at his insistence, then never found the nerve to wear it. She had to cut off the shop tag before she pulled it on.

Turning back and forth before the bathroom's antique cheval glass, she shivered off a sense of *déjà vu*. She smoothed the soft blue cotton over her belly. Her reflection inspired an unexpected smile. Perhaps she'd lost weight over the last few weeks. For once her figure seemed perfect: not fat, just feminine. The scoop neck was low enough to display what cleavage she had. The skirt hugged her legs a few inches above her knee. When she sat it was certain to ride up. But what was wrong with showing off her thigh-muscles? She'd earned them, after all.

In fact, the only problem with the dress was that the bright colour washed out her face. Make-up, she thought, and dug frantically through the cabinet for the bag of cosmetics she hardly ever used. When she'd painted herself as well as she could, she hurried back to the bedroom, gasped at the time and pulled on a pair of lace-top, thigh-high stockings.

Shoes presented another minor crisis. None of her flats seemed to go. Then she spotted Bill's black patent leather heels lying forgotten on the floor of the closet. Oh, why not, she thought. She wiped off the dust with a tissue and slipped them on. Immediately, she felt different: strong, unstoppable – and taller than the five-inch spike heels could account for. As she stalked towards the dressing table mirror, the shoes' metallic clack-clack-clack reverberated up her legs and through her sex. When had her legs grown that long? When had she learned to sway her hips like a feline on the prowl?

Perhaps when I became one, she thought with a secretive smile.

At the dressing table she opened a small velvet box and removed the pearl earrings Jack had given her on her sixteenth birthday. Perhaps it was naughty to wear so many mementoes from other lovers on a date with Storm, but the earrings made her feel confident. Just fancy – when he gave her that present, she'd been a chubby, flat-chested teenager who despaired of any man ever regarding her with admiration. Who'd have thought she'd been tugging at Jack's heart, and not because of how she looked, but because of who she was inside. Though she'd been shy and moody, he'd still found something to love.

A woman could learn a lot from a man like Jack.

She touched one small, dangly earring and studied the effect. These lustrous little drops deserved companions. With a soft sigh, she pulled out another jewellery case. This one held her mother's prized string of pearls from Japan, given to Abby by her father in honour of earning her business degree.

Her fingers shook as she fastened the clasp. She stroked the pearls over her collarbones. She'd seen pictures of her mother wearing them. In looks Barbara Coates had been closer to Sandra than Abby, but her father had always said they'd been much alike in temperament. She was shy and sweet like you, he'd say, but strong inside, the sort of strength that takes folks by surprise. I gave the older girls the flashy jewellery. But these pearls were her favourites and if she'd known you, honey, she'd have wanted you to have them.

Abby's eyes filled at the memory. She hadn't worn this necklace since her father's funeral. She wondered if he'd be proud of the way she was handling her love life. Perhaps not. When he was alive she was his baby, his favourite, despite the price he'd paid to get her. He was stricter with her than with her sisters. But maybe from the distance of wherever he was now he'd understand how much her adventures meant to her, how they'd freed her from a weight she'd been carrying all her life. She was beautiful. She was worth loving. God had not traded her for her mother. What had happened when she was born had never had anything to do with her value as a human being.

She dashed away a tear before it could ruin her eyeliner. She would not run to the bathroom and wash everything off. She wouldn't. Who cared if this was all a bit much for a friendly date? She'd wanted to dress up and she had. If Storm enjoyed it, so much the better, but this was for her.

Storm almost didn't recognise her. She descended the stairs with film-siren slowness. He'd thought she was pretty from the first and with his affection she'd grown beautiful. This, however, was the sort of beauty that stopped men and women in their tracks.

The dress clung to her firm little body like the proverbial second skin, making her breasts seem fuller, her legs endless. And those shoes, those shiny, black, high-heeled shoes; who'd have guessed her ankles were so sexy? Who'd have guessed she could walk like sex on wheels? Like sex on elegant wheels, he corrected, taking in her glossy upswept hair and the pretty little pearls shivering in her earlobes. Her eyes were brilliant pools of green. Her mouth, always kissable, beckoned irresistibly under cover of a pink a few shades darker than her own.

At once, he pictured a few places he'd enjoy collecting lipstick prints. His breath rushed more quickly through his parted lips. A pulse throbbed in his groin, signalling the onset of a swift arousal. She clicked to a halt in front of him.

'Are those for me?' she asked, smiling the way beautiful women have been smiling since the beginning of time.

Numbly, he handed her the nosegay of violets he'd driven halfway up the coast to find.

'They're beautiful,' she said, her golden lashes sweeping over her soft green eyes as she brought them to her nose. 'I'd better put them in water, though. Violets are fragile.'

Storm watched, still dumbstruck, as she clacked with hip-swaying grace towards the kitchen. Her disappearance brought him to his senses. He pressed his palm over his pounding heart. This was bad. He was acting like a schoolboy. He'd never make her fall in love with him this way.

By the time she'd returned, he'd recovered sufficiently to offer her a sky-blue cardigan from the pegs in the hall. 'In case the restaurant is cold,' he explained, thinking he might feel calmer if she covered those two pale swells of breast.

She smiled and folded the sweater over her shapely arm. He stared down at her, awkward, unable to settle on what to do but wanting so badly, so badly.

'Shall we go?' she asked.

'Wait.' He bent to kiss her powdered cheek, which led to the silky side of her neck and the perfumed hollow that marked the beginning of her cleavage. His cock began to lift again but he couldn't quite back away. She smelt of lavender and orange blossom, the same scent she'd been wearing the day they met. 'You look beautiful,' he said, meaning it more than he ever had in his life.

'Thank you.' Her cheeks pinkened with pleasure. 'You look rather dashing yourself.'

He knew she hadn't heard then; knew she hadn't deciphered the love behind the compliment. He wondered at that as he pressed his hand to the small of her back and guided her out of the door.

It seemed so loud to him, he'd have thought the world could hear.

Abby was delighted to hear they'd be taking one of the whale-watching boats to Plymouth. The evening was perfect, clear and cloudless, with the sun a few hours short of setting. Storm draped the sweater around her shoulders to protect her from the spray, then stood behind her and surrounded her with his arms as they both leant over the railing.

They spotted a few humpbacks in the distance, but only one up close – a sleek young male who accompanied the boat halfway across the bay, never more than a few feet from the hull as he surfaced and submerged in long, smooth arcs. His skin was black and shiny, far more beautiful than her pointy-toed shoes. The powerful propulsive drive of his flukes barely caused a wake. He seemed unaware of their presence, not rolling or spy-hopping the way a curious whale would. Nonetheless, the way he shadowed their path proved he must be aware.

He was pitting himself against the boat, Abby decided, and, as far as she was concerned, he was coming out on top. She found the sight of all that power arousing, especially when Storm unbuttoned his charcoal-grey suit jacket and pressed a rather impressive erection into the curve of her buttocks.

'Did you know that whales are one of the few mammals who mate for fun?' he said, low and husky in her ear.

'Aside from us, you mean?'

His breath gave a funny catch. 'Aside from us,' he agreed a second later and wrapped one arm around her waist.

All around them tourists gawked and shrieked at the racing whale, but Abby's world abruptly shrank to a population of two. Storm's fingers crept lower, pressing the soft pad of flesh that crowned her vulva, a pressure that just barely teased the swollen tip of her clit.

'I wish I could fuck you now,' he whispered, rubbing himself harder against her rear.

Abby rolled her lips between her teeth. Her nipples felt like stones, her sex like a pot of honey set in the sun. His second hand crept higher, stroking the lower curve of her breast under cover of the sweater. A whimper broke in her throat. He reached higher with one finger, and higher. He touched her stiffened nipple and flicked it back and forth. Then his other hand reached, stretched, until he pushed the little swell of her arousal into the soft, wet folds that surrounded it. The thin silk of her panties clung to her skin where he pressed.

'Don't,' she breathed, though she didn't move. 'My dress will get wet.'

He groaned against her ear, a low sound of wanting that brought the wetness she'd feared from the depths of her sex. When the whale suddenly dived beneath the boat and surfaced on the other side, neither of them joined the general rush to the other side of the boat.

As soon as they were alone, Abby turned in Storm's arms. Their hips settled together, two complementary puzzle pieces. He gazed into her face as if he meant to memorise her features. 'You are so beautiful,' he said in a strangely hushed tone.

Abby felt as though she were missing something. His eyes were so intent, so luminous. Before she could begin to figure out what lay behind them, however, his arms were gathering her close and his mouth was sinking towards hers.

They kissed with a slow curve and probe of tongues, first into her mouth, then into his, the alternations timed with perfect smoothness like the passage of the whale. Storm rubbed his cock against her, pressing her to the rail and making her straddle the muscle of his thigh. His bulge grew bigger and bigger until his neck and shoulders took on the tightness she'd come to recognise as his I-can't-take-this-another-minute tension.

She knew he wouldn't require more than a few well-placed strokes to get off, but when she offered him a hanky and a hand he shook his head. 'I like to wait,' he said.

'But you're so big!' Abby covered her mouth to hush her own protest.

'I'll button my jacket.'

Abby looked down at the protrusion he was pressing so forcefully into her hip. He was huge – and no doubt frustrated as hell. Idiot man. What was he trying to prove? 'I'm sorry, Storm,' she said. 'But that thing of yours is indecent. I refuse to be seen in public with it.'

He cursed at her, then laughed, then looked around for a shadowed corner as if their lives depended on getting away. He found one behind the staircase that led to the upper deck. They were shielded from view on two sides at least, and with the whale to keep everyone occupied there wasn't much chance they'd be interrupted – not that Storm was in any state to quibble. An unlit ship's lantern swayed on the wall above his head as he carefully drew down his zip. As big as he was, he was apt to do himself damage if he weren't careful.

With a tremor he couldn't hide, he took her hand and pulled it towards the distorted gap in his trousers.

'Please, no handkerchief,' he said, his breath gusting with anticipation. 'I want to come in your hand. I want to feel your skin.'

As soon as the hot, satiny head brushed her palm, Abby wanted that, too. It was wet with pre-come, a warm, slippery fluid that seeped from the tip in a small, but steady flow. She spread it over the crown of his cock, loving this eloquent betrayal of his need. He was so far gone his penis wept with hunger and could not stop.

'Rub me right here,' he whispered, guiding her finger to a constellation of folds beneath the flaring ridge, the very same spot Ivan had been so desperate to have her lick. Her palm still cupped around the head, Abby shivered in memory and rubbed the folds, intrigued by their texture, by the violent quiver of reaction such a light touch inspired.

His head swooped down to kiss her as soon as her finger moved. He took control of the kiss this time, and his tongue did not retreat from her mouth. Holding the back of her head with one hand, he cupped the other over hers to increase the pressure on his cock. She grabbed his testicles and squeezed them through his trousers. He choked a moan into her throat. His hips jerked, his teeth caught her lower lip, and then she felt a series of pulsing bursts against her palm. His seed was warm and sticky. Some of it rolled back down his cock but she caught the lion's share.

As the last of his tension sighed from his lungs, she handed him her handkerchief. He cleaned them both quickly. Her hand was hot when he wiped it on the linen square. He touched the pulse at her wrist and found it racing.

'I'm sorry.' He shoved the hankie in his pocket. 'You're still – This place isn't private enough to –'

She laughed. She knew it went against his principles to leave a woman hanging and it pleased her that he'd been so desperate he couldn't wait. 'Don't be silly,' she said, knowing he'd more than make it up to her. 'I like waiting, too, and, unlike some people, I don't look obscene while I'm doing it.'

It seemed to Storm that he was blundering right and left. First he acted like a tongue-tied schoolboy at the sight of her skimpy dress. Then, when he knew damn well he couldn't reciprocate, he let her give him a thirty-second hand-job on the boat. Thirty seconds at most, he amended, in complete self-disgust. Finally, when she expressed surprise at how nice the restaurant in Plymouth was, he let her see that her reaction had annoyed him.

'I'm not going to take you to some crab shack,' he'd huffed.

She laughed the way women do when they think men are acting like, well, men. This made him so grumpy he ordered for both of them, which he knew was not something an enlightened modern male should do, no matter how superior his taste.

She didn't complain, though, just draped her sweater over the back of the chair and gazed out of the huge picture window. The bill he'd slipped into the *maitre d*'s palm had ensured them a table with a view. 'Look, there's another pod of whales,' she said, pointing towards the sweep of the bay. 'See that big fellow breaching? Oh, what a splash!'

Storm tugged his earlobe. She looked happy. Her cheeks were glowing. Her eyes sparkled. Could she be enjoying herself? He felt so stupid, as though his normally infallible instincts had abandoned him. Apparently, making a woman fall in love was a lot easier when you weren't actually trying to do it.

She spoke of her childhood over the entrée. Her father liked to take them beachcombing at sunrise, she said, and her sister Sandra always overslept, then swore they let her just to be mean. 'Francine was the family tease, after Dad, that is. One morning, she made a tape of Sandra snoring through our wake-up call just to prove we'd tried.' Abby's eyes danced at the memory. 'Sandra hated being proved wrong worse than anything. I thought she'd never speak to Frannie again. Of course, if anyone pestered either of us, Frannie was the first to punch the offender in the nose. Dad called her "his little scrapper".'

'What did he call you?' Storm asked, happy to listen to the stories. He knew such things were the coin of friendship. If Jack Weston was her friend, by God, Storm would be, too.

Abby rolled her eyes. 'Dad called me "his little princess", which annoyed Sandra so much she started calling me Princess Butterball.' Abby chuckled and covered her mouth. 'I was a little chubby. Of course, nowadays, Sandra is so weight-conscious she'll hardly let herself eat a whole stalk of celery.'

'Food was meant to be enjoyed,' Storm said seriously.

'Exactly,' Abby agreed, carving herself another bite of filet mignon. 'Otherwise, what's the point of eating?'

They spent the remainder of dinner discussing their favourite meals and where they'd eaten them, films they'd seen and books they'd read. He discovered they both had a secret passion for hard-boiled detective novels. Surely that was a good omen? Buoyed by the ease of the conversation, he had almost forgotten his earlier missteps by the time they settled in over coffee.

Normally, he listened to women because he knew it

pleased them, but he wouldn't have minded listening to Abby all night. She was funnier than he expected, and had a broader range of interests. In fact, there seemed to be a whole other woman hiding beneath the woman he'd fallen in love with – which made him wonder at himself. How could he have fallen in love with someone he barely knew? What kind of crazy emotion was that? But the stupidity of it didn't matter. He was here with her, the woman he loved, and she was sharing the little events that had made her who she was. Life was good.

Until she unwittingly stepped into his forbidden zone.

'What about your family?' she asked. 'I know you said your parents are dead, but do you have any brothers or sisters?' He shook his head and set his cup in the saucer. He stared at his hands. His fingertips whitened as he pressed them into the starched red tablecloth. Abby reached across the table and stroked his wrist. 'Were you young when they died?'

He shook his head again, feeling the silence lengthen and wondering how long it could go on before the moment was irretrievable. Be a man, he told himself. She gave you a piece of her history. The least you can do is offer up a piece of your own. He cleared his throat.

'It was just my mother and me,' he said, his voice so rough he found it impossible to meet her eyes. 'She was a waitress. We lived in Montreal, in Quebec. I guess you'd call where we lived a project – low-income housing, run-down, kind of dangerous.'

He straightened his silverware, all too aware of Abby's hush. His palms were clammy. He dried them on his trousers and returned them to the table. He strove for an even tone.

'My mother was a weekend drunk. She always made it to work but on her days off, well, let's say she drank most of her tips. I honestly don't know who my father was. She had a lot of boyfriends, most of whom weren't a pleasure to be around. When I got tired of dealing with them, I'd run around the city with my friends. Montreal is a beautiful place, lots of history, lots of water. The Fleuve Saint Laurent, the St Lawrence Seaway, runs right through it.'

Storm sighed and turned his knife upside down. 'I had plenty of freedom. Sometimes I'd stay away as long as a week, sleeping with friends or on the street if it was warm. I missed a lot of school, but I was smart enough to catch up when I dropped back in.

'Anyway, one time when I was sixteen, I went on a two-week walkabout. When I got home, my mother had moved. No forwarding address, no note, just packed up and left. I guess she reckoned I was old enough to take care of myself.' Which I was, he reminded himself, trying to forget the hollow echo as he pounded on the door, the clenching in his stomach as he thought: Incredible. The bitch has finally sunk lower than even I thought she could. And Mr Kozlakis pressing the money he knew they couldn't spare into his hand, the money that had saved him from starving until he could hitch-hike to LA. He clenched his jaw to keep it steady.

'Oh, Storm.' Abby covered both his hands with her own. 'That must have been awful.'

He didn't need to see her to mark her sympathy. Angry for saying more than he'd intended, he fisted his hands beneath her hold. 'I don't need pity,' he said.

Abby's laughter startled him into looking at her. A trail of silver marked one soft pink cheek. His throat tightened.

'You may not need pity,' she said, smiling through the remnants of her tears. 'But, after a story like that, it's pretty hard to hold it back.'

He lowered his head again. 'I'm sorry. I shouldn't have told you all that.'

'Of course you should have.' She squeezed his fists until he forced them to relax. 'How else do people get to be friends?'

But he couldn't help thinking he had done the wrong thing. He should have told her about Mrs Kozlakis, about the little Greek restaurant where she'd taught him how to cook – the happy times, the love. He should have told her about the way the snow frosted the city in the winter like a wedding cake, about hitching to LA and gaping at the palm trees, about finding a job frying burgers the day he arrived and never looking back. He'd made the success of himself only Mrs K had believed he'd make. For that, he needed no pity.

Abby was quiet on the boat trip home. The night was dark and the lanterns were lit. They stood at the rail and she held his hand, but lightly, as if she didn't want to encourage more intimacy. When he walked her to the cottage, she didn't invite him in.

'Friends,' he muttered under his breath as he stomped back to the inn.

Damn her for thinking that's all he wanted, and damn him for letting her. God in heaven, why couldn't he do the right thing the one time the right thing meant the world?

Abby sat at her dressing table, feeling as if she'd been hit by a train. Her fingers trembled as she pulled the tiny pearl teardrops from her ears. She hadn't dared ask Storm in. The emotions that roiled inside her were so strong she was sure she'd give herself away. What she'd feared from the start had happened.

She'd lost her heart to him.

That awful, wonderful story had been the final straw. Knowing that she'd always had a soft spot for a hard-luck tale didn't change her feelings in the least. She understood so much she hadn't understood before –

why he feared commitment, why he didn't trust love, even why he'd devoted himself to the art of pleasing women.

He didn't believe they'd love him for himself.

She set the earrings in their box and stared at her dazed reflection. He was horribly lovable, devastatingly lovable, so lovable the thought of him spending his life drifting from one meaningless relationship to the next made her sick to her stomach. None of which meant she could change him; none of which meant he was any less dangerous to her than he'd been before.

13

Stripping naked for Storm was one thing, Abby thought. Stripping naked for Jack while Storm watched was quite another.

They'd all gathered in Jack's glassed-in studio where he planned to take tonight's photographs. He'd pushed back the furniture and tossed a soft red blanket across the carpeted floor. The shades were lowered. Constructed of thin brown and gold reeds, they'd make an interesting backdrop – or so she thought as she tried to distract herself from her anxiety.

She snuck a look at Storm. Jack told him he wouldn't be incorporated into the pictures until later. Relegated to observer, he leant against one wall with both arms crossed, as though he expected Jack to drag out a mud-wrestling pit. In his snug white T-shirt and jeans, he reminded Abby of a long-haired James Dean. 'Show me,' said his face. 'Prove that I can trust you.'

To see him, you'd never guess he practically twisted her arm to get her here on time.

'Mustn't be late,' he'd said with a too-tight smile.

She suspected he was jealous. Now that she'd admitted to her own feelings, behaving as if she shouldn't take his into account was a lot harder. Jealousy was not a sign of commitment, however, or the desire to extract one. Besides which, their immediate professional future might depend on this influx of cash.

But I'm not doing it for the money, she told herself, turning her eyes back towards Jack. He was certain to create something beautiful. Why shouldn't she and

Storm be a part of that? At the very least, she'd have a memento once he moved on to his next conquest.

She fought a sigh. Jack was busying himself with mysterious equipment realignments: light meters, giant lamps and screens. He was lucky. His face gave nothing away. He squinted into a viewfinder. 'Any time you're ready,' he said with a brief glance in her direction.

Any time I'm ready, what? Abby thought, and twisted her hands together at her waist.

At least Marissa looked as nervous as she felt. Dressed only in a white silk robe, she grabbed Abby's hand and pulled her through the house to Jack's bedroom.

'Those idiots,' she said, pushing her to sit at the foot of his bed. 'Expecting you to rip off your clothes at the drop of a hat.'

What a mother-bear she could be. Abby grinned as Marissa knelt before her and began untying her trainers. Her touch, though impersonal, sent a funny shiver up Abby's legs. Abby noticed the spikes of her short black and henna hair were more unruly than usual. She must have been raking her fingers through it all evening.

'I bet he didn't tell you why you're really here,' she said in that same scornful tone.

Abby opened her mouth to say: 'Of course he did. We're here to pose for his next book.' Then she remembered Storm's suspicions. 'Do you know something I don't, Marissa?'

Marissa pulled one unlaced shoe from Abby's heel, shoved it under the bed, then put both hands on the floor to steady her balance. She looked like a runner about to burst into motion at the starter's gun, head down, body tense. 'I'm pretty sure you're here for me,' she said. 'Jack knows I have a thing for you. He thinks, if he throws us together in an erotic situation and it doesn't work out, I'll have to get over my crush.'

'Oh,' Abby said, unable to think of a single intelligent response.

Marissa pulled off her second shoe and shoved it under the bed with its partner. Beyond that, she seemed unable to move.

Abby studied the top of the other woman's head. From the way Marissa occasionally stared at her, she'd thought she might be bi. But Abby had assumed Marissa didn't want to face the kink in her sexual orientation. She'd never mentioned liking women and, when Gemma called to recommend her for the waitressing job, she hadn't mentioned it, either. Not that she had to; Abby was an equal-opportunity employer and all that.

Aware that she was babbling to herself, she squeezed her knees. 'You mean, you and Gemma –'

'Yes,' Marissa said. 'We were lovers.'

So. Marissa and Gemma had slept together: her old college flatmate and her best waitress. She thought of all the times Gemma had tried and failed to seduce her, how Abby had been ignorant at first, then embarrassed, and finally grateful they could still be friends. Had Gemma told Marissa about those ill-fated attempts? Had the two of them discussed her the way men discuss a woman they want: what a pair of cantaloupes she's got, eh? Abby shook her head. This was so weird.

Without warning, Marissa clasped Abby's calves and pressed her head to her knee. 'Just let me show you,' she said, kissing her skin through a rip in the denim. 'You wouldn't have to do anything. Just let me show you how it can be.'

Abby wasn't sure what made her let Marissa push her gently back on to the bed. Curiosity, maybe, or sympathy, or maybe even annoyance at the men for wanting to turn something that meant so much to Marissa into a show.

Jack's bed didn't have a proper spread. A thick blue-

and black-striped Hudson Bay blanket covered the sheets, half soft, half scratchy. It felt strange against her bare skin as Marissa eased off her oldest pair of jeans. Her panties followed. When they were gone, Marissa slipped on to the bed with her. Oh, God, Abby thought. What now?

'You're shaking!' Marissa exclaimed, and proceeded to stroke her face as if she were a fretful child. 'Don't be afraid. I won't hurt you, Abby. Not ever.'

'I'm all right,' Abby insisted. Oddly enough, she was. She'd shaken just as hard the first time she made love to a man, mostly because she hadn't the faintest idea how she'd react or what she ought to do. But that wasn't the case today. Though she wasn't sure how she'd react, she had a fair idea of what she ought to do: the same as she would for any lover.

She reached up and stroked Marissa's hair, spearing her fingers into the softness that lurked beneath the styling gel. Marissa stilled. Her face tightened and darkened with an intensity that frightened Abby.

'I want to kiss you,' she whispered.

Abby nodded and pulled her closer, feeling as if she were sinking into a strange dream. Marissa's kiss was soft as a feather, much softer than she'd expected, given her sometimes abrasive personality. The tip of her tongue flirted with Abby's lips, tracing the seam and tickling the soft inner margins until Abby relaxed and opened for a deeper entry.

Marissa moaned when their tongues met in the middle.

The low, hungry sound sent a shiver of heat down Abby's spine. Slowly, as though she feared Abby's reaction, Marissa lowered her body. Abby still wore a soft cotton tank top, but Marissa's nipples pressed sharply through her white silk robe. Behind the pebbled nubs, her breasts were firm and soft.

So this is what men feel, Abby mused. She put her arms around the other woman's back. She was so slender. Her muscles, though, were as hard and wiry as a man's. Abby stroked the bumpy line of her spine and thought: how fragile she is, and then, how delicious. To have this power over her own kind was an unexpected thrill. Something opened inside her, a deeply scented flower, both heavy and delicate. Her sex began to pulse. She slid her hands lower and cupped Marissa's rock-hard buttocks. She had no fat here, just lean, hard muscle. Abby squeezed her a little just to be sure. Marissa's cheeks clenched. She squirmed and kissed her harder.

A second later, she lifted her body far enough to yank her robe open. 'I'm sorry. I've got to –' and with a groan of pleasure, she ground her bare pussy over Abby's thigh.

She was wet and hot. Her curls were coarser than either Abby or Storm's and her clit was large enough to feel between her mashing lips. Abby wouldn't have minded touching it, seeing it, but Marissa seemed determined to take the lead. Her hand skimmed down Abby's side, grabbed one cheek and squeezed hard, then cruised around her hip to comb through her pubic curls. She tugged on the lower fringe. 'You're wet,' she marvelled. 'Oh, Abby.'

Her gratitude embarrassed her. She knew if she didn't sidetrack her, Marissa would be crawling down her body and kissing her there. Abby didn't want that; didn't want Marissa to do anything with such worshipful overtones. When she thought back on this later, Abby wanted her to remember they came together as equals.

'Touch me,' she said, calling Marissa's dark, shining gaze back to hers. 'Touch me the way you'd touch yourself.'

Marissa watched her eyes as she slid her fingers

between her lips. One knuckle grazed a sweet spot on the side of her clitoris. Abby shivered. Marissa smiled. Burying her other hand in Abby's hair, she began to pinch the swollen bundle of nerves, pinch and release, pinch and release, until Abby lost her fear that she wouldn't be able to come for her.

Relaxing into her rising arousal, she closed her eyes and raked slow circles around Marissa's buttocks. The other woman's breath came faster. Her hips jerked closer, then drew away as if she'd done something she shouldn't.

'You, too,' Abby said, coaxing her to roll against her thigh. 'You, too.'

Hesitantly, she complied. Her motions were tentative, jerky. Abby suspected she didn't want to reveal the full extent of her excitement. She must have thought it would put Abby off.

But that was no way to make love. Like her big sister Francine always said: 'If it's worth doing, it's worth doing right.' With a squirm and a push, Abby turned them both on their sides and took the other woman's nipple into her mouth.

Marissa cried out and clutched her head. The position felt awkward, but, oh, the sensations that surged through her as she sucked that turgid peak. She could see why men liked this. The appeal was so primitive, especially for Abby, who had never felt the like, not even as a baby. Marissa's skin was smooth as butter here. She rolled the nipple against the roof of her mouth, sucking a little, licking a little, trying to draw it out even further. Marissa's hips worked harder against her thigh, so hard that Abby's muscles began to ache.

'Oh, God,' Marissa gasped and shuddered in orgasm.

The climax seemed to destroy her restraint. She was all over Abby then, pushing her on to her back and kissing her, touching every inch of skin she could reach.

This time, Abby could not prevent her from licking her way to her pussy, but now she was too aroused to care.

Her hips jerked off the bed as soon as Marissa lapped at her straining clit. Marissa had to press her elbows over her inner thighs to hold her down. She used her fingers, too, all over the squirming territory between her legs. They slid up and down her inner lips, probed her sheath, crawled down between her cheeks and pinched the pucker of her anus. None of her lovers had created this sense of total invasion. It wasn't that Marissa knew what a woman liked and they didn't. It was that Marissa had no fear of Abby's body. Abby's pussy might as well have been her own for all the hesitation she showed in exploring it.

Marissa's tongue worried through her slippery folds to find the bare, swollen button. She fluttered the tip against that nerve-laden point, as rapid as hummingbird wings. The sensation was too much, too raw. Abby bit her lip until she tasted blood, straining, straining. Her hands fumbled for Marissa's head, half wanting to push her away, half wanting to drag her closer.

'Oh!' she gasped, abruptly teetering over the edge.

Marissa nursed her orgasm to the very last, sweet spasm, then began to push her towards climax again.

'No,' Abby said, gently lifting her away. 'That's enough.'

Marissa sat up, her eyes worried, her mouth shining with Abby's juices. 'If I did something wrong, I could –'

'You didn't do anything wrong,' she assured her. 'That was wonderful.'

And it had been wonderful. It just hadn't been quite ... right.

She smiled and touched Marissa's cheek with the back of her fingers. She looked beautiful, an exotic, obsidian-eyed goddess in a rumpled silk robe. She deserved to devastate her lovers, not merely please them. 'We should probably get back to the others,' she said.

Marissa grimaced and wiped her face on a corner of her robe. Her eyes searched Abby's again, then slid to the window where ivory lace curtains swayed in a salty breeze. 'They'll be expecting a show, you know,' she warned.

A delightful spark of wickedness supplanted Abby's concern. 'So we'll give them a show.' She laughed at Marissa's double take. 'And then we'll make them give us one.'

'Jack and Storm?' Marissa's eyes widened skeptically. 'No way.'

Abby pursed her lips and shrugged in rebuttal. If nothing else, the last fifteen minutes were proof that stranger things could happen.

Storm ran his finger around the collar of his T-shirt. They'd only been shooting five minutes and already he was sweating like a pig.

'How does this look?' Abby asked, for what had to be the twelfth time.

She and Marissa were tangled together on the soft red throw, white limbs and tan, black hair and gold. Abby lay behind Marissa. One of her hands was spread like a spider around Marissa's pointy breast. The other was draped over her mound. Marissa's face was flushed, her nipples so dramatically erect they had to be half an inch long. Every so often she'd squirm higher on the thigh Abby had pressed between her legs. Storm could see her juices shining on his lover's smooth white skin. Worse, he could see that Abby was not the least bit shocked.

He knew something had happened between the women when Abby went to change. She'd come back flushed and confident, with a twinkle in her eye and not a stitch on her back. Even Jack had paused at her brazen entrance. The thought of what Marissa must have done to cause the change made him crazy: crazy jealous and crazy aroused. Ridiculous, to be jealous of a woman. Abby was as heterosexual as they came. Or so he thought till he spotted the kiss-marks on Marissa's breast.

She was impossible, insatiable, and this flirtatious little game she was playing didn't calm him in the least. He'd long since shoved his hands into his pockets to camouflage his massive erection. Jack and Abby, however, both behaved as if they were arranging fruit.

'Would you rather see her curls?' Abby asked, demonstrating with a slight shift of her hand. 'Or should I cover them completely?'

'It doesn't matter,' Jack said. 'I'll shoot when I see something I like.'

'But –' Abby began.

'For God's sake,' Storm muttered.

Abby fluttered her wide green eyes at him. 'Maybe you could help, Storm. I just can't imagine how this position looks.'

'*Putain*,' he swore. He'd help her get positioned.

Her mouth 'O'd as he pushed off the wall and strode towards her, the innocence of her expression ruined by the flickering attention she gave his bulge. Look your fill, he thought savagely, his entire abdomen pounding. Without warning, he knelt before Abby, shoved her longest finger between Marissa's creamy lips and forced it to rub the protuberant blade of her clit.

Even then she didn't flinch.

'There,' he growled. 'That's a nice position.'

'Hm,' said Jack, as though Storm had moved an apple an inch to the left. 'Storm, why don't you lift Marissa's arm over her head for me?'

Thus he became the photographer's assistant,

manoeuvring the women into the echoes of his most hackneyed male fantasies. The fact that he knew they were hackneyed didn't lessen the effect of each position on his private parts. By the time he'd worked the two into a *soixante-neuf*, his cock felt hard enough to break off. His hands were shaking. Sweat dripped down the sides of his face. The women were hiding smiles each time he drew close to rearrange them.

'I've got enough of this series,' Jack said, but before Storm could sag in relief – or disappointment; it was hard to say which – he added: 'Why don't you strip off and join them?'

The women sat up, eager as puppies for a treat. Jack turned as well and consequently three sets of eyes watched him peel down to his briefs. His skin crawled with awareness. He could feel the head of his cock poking above the waistband. Abby licked her lips. Jack just smiled.

Storm jerked the briefs down and tossed them on to his other clothes.

Marissa whistled with the enthusiasm of a construction worker. To Storm's extreme self-disgust, he blushed. To hell with this, he thought, striding towards the women. They rolled apart for him, then rolled together when he settled between them. He shuddered as their flesh pressed him from either side. He'd been with more than one woman before, but never in an atmosphere so charged. He'd happily have fucked either one of them, repeatedly, for broadcast on the evening news.

Jack snapped a single shot of their huddle, then stepped out from behind the tripod.

'Hm,' he said, studying the composition.

'You've lost your arranger.' Abby's voice dripped honey and smoke.

Jack pinched his lower lip. 'So I have.'

'Perhaps you'll have to do it yourself,' Marissa said.

'Oh, no,' Storm said, though he knew he'd be better off keeping quiet.

Jack grinned at him. Abby nipped the meat of his shoulder. 'You had your fun,' she said. 'It's only fair you let us have some, too.'

Storm sighed. When she put it like that, how could he refuse?

At first, Jack's touches were professional – and indirect. He moved the girls so that their breasts rolled on to his ribs or their hair mingled over his groin. He placed Abby's hand over his pectoral, Marissa's thigh across his belly. After a while, though, he began to touch Storm himself, lifting his arm, tilting his head. More than once he dragged his hand down the length of his spine, which made him shiver but had nothing to do with getting him into position. In the end, the pretence of picture-taking was swept aside and the girls joined in, moving him this way and that, like a bendable mannequin for an X-rated shop window.

'This pose is nice,' Marissa said.

They had him straddling both girls' hips. His cock hung down between their bodies, hot and thick, fighting its own weight. It didn't feel like a part of him anymore, more like an alien invader. He was ready to plunder, ready to fuck till morning. Unfortunately, the rules of this game didn't seem to allow for anything but torment.

He swore in French, not wanting to scare the women with the violence of his need.

Abby must have guessed his meaning. She ran the back of one finger over his cock's dangling head. Storm groaned at the fleeting touch. She showed the fluid she'd gathered to Marissa. Marissa grinned and pulled the finger into her mouth, sucking it in and out long after it was clean.

Abby flushed. Marissa chuckled. She was rubbing

Storm's nose in it. She'd fucked Abby. He knew it. 'I feel you, too,' he said. 'Both your juices, all over my skin.'

Abby shivered, then Marissa, as if the tremor were catching. He savoured his victory, but only for a moment because Jack was guiding them into their next position. The way he handled Storm was different now. It was more caressing, less businesslike. The change made him nervous. He tried to be a good sport, but when Jack's hands ventured over his balls he couldn't help grabbing the man's wrist.

'Bad,' Abby scolded, squirming out of the tangle to face him. 'Marissa and I posed for you, didn't we?'

Storm couldn't answer, merely pant.

She touched Jack's wrist, the wrist that Storm had trapped, then cupped the fingers that cradled his scrotum. Neither Storm nor Jack let go, though Jack did resettle his fingers and give him a squeeze. Storm tried not to squirm, but the touch was excruciatingly pleasant. Jack's hand was so much bigger than a woman's. His palm was rough, with a working man's calluses. He knew a few tricks, too. One of his fingers slipped behind Storm's scrotum to rub the internal root of his cock. Already stiff as iron, his skin tightened a fraction more.

Seeing the tiny surge, Abby lifted her hand and tapped the bulging crown with the tip of her finger. The blow fell just hard enough to sting. He groaned a plea for mercy.

'You seem to be enjoying this,' she said. 'Are you sure you want us to stop?'

He looked at the question in her eyes, then at the quiet smile in Jack's. His body tingled from head to toe, driven to a rare pitch of arousal. He wanted to come; wanted to throw himself over the abyss and fuck the lot of them. He simply couldn't bring himself to say so out loud.

Abby must have read the conflict in his face. The

corners of her mouth curled upwards. 'Perhaps I could make this easier for you,' she said. She stepped away to rummage in one of the boxes that sat against the wall. She emerged with a tangled black extension cord. Storm's heart began to race as she wound it around her arm. The cord reminded him of his shiny latex ties.

'Oh, no,' he said, shaking his head. 'No, no.'

But he remained where he was as if his knees had been glued to the floor. She wouldn't bind him, not in front of the others. That was his private vulnerability, not meant to be shared with anyone but her.

His body hair stood on end as she looped the cord around his chest.

'Say no like you mean it,' she whispered, her lips brushing his ear.

Storm shut his mouth and swallowed.

Marissa helped Abby tie him up. He closed his eyes under the euphoria of two women's hands trussing his arms to his torso. One pair of hands was long and hard, the other small and soft. One stroked, one pinched, and both were covered in warm, silky skin. As they tied him, breasts nudged him between the confining strips, and thighs, and arms, and damp, clutching pussies. They rubbed against him, both of them, and left their sex marks on his skin.

The effect was so devastating he almost forgot that Jack was there, waiting.

The women fell away once they'd finished binding him. His arms were immobilised, but the rest of him was free. The final loop of the cord pressed the base of his cock in the front and the curve of his buttocks at the back. His blood beat hard beneath the constriction. It rushed in his ears. He felt dizzy, as if he might fall, but also as if he wanted to fall, no, wanted to plunge down an endless cliff. Could they see how he felt? Could they tell what they'd done to him? The uncertainty was like a pinch administered to a pleasure centre, painfully arousing. He dreaded moving any further into the mystery. His body, however, would not tolerate inaction. Reluctantly, he opened his eyes.

Jack stood above him, naked now, his hands on his hips. His long, curving cock jutted towards Storm's face as though daring him to do something about it. He stared at it for a moment, mesmerised by its unusual configuration, by its vigorous throb. As he watched, a bead of moisture seeped from the pointy tip. The man wanted him – badly. Unnerved, Storm's eyes slid upwards, past the flat belly to the cloud of silver hair that covered the other man's chest.

The colour sparked something in his subconscious. He looked into Jack's face, saw the smile lines, the confidence, the reined-in excitement.

He's old enough to be my father, he thought before he could push the awareness away. He didn't want to be thinking that. He was too old to be thinking that. But the silver hair, the secrets in his eyes ... He knew things that Storm might know, too, when he reached that age.

As though sensing his agitation, Jack reached out and stroked his cheek. How can he be so unselfconscious? Storm wondered. How can he swing from man to woman without a qualm?

'Tell me what you'd like,' Jack said, but Storm couldn't answer. 'This?' he suggested, and rubbed the tip of his crooked cock across Storm's shaking lips.

All he had to do was open them. It would never be easier than now, when his whole world throbbed with sexual meaning. He moaned and drew the first few inches inside. Ah, it was so smooth, so warm and silky. It tasted of salt and something else – his seed. Yes, it tasted of oysters, even had the same slippery charm.

Intrigued, he sucked gently, then lapped the crown with the flat of his tongue. The cock shivered in his mouth.

Is this what women feel, he wondered, this sense of both servility and power?

A body pressed behind him – Abby's, he knew from the soft, round swell of her breasts. She wound her arms around his waist and took his cock in her hands. She stroked him as he sucked, gently, so gently up and down the sides, only enough to keep him hard and high. Her touch soothed him. She was here. She would not let things go wrong.

Somewhere in the distance a camera shutter snapped. Marissa, he thought, glad she'd pulled away. He'd enjoyed her edgy touch, but now he wanted Abby to himself. And she liked this, he reminded himself, as if the pebble-hard press of her nipples weren't reminder enough. Buoyed by her excitement, he intensified the pull of his cheeks. Jack's breath sighed out of him. He began to thrust, not too deeply to bear but deeper than Storm had taken him on his own.

'Steady,' Jack said, bracing his head with one hand. His fingers burrowed through Storm's hair. Storm realised Jack wanted to control the rhythm – which left nothing for him but tongue work.

But that was all right. Storm could wreak plenty of havoc with that. He knew what he liked anyway. With a private grin, he kept his tongue wet and his lips tight, creating a slight vacuum for the other man to work against. He made sure the sweet spot under the head got a good, hard massage with every pass.

'Damn,' Jack said admiringly, on the fifth repetition of the stunt. He gripped the base of his cock between forefinger and thumb, pulling the penile skin towards his belly as taut as it would go. The gesture warmed Storm's pride.

Oh, yes, he thought, knowing that trick himself. You pull it tight, old man. You make sure you can feel every lick just as clearly as you can. To reward him for the compliment, he ran his tongue around the head and dug it into the tiny hole.

Jack moaned and thrust faster. The shutter snapped wildly, like a communal pulse run amok. Abby craned her chin over Storm's shoulder. He could feel how excited she was. Her heart was racing, her body damp and hot.

'Look at him,' she whispered. 'Oh, look.'

He looked. Jack's balls were drawn up high against his body and a thick blue vein pulsed under the skin of his belly. His cock glistened as it left Storm's mouth, veering strongly left. The pressure of his lips could no longer pull it straight.

Soon, Storm thought, and hummed his anticipation into the smooth, driving flesh.

Jack clutched his shoulders at the tiny vibration. Storm wrapped his tongue over the head and hummed again. Jack shuddered. Abby gasped for breath and held it. One of her hands left Storm's groin and touched his cheek. He knew she could feel Jack pushing in and out, and knew Jack could feel the light pressure of her fingers.

'Christ,' Jack swore.

The old man's shaft gave a single, warning throb. He chuffed out a grunt, thrust one more time to the verge of Storm's throat, then grabbed his cock and wrenched it free. His seed struck Storm's chest in pulsing sprays of heat. If Storm had had the breath for it, he would have laughed. It seemed the old man had a touch of shyness after all.

But that didn't matter now. Breathing as hard as if he'd run a race, Storm turned to Abby. Her face was pink. Her breasts trembled with the pounding of her heart. He grinned at her, relieved that it was over, but pleased with himself, too.

He cocked his head towards his groin. 'Want to finish what the old man started?'

'Do I ever!' She laughed and toppled him back on to the red blanket. Trussed as he was, he fell hard. In seconds she'd straddled him and was positioning him for entry.

'Hey!' He twisted between her legs. 'Aren't you going to untie me?'

'What for?' She wagged his cock back and forth. 'I've got the best part right here.'

But he couldn't let her ride him, not under the watchful eye of the camera. With a grimace and a squirm, he worked the cords up to his chest and yanked them over his head.

'Cheater,' she said, but she laughed as he pushed her under him and rolled them both in the blanket.

He sank into her with a noisy sigh. 'There,' he said. 'That's where you belong.'

'A woman's place?' she gasped, but he couldn't keep up the banter with her flesh so warm around him.

'I ache,' he whispered, for her ears only, 'and you feel so good.'

She smiled and pulled his head down for a kiss. At once their hips began to rock, the rhythm shutting out the world. He sucked her tongue into his mouth, then lost his breath and had to bury his face in her tousled hair. Ah, she was sweet. He kissed her again, and again broke for air.

'I ache,' she mouthed, and guided his hand down between their bodies.

Her back arched as he stroked her, slowly at first and then with real speed and pressure. He couldn't wait for her. She had to hurry. The afternoon caught up to him in a rush and he was ready to burst from the accumulated tension. He needed to pour it into her. He needed to let go so badly his bones hurt.

'Oh, yes,' she said, her thighs shifting and gripping on his hips. 'Oh, yes.'

He came before the 's' finished hissing – couldn't stop it if he tried. His head jerked back. His hips snapped forwards. A delicious flare of pleasure licked through his groin and then the seed burst from him so hard it felt as if it were being suctioned free. The glow spread down his thighs and up his torso, warming him as he sagged helplessly down. His arms were shaking too badly to hold his weight.

'Shh,' she said, stroking his back. His cock slipped free by itself, completely spent.

'But you didn't –' He touched her swollen clit.

'No.' Shyly, she shook her head. 'Take me home. I'll come for you there.'

'As many times as I want?'

She grinned and shoved his sweaty chest. 'As many times as you can handle, big boy.'

With that promise, Storm felt a measure of strength return.

Abby returned to the bedroom to dress. Storm could have gone with her but some formless urge held him back, something unsettled, unanswered. He looked around the empty studio, smelling dust and sex and books. Marissa had wandered outside. Satisfied that Abby was safe, he pulled on his jeans and followed the old man into the kitchen. There he leant back on the counter by the sink, watching him pull the makings of a sandwich from the cabinets: rye bread, mustard, a tin of smoked ham. Bachelor's fare.

'You're in love with Abby, aren't you?' Storm said. He didn't know when the knowledge had come to him, but once uttered the statement had a ring of truth. Jack set the bread knife down and smiled his cocky, old man smile. Storm wasn't fooled. 'You are. I say the words and tears come to your eyes.'

As though Storm's accusation required a change of strategy, Jack turned and took two beers from the refrigerator. He cracked one open and handed it to Storm. Any other man would have been embarrassed; Jack merely looked amused.

'My fondness for Abby goes way back. For a while, I thought my sexual feelings had died with my wife. And if you think it's easy to discover that's not the case, you've never been in love.' He opened his own beer and watched a curl of vapour rise from the dark brown mouth. 'I went through hell wanting Abby so, yeah, I'm in love with her. But I also love her. I watched her grow up. She'll never lose me, no matter who she sleeps with.'

Storm lifted his beer and realised his hands were shaking. This man had a history with Abby, a long history that he could never duplicate. He'd shared Abby's home, Abby's holidays, Abby's family. Storm could hardly comprehend what those things meant. 'Are you going to fight me for her?' he said.

Jack laughed, but stopped when he saw the anger in the younger man's face. 'I had one big love in my life, son. A woman like Abby shouldn't have to settle for second place.'

'Are you so sure that's where she is?'

Jack cocked his head at him. 'I have to wonder why you'd ask a question like that, considering the stake you might have in the answer.'

'Why did you . . .' Storm rested the bottom of his beer on his waistband. A drop of condensation rolled off the chilled bottle and past his navel. 'Why did you want me to suck you off?'

'Rather worry about that, would you?' Jack returned to his sandwich making. Storm saw that he was constructing two. With great deliberation, he smoothed a swath of mustard across the bread. 'I guess I've reached a point in my life where I don't want one thing anymore. Not one woman. Not one sex. A lot of people have the potential to be that way, but they don't let themselves.' He cut two thick slices of ham, laid a square of Swiss cheese on top of each, then a leaf of romaine, and then closed each sandwich off with a second slice of bread. He handed one to Storm.

Storm couldn't help thinking how few meals anyone had prepared for him. He took a bite. It wasn't what he would have made for himself, but it tasted good.

'Abby cooked for me,' he said, out of the blue. 'The first night I got here.'

'Yeah,' said Jack, and turned his smile towards his own sandwich.

I could end up like him, Storm thought. It would hardly take any work at all. He'd be an old, randy guy who loved women and knew a lot about what made them tick. Maybe he'd even be happy like Jack – contented.

And maybe, like Jack, he'd have one big love in his past that all the rest would have to measure up to.

Marissa sat on the end of the pier, swinging her legs over the water. Crickets chirped loudly in the dark and insects dive-bombed the grease-spattered lantern that hung from the piling to her right. Moths and flames – there was a metaphor in there somewhere, but she really didn't care.

She wondered why she wasn't crying her eyes out.

She played the moment back in her mind, the moment Storm turned to Abby and everyone else in the room disappeared. Her finger had frozen on the camera shutter. Even she knew that to press it again would have meant violating something very, very private.

They'd looked so beautiful under the blanket, graceful, as if they were dancing instead of fucking.

Maybe that was what being in love did to a person.

Marissa sighed and pulled a thread from the bottom of her cutoffs. She'd given it her best shot, but nothing she'd done had come close to putting that look of adoration on Abby's face. As far as she could tell, Abby hadn't even come for Storm.

Go figure, she thought.

The creaking of a plank warned her of Jack's approach.

'Hey,' he said, and lowered a warm pizza box on to her lap.

'You better have brought beer with that,' she warned.

He chuckled and set a frosty Sam Adams by her hip. She noticed he wasn't eating. He didn't like pizza as she recalled, though he knew she did. This was probably his version of giving a girl flowers.

He let her wolf down two slices of pepperoni with extra cheese before he spoke. 'Are you all right?'

'I'm peachy.' She fished out another piece and bit off the end. 'You knew this would happen, didn't you?'

He tilted back his beer and took a long swallow. 'I notice you're not crying.'

She shrugged. 'Can't fight true love.'

That comment earned her another silence. A fish splashed invisibly in the bay. 'You'll find it,' he said.

I might, she thought, too ornery to say so out loud. She almost believed it, too, though God alone knew why. Maybe because her heart felt free again. She'd lost the last of her hope, and had lived to tell the tale.

'What about you?' she said, survival making her cocky.

Jack stopped with his beer an inch from his mouth. 'I'm too old for that nonsense.'

'Right,' she said. 'That's why you're still carrying a

torch for your wife.' This time he set the bottle on the pier. Marissa faced down his stare. 'Why else would you be screwing every half-likely prospect who crosses your path? My guess is as long as you don't settle down, you feel like you're being true to her memory. I mean, you feel guilty about wanting Abby, don't you? That's why you won't fight Storm for her.'

Jack broke their locked gaze first. He looked down at his beer and scratched a corner of the label from the neck. 'Not everyone was meant to settle down.'

'Not everyone has the balls to try,' she sauced back.

He laughed loudly as if her remark had broken through some barrier. 'You've got that right, sweetie. Settling down takes balls and then some.'

Abby's hand fell limply to the mattress, a casualty of her latest orgasm. 'I'll give you one thing,' she panted. 'You've sure got balls.'

Storm lifted his head from her pussy and crawled up to pillow level. She didn't sound angry, but with all he had at stake it didn't hurt to be careful. 'What do you mean?'

'I mean what you did with Jack tonight. That was very brave.'

'Oh, that.' He tucked her head into his shoulder. 'It wasn't bad.'

She nuzzled his chest. 'Even so, I'm sorry I pushed you into it.'

'I can't pretend I didn't enjoy it. There's been a time or two when I've been curious.'

'But you wouldn't want to do it every night.'

'No,' he said, then considered his answer. Would he want to do it again? He'd hardly satisfied all his curiosity. Of course, trying it again might mean letting Abby satisfy her curiosity, too. She seemed to have plenty of that. He frowned at the ceiling. The clock ticked on the bedside table. He counted to twenty, willing his annoyance to recede.

'What about you?' he asked. 'Would you want to do it every night?'

'No,' she said.

His shoulders gave up their tension with an audible pop. 'Good,' he said, 'because I like having you to myself.'

She hugged him closer, hardly a resounding endorsement of his position, but one that gave him hope.

His words played through Abby's mind: I like having you to myself. I like having you to myself. She ground her teeth together to force them from her consciousness. Those words didn't mean 'I love you.' They didn't mean 'be mine forever.' All they meant was that Storm had a possessive streak – which she'd guessed from the start.

He's not in love, she told herself. Don't you believe he's in love.

And that was the pleasant mantra to which she fell asleep.

14

'I'd like to double-check the trim colour with you,' the crew foreman said.

Abby stared at the faded patches on either side of his denim zip. He must have big balls, she thought, big everything – or maybe he was half-hard. Maybe he was as desperate for distraction as she was. Storm was driving her insane. Every time she turned around he was doing something sweet: opening a door for her, giving her a neck rub. The day before he'd replaced a broken hinge on her closet door. He was not a handy-man. He had bruises on his bruises by the time he finished, but he didn't let her hear a single curse.

She felt as if she were under siege, as if, having won her heart – whether he knew it or not – he now wished to permanently chain her affections.

Yes, chain me, she wanted to say. But she was certain the moment she even looked as though she might request such a thing he'd head for the hills. What was he trying to do to her?

'Miss Coates?'

Abby's head snapped up. 'I'm sorry. What did you say?'

The foreman's gaze fastened on hers. He had pretty amber-green eyes. He was tanned and handsome with short curly hair that was almost the same colour as his skin. His cutoffs stopped midway down thighs in which every thick muscle was delineated. His chest strained the buttons of his stained blue shirt. She doubted she'd be able to encompass his neck in her hands. He was a bull, a hot-eyed, cocky bull. Or was she just imagining that he looked at her as if he wanted to hump her in the east pasture? Her eyes slid to his groin again. Yes, indeed. The faded denim was stretched to its limit now, pushed out by a truly gargantuan erection. It looked to her as if his love tool was primed for action. She fought a snicker as a pulse of interest flickered between her legs. Perhaps this was the distraction she'd been hoping for.

As though he sensed her thoughts, the foreman propped his hands on the front of her desk and leant towards her. Beneath the rolled-up cuffs of his shirt, his forearms were corded with muscle. The smell of his sweat was almost as heavy as his aftershave. He wore Old Spice: not subtle, but effective.

'You are so damn hot,' he said in a low, hoarse voice that sent heat spiralling through her nipples. 'You're like one of those desserts that crazy chef of yours is always setting on fire, all sugar and flame.'

'Really?' she said, charmed by his metaphor. Had she found a diamond in the rough? Was this the start of another rewarding adventure? She leant back in her chair and folded her hands over her belly. 'How fascinating.'

Her outwardly cool tone snapped some restraint within the man. She supposed he wasn't used to having to ask for anything, or denying himself something he wanted. He rounded her desk in three strides, grabbed the arms of her chair and shoved it back against the window. 'You want to fuck or what?'

His words drew a hot surge of fluid from her sex. With an effort, she clung to her pose of indifference. 'Not quite housebroken, are we?' she said, amazed at her own daring. She didn't know this man; had no idea what he might do. But after so many years of doubting herself, she'd grown drunk on her new power – too drunk to rein herself in.

The foreman's jaw worked, anger and lust sparking in his pretty green eyes. He was so close she could see the stubble growing on his chin and the sweat beading his upper lip. What a gorgeous Greek face he had; so arrogant, so manly. Abby was going to enjoy this.

'No, I'm not housebroken,' he said. 'I'll fuck you hard and I'll fuck you deep and, believe me, you'll thank me when it's over.'

She smiled mockingly.

'Bitch,' he said, and kissed the smile from her face. His hands went straight for her breasts, reaching up under her silk blouse and swallowing them in his big, calloused palms. He squeezed them hard and moaned, his face softening with pleasure. What children men were, what wonderful, predictable children.

She grabbed the back of his neck and pushed her tongue into his mouth. For an instant, he stiffened, then took over the kiss with a vengeance, just as she'd known he would. He yanked her out of the chair, cupped her buttocks in one hand and ground her pussy over his bulging groin. She clung to his shoulders and wrapped one thigh around his hip, which gave him even better access to her softness. He pushed his cock at her in hard, sensation-hungry jerks, obviously frustrated by the barriers between their pleasure zones. Abby enjoyed his struggle immensely – he was so enthusiastic, and so flatteringly hard – but thirty seconds were enough to convince him they needed a change of strategy.

'You're a hot fucking bitch, aren't you?' he panted, his vocabulary limited, but effective. 'Lucky for you, I'm man enough to handle it.'

He tore off just enough clothes to fuck: his zip, her panties. She wore a sheer georgette skirt with big red peonies on it. The folds flew in the air as he shoved her on to her desk. He was bigger than she was, but she was no ninety-pound weakling. She shoved back and squirmed free. She went to her knees, yanked his zip wider and pulled his jeans over his hips, exposing a swath of skin the sun had never touched. His cock was enormous, brick-red and topped with a glans the size of a baby's fist. If she hadn't already encountered Bill's big piston, the sight would have frightened her. Instead, she blew lightly into his thick, curly thatch of pubic hair. Then she moved closer.

'Not there,' he said as she mouthed the loose skin of his scrotum.

Obviously, he wanted to go straight for the kill – slam, bang, pow. She, however, wanted to watch him squirm. Storm had taught her that pleasure and now she didn't like to forego it. She sucked one plump testicle into her mouth and coddled it with the flat of her tongue.

'Bitch,' said the foreman. His hips rocked closer as his hands tried to shift her on to his cock. When his tugs grew more insistent, she threatened him with the edge of her teeth. 'Bitch,' he said again, but she was beginning to think it a compliment. She chuckled. His cock was so hard it was bobbing against his belly.

She nuzzled her way from his balls to his root, then worked her way up the pulsing raphe. The silky smoothness of the big, ruddy glans made her moan. She marvelled at how she'd grown to enjoy this act. She licked the head, slow, lapping strokes as if he had an ice cream cone for a cock. She swirled around the ridge and blew lightly into his come-hole.

'Fuck,' he said. He took hold of himself, surrendering to the moment, preparing to guide his penis into her mouth.

Instantly, she backed away and hopped on to her desk. He gaped at her, furious, amazed. Before he could advance on her, she opened a drawer and tossed him a condom. 'Extra large,' she said with a cocky wink. 'Reservoir tip.'

He grumbled under his breath but he had it on in seconds flat.

'Now we're ready,' she said, and started inching her frothy skirt up her thighs. He watched her show and licked his thick, sensual lips, red now from their kisses. His cock hardly needed encouragement but he couldn't keep his hands off it. Slowly, lovingly, he pumped the shaft with his right hand and kneaded his denim-covered thigh with the left. His balls hung outside his cutoffs, thrust higher by the open zip. They were red beneath their hairy flesh, red and full. He was like an animal, she thought, nothing on its mind but the most basic physical pleasure. Indeed, when the first gleaming curls of her mound appeared, he shoved her legs apart, aimed himself, and pressed for his goal.

As big as he was, he took a minute to ease fully in. 'You're a tight one, aren't you?' he said.

'If you say so,' she teased, but she liked the compliment. She liked the way he filled her, too. She kicked off her shoes and planted her heels on the desk to aid his progress. He slid in the final millimetre.

There was no slowing him then. His thrusts came fast and furious, and displayed a good deal more energy than technique. She had to show him how to touch her clitoris; had to threaten to stop if he didn't. He got the idea then – even seemed to like the way his touch made her clench and squirm around him. Still not satisfied with the arrangement, she wet her finger in her juices and stuck it up his arse.

He froze mid-stroke. 'Lady, are you crazy?' he hissed. 'You think I'm some kind of homo?'

She grinned at his outrage. He could protest all he

wanted, but he'd started throbbing like a jet engine the minute she'd breached him.

'I think you're a man with nerves in his butt,' she said, 'just like anyone else.' To prove it, she wriggled her finger a little deeper. His sphincter quivered. He cursed and turned red and started dripping sweat.

'Fine.' His voice had a funny squeak in it, like a rusty hinge. 'Do whatever the hell you want.'

She did, oh, she did. She did what she wanted until she came not once, but twice – big, deep, muscle-wrenching orgasms. Her contractions pulled him past the point of no return.

'Fuck, fuck, fuck.' His face twisted as he began to spasm. She worked her finger deeper and found his joy spot. His eyes widened in shock. He grunted and cursed again, then jerked inside her, a long reverberation of pulses that left him panting for air. He collapsed on top of her before he'd finished coming. His cock twitched in sync with his moans.

Once it was over, her mood dropped like a stone. What was she doing? Why was she lying here under this crude, sweaty man who cared more for his favourite hammer than he did for her? Jack she could understand, even the three musketeers, but this – had she lost her mind?

She couldn't suppress a sigh of relief when he finally gathered himself and pushed off her. With a grimace of distaste, he twisted the condom shut and chucked it in her waste bin.

'I'll give you this,' he said as he tucked himself back in his jeans. 'You're a much better lay than your sister.'

Abby blinked and shook her head. 'Excuse me?'

The foreman yanked up his zip. 'I said you're a better lay than your sister. Bit of a whiner, isn't she?'

Abby clenched her fists. 'You had better be talking about my sister, Sandra.'

'Right,' he said with a cocky grin. 'Two down and one to go.'

Abby's body went cold. Good Lord, she thought. He planned to screw me all along. He probably made a hobby of fucking complete sets of sisters. Some diamond in the rough. She pressed her hand over her clenching stomach. 'If you go anywhere near Francine...' she began, but couldn't finish. Exactly how did a five-foot-two-inch, law-abiding woman threaten a two hundred pound man with no scruples?

The foreman raked his meaty hand back through his curls. 'Yeah, I know she's married,' he said. 'But hey, people make their own decisions.' While Abby spluttered, he patted his back pockets as if looking for something. He pulled out a crumpled envelope. 'I meant to give this to you before. It's from my boss.'

Given the circumstances, Abby had to read the letter twice before she took in its meaning.

'Shit,' she said, and didn't feel the least compulsion to apologise for her language. 'Your boss and I agreed I'd pay these charges as I went along.'

'You should have got it in writing.'

'But why is he asking for more money up front?'

The foreman examined his thumbnail. 'Guess he heard you're having financial difficulties.'

'Shit,' she said again. The pieces fell together. 'Sandra told you something, didn't she?'

The foreman grinned. 'She has got a big mouth, though she doesn't use it nearly as well as you do.'

'Don't remind me,' she muttered, wishing she could take back every twinge of pleasure she'd given him. The bastard. He must have run straight to his boss with the tale.

'Hey,' he said, with a shadow of what might have been remorse. 'It's not personal. It's business.'

Abby forced herself not to spit in his face. Cape Cod was a small place. She might end up hiring another construction firm, but for now it was best not to burn any bridges. 'I understand,' she said with a clenched smile – the best she could manage. 'I'll just have to work this out with your boss.'

The foreman nodded approvingly and glanced at his watch. 'So, we'll, uh, do this again sometime.'

'When hell freezes over,' she snapped.

Luckily, the foreman laughed.

She guessed he'd heard that kind of thing before.

She stormed into the kitchen smelling of sex. Storm set the shrimp he'd been cleaning on a bed of ice. Schooling his face to hide his dismay, he washed his hands, dried them on his apron and turned.

She was flapping a piece of paper in his direction. 'Would you look at this. Would you *look* at this!'

He looked at her. Her top, a scoop-necked silk shell, was a bright poppy red. He couldn't remember her wearing anything so vibrant before. Sweat dampened the neckline. Both her shirt and skirt were creased as though someone had been lying on top of them.

His heart sank. The clothes might have made him suspicious, but the creases told their own sordid story. She'd been fooling around again. He'd done everything he could think of to keep her satisfied. He'd loved her till the sun came up. He'd brought her breakfast in bed. He'd fixed the blasted hinge on her closet door, and she still couldn't be faithful to him. Never mind he hadn't asked her to be faithful. She ought to want to be.

Mon Dieu, he thought, covering his face with his hands. Why doesn't she want to?

'Storm?' She took a step closer. 'Are you all right? Do you need help with the prep work?'

He dropped his hands. To hell with it, he thought. I give up. 'I'm fine,' he said out loud. 'Let me see what you have here.'

He took the letter.

'I can't believe it,' she said as he ploughed through the business-speak. 'Sandra was sleeping with the foreman and blabbed to him about our money problems. I swear, the woman needs a muzzle.'

He folded the letter and gave it back to her. 'How do you know it was Sandra?'

Abby blushed to the roots of her dishevelled hair. Had she heard it from the foreman? Was he the bastard who'd left her looking so rumpled? Jesus. Storm had seen the man. Jack he could understand. The three musketeers genuinely seemed to care for her. Marissa he chalked up to curiosity. But the fact that she'd screw that musclebound, chauvinistic dolt made him want to smash something. Clearly, her taste was degenerating. Rapidly.

'Never mind how I know.' Squirming under his censorious gaze, she tried to smooth her hair back into what had once been a nice French braid. 'The important thing is I don't know how I'm going to pay this bill. Even if I do find a way, as soon as the renovation is finished, I'll need to hire more employees to cover the second dining room. And you'll need a full-time assistant, instead of me just pitching in when I get a minute.'

Storm sagged back against the double sink. Now she didn't want to work with him, either? 'I like it when you pitch in.'

Even to himself he sounded disgustingly forlorn. His tone brought her up short.

'Well, thank you,' she said. 'But you really do need an assistant and I really don't know how I'll pay for this or my mortgage.'

'What about the money Jack is going to pay you for modelling?'

She huffed that suggestion away. 'I can't let him pay me for what we did the other night. I doubt he got a single picture he could use.'

'But he promised you —'

'That doesn't matter,' she said. 'I can't hold him to it.' Abruptly, her big soft eyes swam with tears. 'Oh, Storm. I'm so sorry. You came all the way out here and you worked so hard. You really turned the business around. Now, instead of rewarding you, all I've got to offer is a big, fat mess. Hell —' she grabbed her hair in both hands and pulled '— I'll probably have to declare bankruptcy.'

Storm's heart stumbled for a second, then began to race. This was his moment. She was on her financial knees. He was sure Jack would insist on paying her for her work, but she didn't know that. She didn't love Storm. She probably wouldn't ever love him. If he gathered his bruised and battered balls off the floor, now, this minute, he could fulfil at least one of his dreams.

'I'll buy you out,' he said.

The steadiness in his voice amazed him — and her, too. Her hands ceased tugging her hair. She stared at him. 'You'll buy me out?'

The moment hung in the air, like the eerie hush before an earthquake. Her eyes held only confusion, but any second she might sum it up: how strange it was that a chef would slave for a restaurant he could afford to buy, and how suspicious that he would wait for this particular convergence of events to make an offer.

So what, screamed his wounded ego. This is your dream, your chance to make a real home for yourself.

But cold sweat broke out across his back at the thought of seeing his betrayal through her eyes. They wouldn't even be friends then, not even friends. Anyway, what sort of home would this inn be without her in it? She might not be the Currier & Ives companion he'd secretly dreamt of, but she was the only woman who'd ever touched the deepest part of him. Did it really matter if she neither knew that nor cared? What kind of man was he?

He gripped the sides of his apron and tugged it straight. He took a deep breath.

'I mean...' His voice wasn't steady anymore. He cleared his throat. 'I mean, I think I could afford to buy one of your sisters' shares. If I had a stake, it would make sense for me to help you clear your debts. Isn't Sandra the one who always thinks she's broke? Perhaps she'd like to have cash in hand.'

'I'm sure she would,' Abby said.

She covered her mouth with both hands. He noticed they were trembling. He wanted to soothe that tiny tremor. He, himself, no one else – he wanted to be responsible for its ease. He wanted to be responsible for her happiness. The thought was ridiculous. No one could be responsible for another's happiness and yet to be responsible for even a fraction of her joy in life seemed a worthy goal, as worthy – no – *more* worthy than anything he had done with saucepan and flame.

Clearly, this love business changed one in the strangest ways. He had no hope of romantic success, none, but he was lightheaded, ecstatic at the thought of rescuing her. But Abby had pulled herself together. He had to pay attention.

'Gosh, Storm,' she said. 'Are you sure you want to be partners with a woman who's a hair's breadth from going under?'

'Yes, I am.' He straightened his shoulders. 'You're in a tough spot right now, but once you – once *we* get past it – I think we'll have smooth sailing. We work well together. I think we'll make a great team.'

'I don't know.' She smoothed the waistband of her skirt, her eyes earnest and worried – worried for him, he realised with a delicious little pang. 'A partnership is such a big commitment. It's almost like a marriage.'

'Maybe I wouldn't mind that either.'

He didn't know where the words had come from, but once uttered he refused to withdraw them. He set his jaw. Abby paled. When she spoke, her voice had a breathy squeak to it. 'What did you say?'

His heart was pounding madly but he managed a smile nonetheless. She wasn't laughing, and she didn't look horrified. Maybe it wasn't hopeless. He dried his clammy palms on his thighs. 'I said I wouldn't mind marrying you.'

'Oh, gosh.' Abby fumbled behind her for a stool, then practically fell off it trying to sit down. He took her elbow to help her settle. Her eyes were huge, as startled as if he'd told her he'd flown here from another planet. 'So I guess . . .' She swallowed and folded her hands atop the workstation's battered cutting board. 'I guess you meant that *je t'aime* stuff, after all. You did mean it, didn't you? This isn't just your idea of a business merger?'

'No.' Feeling somewhat giddy, he gathered her hands in his. 'I meant it, though I wasn't ready to admit it at the time. But what about you, Abby? How do you feel about me?'

The tip of her nose turned pink. 'Well, I, I'm very fond of you. I suppose I probably might love you, too.'

He threw his head back on a laugh and pulled her into his arms. How very extraordinary this was. Here she was, stinking of another man's cologne, and he felt so happy he thought he might float right off the ground. It didn't matter. He would scrub her clean. He would love her till she stank of nothing but him. Ah, she loved him. He was home now.

'Abby, Abby, Abby.' He rocked her from side to side. 'We're going to be so happy.'

'Wait, Storm, please.' She pushed free of his embrace. 'I said I loved you. I didn't say I'd marry you. We hardly know each other. But I will tell Sandra you're interested in making an offer.'

He stepped back as if she'd struck him. 'Is it because of the other men? You can't bear to give them up?'

Abby caught her breath in shock. His awareness that she'd been with other men did not come as a complete surprise. The depth of his distress did. The skin around his lips was white. Tears shimmered in his eyes. Not wanting to embarrass him, she looked down at her hands. 'The other men bother you?'

'Yes, they bother me!' He paused to gather himself. His speech grew stiff and formal. 'Whether or not you choose to accept my proposal of marriage, if you wish for us to go on as we are, I would like you to ask me before you sleep with other people and I would like the right to say no.'

'The right to say no,' she repeated, meeting his gaze. No tears threatened now. In fact, his expression was quite formidable. 'And will you choose to exercise that right?'

'I imagine I will, at least for a while.' A faint smile touched his sensitive lips. 'My association with you seems to have left me unusually insecure.'

That set her back on her heels. Her other lovers had made him feel insecure, the great Casanova? She could see how he might be possessive, but insecure? She never would have guessed it, or dared to try such a ploy if she had. It was so underhanded, so childish. All the same, the fact that she, Abby Coates, had succeeded in humbling Storm Dupré inspired a primitive – albeit guilty – satisfaction.

Pricked by the guilt, she shook the crowing pleasure

from her mind and considered his demand. Could she confine her amorous intrigues to him and him alone? She shook her head at her own question. Of course she could. Bill hadn't been half the partner Storm was and she'd never cheated on him. The real question was: did she want to?

She thought back on the past few weeks. She remembered Storm and Jack and Horace and Peter and Ivan – and Marissa, of course. She remembered tying and being tied, watching and being watched. She remembered sand and sunshine and racing whales and sighs at midnight. She remembered dildoes and vibrators and a dusty electric cord. She remembered fear and courage, pleasure and regret. It had been a wonderful rollercoaster ride, and maybe someday she would want to soar into that boundless place again. Jack she would miss, but whether they slept together or not, they would always be friends.

Storm was the only lover whose absence would break her heart.

'I won't let you dictate my every move,' she warned.

He must have heard the whisper of surrender. He caught her arms and pulled her close. 'I wouldn't try to, love. Just give me your word that you'll ask before you go tomcatting. That will be good enough for me.' He buried his face in her hair and mumbled, 'I'll give you my word as well, you know.'

'Mm,' she said. 'What about your motto? You know: no commitments, only pleasure.'

Storm smiled against her temple and kissed her hair. 'Very well,' he said. 'I will allow actions to speak in place of promises.'

Abby let herself believe him then. Her shoulders relaxed. She wrapped her arms around his waist and hugged him. How extraordinary this was. How safe she felt and how hopeful. Never in a million years would she have predicted this moment. Not that she was going to take her future for granted. They still had plenty of things to work out, plenty. And speaking of which . . .

'There's one thing I need to know before I consider either of your proposals.'

'Yes?' He rubbed her back in a long, slow stroke that made the blood heat in her veins.

'I could never commit myself to a man whose real name I didn't know.'

'What?'

'I know your mother didn't really name you Storm.'

He sighed. A chip of ice crackled in the sink. 'Eugene,' he said.

'Eugene.' She rolled it around her tongue. 'Eugene Dupré. I like it. May I have your permission to call you Eugene in private?'

'Does this mean you'll think about marrying me?'

She hid her grin against his chest. 'We'll see.'

He cursed in French, always a good sign. 'Are you trying to make me insane?'

'But I know you like to wait. How could I deprive you of that pleasure in this of all things?'

'Tu es méchante,' he said with great ferocity. 'You are wicked.'

'Well, you know, Eugene –' she tipped her head back and blinked innocently into his eyes '– lately, I have been working on it.'

Epilogue

The food critic from *The Boston Globe* wasn't expecting much of The Coates Inn – a glorified crab shack at best. But the invitation had piqued her interest. On its front was a truly stunning photograph of a naked woman with a circle of oysters on her flat, tanned belly. Her daughter, Nan, immediately pronounced the model scrumptious, despite the fact that nothing rude was showing. Elise had found the picture tasteful, but the oysters glistening on their pearly half-shells made her mouth water. Oysters were a particular vice of hers. She could have eaten them by the bushel.

So she decided to come and here she was – unannounced, of course.

To her surprise, the inn was lovely, a fine example of old Cape architecture. She felt at home just walking through it. A pretty waitress led her up to the second-floor dining room and sat her next to a window with a view of the gently frothing ocean. The jangle of the city fell away as she gazed through the diamond-paned glass.

She forgave the owners the faint smell of plaster.

The waitress filled her glass and ran through her patter on the menu. Elise couldn't help noticing she was just about Nan's age. She had a nose ring and a small tattoo of a beach rose on her shoulder, but she was neatly dressed and friendly. All in all, she seemed much less dangerous than most of Nan's friends. Elise found herself wishing for some polite way to ask a total stranger if she swung a bit to the left.

Too bad lesbians didn't have earring codes the way gay men did – or used to. It would have made a mother's job much easier. With a futile inner sigh, she set the menu aside and asked the waitress what she'd recommend.

'Everything is good,' she said, her pencil poised above her pad. 'In fact, the only thing I wouldn't recommend –' she lowered her voice conspiratorially '– is eating here alone very often.'

Elise furrowed her brow and slid her bifocals down off the top of her head. She hated wearing them. They made her look old, which she wasn't. She was a bright, pass-for-fortyish woman with a lifetime of experience and plenty of healthy appetites, appetites that had – thank the Lord – survived the death of her dear, dear husband two years earlier.

Bifocals or no, she wasn't old. The spectacles did, however, help her see the world more clearly. Now she saw the waitress had a distinct twinkle in her eye. 'Why do you say I shouldn't eat here alone?' Elise asked. 'Is this a pick-up joint?'

'No, no.' The waitress laughed. 'But you may find yourself wishing it were by the time you're finished eating.'

She wouldn't say more but, in truth, her teasing charmed. How Elise wished Nan would hook up with a nice girl like this! Elise wasn't holding out for a doctor or anything so bourgeois. Any chit with a job, a brain, and a modicum of tact would have suited her.

Oh, well. Short of moving to the Cape, she couldn't see any way to further this particular matchmaking scheme. Not that moving to the Cape would be a hardship, she thought, gazing contentedly at the ocean vista. She could start compiling that cookbook she'd always meant to edit: *Hardwicke's Best of New England Cuisine*.

She'd need a good photographer, of course, and a presentation chef, but in an arty community like this one, she was sure she'd find herself tripping over them.

She was still braiding happy thoughts when the appetiser arrived. A paper-thin slice of salmon with a whisper of seasoning, it could only enhance her mellow mood.

Superb, she thought, letting it melt in her mouth and slip slowly down her throat. She settled back in her chair and wriggled her toes. Good food always made her feel sensual and this was better than most. She could hardly wait to see what the chef did with the Oysters Rockefeller.

Tingling with happy anticipation, she gazed around the crowded dining room. The tourist season was young yet, but business seemed brisk, and most of the customers looked as happy as she felt. Two seventy-year-olds cooed like teenagers at a table across the way. She loved seeing that. She and Aaron would have been like that, if they'd had the chance. She smiled. Funny how time and knowing you'd been loved could change a wrenching pain into a sweet nostalgia. She'd been very, very lucky and, who knew, perhaps someday she'd be lucky again.

Her gaze travelled onwards, noting a table of three laughing men, one fat, one thin and one bulked up like a body-builder.

Then an older gentleman sitting alone at the next table over caught her eye. Dressed like a fisherman in a worn cotton shirt and jeans, he was scribbling in a cheap spiral notebook. Normally, neither of these things would have attracted her attention. He looked very fit, though, and his face bore an expression of such concentrated intelligence that she immediately wanted to know all about him.

Who was he? What was he writing? And why wasn't some lucky, laughing matron fixing him dinner at home?

She must have been staring very loudly because after a few seconds he looked up, stared back, and winked at her – winked at her, for goodness sake! Her hand fluttered to her throat. She looked away, of course. Appetites or not, Elise Hardwicke did not flirt with strangers. It had been a nice wink, though, and a very nice face that housed it: a humorous, weathered face with a look of gentle wisdom.

A good face to wake up to, she thought, then scolded herself for acting like a twit. The man had merely winked. He probably thought she was being rude.

When she looked up a minute later, however, he was staring at her.

Oh, why not, she thought, and this time she winked at him.

Author's Note

Naturally, everyone has their own opinions about the validity and uses of different aphrodisiacs. My sources for this book included:

Secrets of Venus: A Lover's Guide to Charms, Potions and Aphrodisiacs by Vera Lee, PhD; *Aromatherapy for Lovers* by Tara Fellner; and *Intercourses: An Aphrodisiac Cookbook* by Martha Hopkins and Randall Lockridge.

These fine authors cannot, of course, be blamed for my mistakes.

Visit the Black Lace website at
www.blacklace-books.co.uk

**FIND OUT THE LATEST INFORMATION AND TAKE
ADVANTAGE OF OUR FANTASTIC FREE BOOK OFFER!
ALSO VISIT THE SITE FOR . . .**

- All Black Lace titles currently available and how to order online
- Great new offers
- Writers' guidelines
- Author interviews
- An erotica newsletter
- Features
- Cool links

BLACK LACE — THE LEADING IMPRINT
OF WOMEN'S SEXY FICTION

TAKING YOUR EROTIC READING
PLEASURE TO NEW HORIZONS

BLACK LACE

LOOK OUT FOR THE ALL-NEW BLACK LACE BOOKS – AVAILABLE NOW!

All books priced £6.99 in the UK. Please note publication dates apply to the UK only. For other territories, please contact your retailer.

KING'S PAWN
Ruth Fox
ISBN O 352 33684 6

Cassie is consumed by a need to explore the intriguing world of SM – a world of bondage, domination and her submission. She agrees to give herself to the inscrutable Mr King for a day, to sample the pleasures of his complete control over her. Cassie finds herself hooked on the curious games they play. Her lesbian lover, Becky, is shocked, but agrees to Cassie visiting Mr King once more. It is then that she is initiated into the debauched Chessmen Club, where she is expected to go much further than she thought. **A refreshingly honest story of a woman's introduction to SM. Written by a genuine scene-player.**

TIGER LILY
Kimberley Dean
ISBN O 352 33685 4

When Federal Agent Shanna McKay – aka Tiger Lily – is assigned to a new case on a tough precinct, her shady past returns to haunt her. She has to bust drug lord, Mañuel Santos, who caused her sister's disappearance years previously. The McKay sisters had been wild: Shanna became hooked on sex; her sister hooked on Santos and his drugs. Desperate to even the score, Shanna infiltrates the organisation by using her most powerful weapon – her sexuality. **Hard-hitting erotica mixes with low-life gangsters in a tough American police precinct. Sizzling, sleazy action that will have you on the edge of your seat!**

Coming in May 2002

SLAVE TO SUCCESS
Kimberley Raines
ISBN 0 352 33687 0

Eugene, born poor but grown-up handsome, answers an ad to be a sex slave for a year. He assumes his role will be that of a gigolo, and thinks he will easily make the million dollars he needs to break into Hollywood. On arrival at a secret destination he discovers his tasks are somewhat more demanding. He will be a pleasure slave to the mistress Olanthé – a demanding woman with high expectations who will put Eugene through some exacting physical punishments and pleasures. He is in for the shock of his life. **An exotic tale of female domination over a beautiful but arrogant young man.**

FULL EXPOSURE
Robyn Russell
ISBN 0 352 33688 9

Attractive but stern Boston academic, Donatella di'Bianchi, is in Arezzo, Italy, to investigate the affairs of the *Collegio Toscana*, a school of visual arts. Donatella's probe is hampered by one man, the director, Stewart Temple-Clarke. She is also sexually attracted by an English artist on the faculty, the alluring but mysterious Ian Ramsey. In the course of her inquiry Donatella is attacked, but receives help from two new friends – Kiki Lee and Francesca Antinori. As the trio investigates the menacing mysteries surrounding the college, these two young women open Donatella's eyes to a world of sexual adventure with artists, students and even the local *carabinieri*. **A stylishly sensual erotic thriller set in the languid heat of an Italian summer.**

STRIPPED TO THE BONE
Jasmine Stone
ISBN O 352 33463 O

Annie has always been a rebel. While her sister settled down in Middle America, Annie blazed a trail of fast living on the West Coast, constantly seeking thrills. She is motivated by a hungry sexuality and a mission to keep changing her life. Her capacity for experimental sex games means she's never short of partners, and she keeps her lovers in a spin of erotic confusion. Every man she encounters is determined to discover what makes her tick, yet no one can get a hold of Annie long enough to find out. Maybe the Russian Ilmar can unlock the secret. However, by succumbing to his charms, is Annie stepping into territory too dangerous even for her? **By popular demand, this is a special reprint of a free-wheeling story of lust and trouble in a fast world.**

Coming in June 2002

WICKED WORDS 6
A Black Lace short story collection
ISBN O 352 33590 O

Deliciously daring and hugely popular, the *Wicked Words* collections are the freshest and most entertaining volumes of women's erotica to be found anywhere in the world. The diversity of themes and styles reflects the multi-faceted nature of the female sexual imagination. Combining humour, warmth and attitude with fun, filthy, imaginative writing, these stories sizzle with horny action. Only the most arousing fiction makes it into a *Wicked Words* volume. **This is the best in fun, cutting-edge erotica from the UK and USA.**

MANHATTAN PASSION
Antoinette Powell
ISBN O 352 33691 9

Julia is an art conservator at a prestigious museum in New York. She lives
a life of designer luxury with her Wall Street millionaire husband until,
that is, she discovers the dark and criminal side to his twilight activities –
and storms out, leaving her high-fashion wardrobe behind her. Staying
with her best friends Zoë and Jack, Julia is initiated into a hedonist circle
of New York's most beautiful and sexually interesting people.
Meanwhile, David, her husband, has disappeared with all their wealth.
What transpires is a high-octane manhunt – from loft apartments to
sleazy drinking holes; from the trendiest nightclubs to the criminal
underworld. **A stunning debut from an author who knows how to
entertain her audience.**

HARD CORPS
Claire Thompson
ISBN O 352 33491 6

This is the story of Remy Harris, a bright young woman starting out as an
army cadet at military college in the US. Enduring all the usual trials
of boot-camp discipline and rigorous exercise, she's ready for any
challenge – that is until she meets Jacob, who recognises her true
sexuality. Initiated into the Hard Corps – a secret society within the
barracks – Remy soon becomes absorbed by this clandestine world of
ritual punishment. It's only when Jacob takes things too far that she
rebels, and begins to plot her revenge. **Strict sergeants and rebellious
cadets come together in this unusual and highly entertaining story of
military discipline with a twist.**

Black Lace Booklist

Information is correct at time of printing. To avoid disappointment check availability before ordering. Go to www.blacklace-books.co.uk. All books are priced £6.99 unless another price is given.

BLACK LACE BOOKS WITH A CONTEMPORARY SETTING

☐ THE TOP OF HER GAME Emma Holly	ISBN 0 352 33337 5	£5.99
☐ IN THE FLESH Emma Holly	ISBN 0 352 34498 3	£5.99
☐ A PRIVATE VIEW Crystalle Valentino	ISBN 0 352 33308 1	£5.99
☐ SHAMELESS Stella Black	ISBN 0 352 34485 1	£5.99
☐ INTENSE BLUE Lyn Wood	ISBN 0 352 34496 7	£5.99
☐ THE NAKED TRUTH Natasha Rostova	ISBN 0 352 34497 5	£5.99
☐ ANIMAL PASSIONS Martine Marquand	ISBN 0 352 34499 1	£5.99
☐ A SPORTING CHANCE Susie Raymond	ISBN 0 352 33501 7	£5.99
☐ TAKING LIBERTIES Susie Raymond	ISBN 0 352 33357 X	£5.99
☐ A SCANDALOUS AFFAIR Holly Graham	ISBN 0 352 33523 8	£5.99
☐ THE NAKED FLAME Crystalle Valentino	ISBN 0 352 33528 9	£5.99
☐ CRASH COURSE Juliet Hastings	ISBN 0 352 33018 X	£5.99
☐ ON THE EDGE Laura Hamilton	ISBN 0 352 33534 3	£5.99
☐ LURED BY LUST Tania Picarda	ISBN 0 352 33533 5	£5.99
☐ THE HOTTEST PLACE Tabitha Flyte	ISBN 0 352 33536 X	£5.99
☐ THE NINETY DAYS OF GENEVIEVE Lucinda Carrington	ISBN 0 352 33070 8	£5.99
☐ EARTHY DELIGHTS Tesni Morgan	ISBN 0 352 33548 3	£5.99
☐ MAN HUNT Cathleen Ross	ISBN 0 352 33583 1	
☐ MÉNAGE Emma Holly	ISBN 0 352 33231 X	
☐ DREAMING SPIRES Juliet Hastings	ISBN 0 352 33584 X	
☐ THE TRANSFORMATION Natasha Rostova	ISBN 0 352 33311 1	
☐ STELLA DOES HOLLYWOOD Stella Black	ISBN 0 352 33588 2	
☐ SIN.NET Helena Ravenscroft	ISBN 0 352 33598 X	
☐ HOTBED Portia Da Costa	ISBN 0 352 33614 5	
☐ TWO WEEKS IN TANGIER Annabel Lee	ISBN 0 352 33599 8	
☐ HIGHLAND FLING Jane Justine	ISBN 0 352 33616 1	

❏ MINX Megan Blythe	ISBN 0 352 33638 2
❏ PLEASURE'S DAUGHTER Sedalia Johnson	ISBN 0 352 33237 9
❏ JULIET RISING Cleo Cordell	ISBN 0 352 32938 6
❏ DEMON'S DARE Melissa MacNeal	ISBN 0 352 33683 8
❏ ELENA'S CONQUEST Lisette Allen	ISBN 0 352 32950 5

BLACK LACE ANTHOLOGIES

❏ CRUEL ENCHANTMENT Erotic Fairy Stories Janine Ashbless	ISBN 0 352 33483 5	£5.99
❏ MORE WICKED WORDS Various	ISBN 0 352 33487 8	£5.99
❏ WICKED WORDS 4 Various	ISBN 0 352 33603 X	
❏ WICKED WORDS 5 Various	ISBN 0 352 33642 0	

BLACK LACE NON-FICTION

❏ THE BLACK LACE BOOK OF WOMEN'S SEXUAL FANTASIES Ed. Kerri Sharp	ISBN 0 352 33346 4	£5.99

To find out the latest information about Black Lace titles, check out the
website: www.blacklace-books.co.uk or send for a booklist with
complete synopses by writing to:

> Black Lace Booklist, Virgin Books Ltd
> Thames Wharf Studios
> Rainville Road
> London W6 9HA

Please include an SAE of decent size. Please note only British stamps
are valid.

Our privacy policy
We will not disclose information you supply us to any other parties.
We will not disclose any information which identifies you personally to
any person without your express consent.

From time to time we may send out information about Black Lace
books and special offers. Please tick here if you do <u>not</u> wish to
receive Black Lace information.   ❏

Please send me the books I have ticked above.

Name ....

Address ....

....

....

....

Post Code ....

Send to: Cash Sales, Black Lace Books, Thames Wharf Studios, Rainville Road, London W6 9HA.

US customers: for prices and details of how to order books for delivery by mail, call 1-800-343-4499.

Please enclose a cheque or postal order, made payable to Virgin Books Ltd, to the value of the books you have ordered plus postage and packing costs as follows:

UK and BFPO – £1.00 for the first book, 50p for each subsequent book.

Overseas (including Republic of Ireland) – £2.00 for the first book, £1.00 for each subsequent book.

If you would prefer to pay by VISA, ACCESS/MASTERCARD, DINERS CLUB, AMEX or SWITCH, please write your card number and expiry date here:

....

Signature ....

Please allow up to 28 days for delivery.